Saltwater
Flyfishing

Saltwater
Flyfishing

BRITAIN AND NORTHERN EUROPE

Edited by Paul Morgan

WITH CONTRIBUTIONS BY

*Asgeir Alvestad   Roger Baker   Claus Bech-Petersen
Barry Ord Clarke   Nick Cosford   Gary Coxon   Richard Davies
Alan Hanna   Jan Hansen   Stan Headley   Kim Jacek   Martin James
Peter James   Martin Jørgensen   Wolfgang Küter   Mike Ladle
Marco Sammicheli   Rudy van Duijnhoven   Bjørnar Vihovde*

AND EXTRACTS FROM THE EARLIER WRITINGS OF

*A.F. Bell   John Bickerdyke   R. Bowden-Smith
Stephen Johnson   R.N. Lochhead   Sidney Spencer*

COCH-Y-BONDDU BOOKS

ISBN 0 9528510 9 1

First published in 1998 by Coch-y-Bonddu Books

Designed and typeset in Garamond by Jonathan Ward-Allen
Published and distributed by Coch-y-Bonddu Books
Machynlleth, Powys SY20 8DJ
Telephone 01654 702837
Fax 01654 702857
Printed and bound in Great Britain by
Biddles Ltd, Guildford and King's Lynn

CONTENTS

PART V - POLLACK AND COALFISH

PART VI - COD, GARFISH & OTHER SPECIES

PART VII - SALMON IN THE SEA

PART VIII - FLYFISHING AROUND EUROPE

PART IX - TACKLE AND METHODS

PART X - BIOGRAPHIES AND BIBLIOGRAPHIES

ACKNOWLEDGMENTS

My thanks go to all of the following for their help and assistance:

The contributors; especially for their enthusiasm and willingness to share their knowledge with others.

Rudy van Duijnhoven, Barry Ord Clarke, Peter James and Crystal River for their photographs, and Peter James for the use of his terrific cartoon illustrations.

Mrs Brenda Johnson for permission to use the extract from Stephen Johnson's *Fishing with a Purpose*.

Trout Fisherman magazine and photographer Rod Calbrade for the use of pictures of our mullet-fishing expedition.

Mark Bowler of *Flyfishing & Flytying* magazine for the use of previously published material on bass and shark fishing.

Cassell Plc for permission to use the extract from Sidney Spencer's *Newly from the Sea*.

Henk Verhaar, listmeister of Eur-flyfish@, and his list-members, for their help, advice, encouragement and contributions.

Jon Ward-Allen for his design, layout and exceedingly good cheese, tomato and spring onion toasted sandwiches.

The Bass Angler's Sportfishing Society for material by Nick Cosford and illustrations by Peter James which have previously appeared in the *B.A.S.S. Magazine*. And for the society's collective efforts to get bass recognised as a game fish and to ensure their adequate legal protection.

Fellow booksellers Ron Coleby and John Scott for help in solving bibliographical puzzles, particularly about the authorship of *Fly-fishing in Salt and Fresh Water*, as well as Lennart Widmark, Richard Hunter, Ken Callahan, David Burnett and many others who have helped me with the snippets of information which have gone to make up the book.

The illustrations of fish are from *The Fishes of Great Britain and Ireland* by Francis Day, and the cover illustration is by George Sheringham and is from *The Book of the Fly Rod*.

I have made every effort to contact the holders of copyright in respect of writings used in this book. In some cases I have failed. Should any reader hold the copyright for any of this material would they please contact the publisher.

PART I
INTRODUCTION

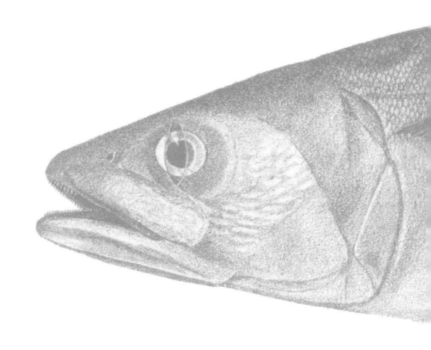

1
FOREWORD

Paul Morgan

There is nothing new about flyfishing in the sea. As long as man has fished with feathers and hooks, he must have used them to angle for mackerel and bass. Before the turn of the century the long rod, casting line and artificial fly would have been as efficient a way of taking inshore predatory fish as any other. The all-round angler of the day would have used whichever method was appropriate at the time.

However, many branches of flyfishing were sidelined during much of the twentieth century. Apart from the fashionable and exclusive salmon and chalk-stream trout fishing, flyfishing was largely taken over by the efficiency of modern bait-casting tackle, and by the nineteen-fifties the average angler was far more likely to fish with bait or spoon than with the fly. This was especially marked in sea angling, where the ability to cast long distances with the improved multipliers and fixed spool reels was considered all-important.

From about 1960 this trend began to be reversed. In Britain this was largely due to the opening up of the large water-supply reservoirs to angling, and to the consequent accessibility of inexpensive trout fishing throughout England especially. For the first time many ordinary anglers had the opportunity to flyfish, and, thanks to pioneering flyfishermen/authors like Tom Ivens, Brian Clarke and Dick Walker, an explanation and rationale which enabled them to succeed.

By the 1980s, in Britain and America, there were large numbers of competent flyfishermen, sated with bag-limits and put-and-take trout fisheries. With increasing leisure-time they began to look further afield for a more satisfying, perhaps more aesthetic, way of following their pursuit. Many returned to - or discovered for the first time - river and stream fishing, angling for grayling and sea-trout, and traditional angling methods and materials. Split-cane flyrods and silk lines began to reappear.

Across the Atlantic the search for new and different flyrod quarry was much easier. There, a larger proportion of predatory, fly-taking, fish, both in fresh and saltwater, enabled flyfishers to widen their horizons enormously. On the east coast especially, anglers turned more to the sea. In the Southern states new fisheries grew up, mainly in Florida, for

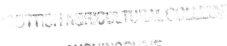

bonefish, tarpon, redfish and others. Further north flyfisherman were fishing the surf for striped bass and bluefish. Gradually new methods and materials were developed for saltwater fly-tying and flyfishing, and books and magazines on the subjects began to appear to satisfy the growing demand.

In northern Europe an existing flyfishing tradition has been given a boost by the Danish trout stocking policy which has led to a terrific population of sea-trout in the Baltic Sea and created a major new saltwater fly-fishery. Anglers from Germany and the Low Countries, with little flyfishing background but with a pioneering spirit, have joined the Scandinavians in this. Indeed, Belgium and Holland, with hardly any recognised game-fisheries, have gained a reputation for skilled and innovative fly-tying and flyfishing.

Through international magazines, television and the internet most anglers now know of the possibilities of exciting and exotic fishing in far corners of the globe. Relatively cheap travel enables many British and Europeans to fish in the Caribbean and even further afield. Flyfishing is now a truly international pastime, with new playgrounds being opened up in Alaska, South America, Africa, the north and far east of Russia, the Pacific Islands - wherever sporting fish are to be found.

BUT. Exotic flyfishing is unavoidably commercial. It is invariably expensive. It is almost exclusive to the well-off, middle class, middle-aged angler. The ordinary angler may be able to afford a foreign trip, but is usually a once a year, or even a once in a lifetime, extravagance.

Anglers wondering what to do for the other fiftyone weeks of the year are slowly waking up to the enormous potential for sport which has been on their doorsteps all along. In our freshwater lakes and rivers, and our estuaries and bays, teem many sporting species of fish. We are rediscovering the thrills of flyfishing for pike, the frustrations of sight-casting to mullet and carp, the take of the bass and the unstoppable dive of the pollack.

What this book sets out to do is to explain that good, inexpensive flyfishing can be had, in the sea, all around the coasts of Europe. It can be very easy, as when casting to a frenzied shoal of feeding mackerel or bass. It can be really challenging, as when stalking shoals of timid mullet. It is always exciting.

Every stillwater trout fisherman already has the equipment necessary to fish for these species. It is something which can be done during a family break at the seaside. Early in the morning or late in the evening (the best times anyway), with a minimum of tackle, the holidaying angler can sneak away and be in with a good chance of excellent sport.

This is not intended to be a technical book. Individual contributors have described their fly patterns and equipment, but it is presumed that the reader will have access to the appropriate fly-tying manuals and magazines. A reading list of saltwater fly-tying books is to be found at the back of the book. Most flyfishing shops now advertise a range of professionally tied flies for saltwater.

One of the great attractions of flyfishing in the sea is its lack of regulation. Its comparative freedom from bureaucracy, from petty rules and restrictions.

There are legal size limits for fish, and in some circumstances licences are required, but generally fishing in the sea is not as surrounded by laws and bylaws as freshwater fishing.

I enjoy eating the fish that I catch and this is an important part of the whole exercise for me. Some of the quarry species of the saltwater flyfisher are plentiful and good to eat. A basket of mackerel, a beautiful sea-trout or a fat cod brought home for the table form an admirable culmination to a fishing expedition.

Some of our quarry species, however, are slow-growing and very vulnerable to over-exploitation. In Britain bass are the principal example, but this can also be relevant to mullet, sea-trout and other species. When fish are scarce, or when fishing pressure is high, we should act responsibly, returning all or most of our catch. Providing we are aware of the need for sensible conservation practice, we can take a modest harvest from a strong population of fish without any qualms.

2

SETTING THE SCENE

Stan Headley

The air is cold, the sea is grey, and the wind blows through, rather than around, the lone figure. He surveys the long stretch of the bay in the thin, cold light of the March morning. Apart from wind and wave, nothing stirs. To the uninitiated, there are no outward signs that this is the place or that this is the time. But the watcher knows. At this state of tide, fish regularly frequent this lonesome place of cold salt water.

As the tide ebbs away from the bay, revealing banks of bladder-wrack, sand and shingle, the angler wades quietly, heron-like, through the shallow water. The high headland to the south causes the wind to veer and push frisky waves in towards the shore, masking his approach. The sun, low to the south-west, throws his shadow back across the dry stones and dead shells. The fish will not see him, or sense his stealthy movements, until it is too late.

A fairly long line is shot out to the edge of a dark patch of water - a darkness betraying a still sunken patch of weed lying in knee-depth water. The angler takes a long pull of line to make his fly rise and swim alongside the sunken wrack. A heavy bulge of water builds up behind the fly, betraying the close inspection of a quality fish, and more line is quickly retrieved to give the fly the impression of fearful flight. A deep swirl develops on the water surface, the rod first slams down, then rises sluggishly as the fish pulls away and the angler strikes back.

Out of the water erupts a shimmering platinum bar, surrounded by a halo of iridescent spray - an indelible memory painted by the early March sunshine. Out and away surges the fish, occasionally skipping across the surface like a skimmed stone, whilst the gathered line lashes and writhes like a beheaded snake in the water between the anglers legs, then quickly away to follow the fish.

Will he (a much-wanted fish is always 'he') run for cover? Will the line snag in the swaying wrack? Will the hook-hold fail or, almost unthinkable, the hook-knot slip? Rampant pessimism and misery vie for dominance in the mind. The pre-triumphal angst of the angler is similar to the post-coital depression of the lover. The feeling of "so close, yet so far away" are never more acutely experienced as when a violent, heavy fish freshly

struggles on a mere wisp of insubstantial gossamer. If he (the fish) is pan-
icked and then lost, he'll sprint from the area taking the rest of the shoal
with him. No matter how diligent the hunt, those fish will not be found
again that day, and all will be in vain.

But no. Miraculously, given the background of weedy snags and sharp-
edged stone, the fish ignores all pathways to freedom and fights ever closer to the angler's legs. One last desperate bid for escape is made and, in an
effort to rid himself of the mysterious restriction, he lashes his head from
side to side, tearing the water into foam and spray. But it is hopeless - slid-
ing over onto his side, the waiting net engulfs him.

Centuries slip away, and the lone figure reverts to his ancestral type - the
hunter in the wilderness. Senses become almost painfully acute, the thin
veneer of civilisation frail and tenuous, the demands of modern life temporarily ludicrous and unimportant. Whatever outward displays of victory are shown, they are for the sea-birds and seals to witness alone. The
transition has been successfully made, and the wildest of all wild things
conquered. The fish is dead, and he will be taken home for the feast. The
act of killing one good fish is an affirmation of our true nature and her-
itage, to slaughter a host is to deny it.

Never thinking to step back into the tide - more fish will only dull the
taste of victory - the angler safely gathers his trophy, trudges away from
the sea, through the dry, crunching weed and shells. The day is complete.
The wind is left alone in the bay. A sea-trout has been taken from the sea.

3

SALTWATER FLYFISHING ONE HUNDRED YEARS AGO

John Bickerdyke

*Natural Flies taken by Sea Fish - Fly-fishing for Herrings - The Whitebait Fly -
Fly-fishing for Salmon and Sea Trout in Salt Water - The Slob, or Estuarine Trout -
Fly-fishing for Shad, Mullet, and Sand Eels, &c.*

The amateur sea fisher should at the outset understand that fly fishing, as anglers use the term, is not necessarily the casting of a natural fly, or a bait designed to represent a natural fly. If we use a bait made of such material as feather, fur, coloured silks, tinsel, or combinations of these materials, and cast it out by means of a fly rod, we call such casting fly fishing. In the sea, though there are a large number of fish which may be caught on certain artificial and natural baits conveniently cast out by means of a fly rod, the species which will, so far as we know, rise to a fly tied to represent the natural insect, are very few. Couch, the great Cornish naturalist, states that garfish will feed on the black flies which, on calm days, may sometimes be observed on the surface of the sea. In fact, he puts the question beyond doubt by stating that on an autopsy being made, the stomachs of these fish were found crammed with the flies. Herrings are sometimes taken on artificial trout flies, and so we may presume would rise to the natural fly when they have an opportunity, as would sometimes occur when they crowd into inlets of the sea - more particularly on the

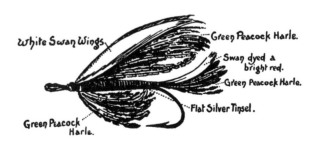

The Whitebait Fly

16

coast of Scotland in the autumn. Sometimes small herrings are seen rising to flies in salt water pools near the mouths of creeks and streams. There is not much doubt, too, that sand eels rise to natural flies, and probably smelts may be included in the list. Last, but very far from least, comes the sea trout; but in salt water he is much more partial to what are termed fancy flies and baits of various kinds than to artistic imitations of the natural insect.

I have already mentioned the habits of certain sea fish which come to the surface and feed on the young of the herring and sprat. When these fish can be approached, there is no more killing fly for them than one I had dressed to represent a whitebait, and have, therefore, named it the "whitebait" fly. The illustration and descriptive lettering show exactly how this fly should be dressed, and the size shown is generally a very useful one. It may, however, be made twice or even three times as large for large pollack and bass. The silver body and white wing represent the white belly and silver sides of the fly, while the green peacock harle is a very good imitation of the greenish colour of the back of the little fish.

Those who wish to be extremely realistic may fix the white wing below the body, have the harle on the back, and tie the two together beyond the bend of the hook, but I have not found a fly so tied kill any better than the pattern first described. For calm and very clear water these flies should be tied on hooks about half this size, say a No. 7.

Those who are accustomed to freshwater fishing will hardly need to be told that on rough, dark days large flies should be used, while on bright, calm days a very much smaller one is usually more killing. When the fish follow a fly without seizing it, a smaller size should also be tried. I have had splendid sport with the whitebait fly at Filey Brigg, catching over half a hundredweight of fish in a very short time - in fact, hooking and landing them as fast as it was possible to do so. This is one of the best flies that can be used for mackerel, though, as I have already said, the strip of fish skin is infinitely superior to it or any other fly. If it is allowed to sink nearly to the bottom among the shoal of codling, some of these fish will certainly be caught. Among other favourite flies for bass are any gaudy salmon flies, such as Jock Scott, Thunder and Lightning, Blue Doctor, &c.

In some places salmon will at times take a fly in salt water, not merely in tidal pools of river, but actually in an arm of the sea. The most remarkable instance of the kind which has come under my notice occurred in Loch Roag, the great sea loch on the west side of the Island of Lewis, a small island on this inlet of the sea celebrated as having been the home of Mr Black's charming heroine, Sheila, Princess of Thule. A river connecting a chain of lakes runs in at the head of the loch, and teems with salmon.

Both salmon and sea trout, when waiting in the sea loch before running up into fresh water, are at times taken in considerable quantities with an artificial fly. In one week, at the end of July, sixty fresh run salmon were taken in salt water by five rods. There is also a piece of water off Sutherland, called the Fleet, which lies between Dornoch and Goldspie, and there the salmon are regularly fished for in salt water with the artificial fly.

Sea trout sometimes rise extremely well in salt water, not out in the open sea, but in sea lochs or arms of the sea, in which they remain for some time before running up the tributary streams for spawning purposes. They are mostly found lying close to the shore, on the edge of seaweed, in rather shallow water, and are more easily approached by wading from the shore than from a boat. But though they will take a fly, better sport is often had by casting other baits. In Norway it is a common practice to row round the edge of the fjords, trailing a rather gaudy, medium sized salmon fly, to the hook of which is fastened two or three earth worms. No swivels are required on the line, but three or four inches of lead wire may be twisted on the line to sink the fly. Otherwise exactly the same cast is used as is required for artificial fly fishing in rivers. I have not fished for sea trout in Orkney, but a friend of mine who lives in that part of the world tells me that the only fly he has found to kill sea trout in salt water up there is a Palmer, tied with a fiery brown cock's hackle. He believes the trout take it for a sandhopper. Sometimes a speckled grey wing feather is added. He finds that the very bright gaudy flies used further south are of little avail.

There are four salmon flies which, dressed on small hooks, I can recommend for sea trout. They are the Durham Ranger, Thunder and Lightning, Lion, and Jock Scott. Blue and Silver Doctors and Alexandras are also useful flies. In estuaries a miniature salmon fly is sometimes very killing. By miniature I mean one of a size not usually found in tackle shops. A hook as small as No. 5 new scale, No.10 Redditch scale, may be used. I saw a splendid bag of large sea trout made with a Blue Doctor tied on such a hook, when larger flies were found absolutely useless.

When sea trout are rising extremely short, and being pricked repeatedly without being hooked, it is a good plan to try what a smaller fly than the one on the cast will do.

One year, being much bothered with short-rising salmon, I devised a special form of double hook, very long in the shank and small in the bend, which has been found to answer extremely well. It is quite as useful for sea trout as for salmon, and I have caught sea trout up to 12lb. on flies and hooks no larger than that shown in the illustration.

It must not be supposed that sea trout are without shyness or fear of

Salmo Irritans Hook
(designed by the Author)

man, because they happen to be in salt water. Splashing of the oars, careless wading, or the sight of an angler perched on a rock and showing boldly against the sky, are all adverse conditions to success.

A fish closely allied to the sea trout is the estuary trout (Salmo estuarius), called slob trout in Ireland. This at times takes ordinary trout flies very well in the salt water at the mouths of rivers. These fish are believed to be ordinary river trout which, owing to a scarcity of food in the neighbourhood of their birthplace, descend from time to time to the estuary for the better feeding it affords. They are not so silvery as sea trout, but more so than these brown trout, Salmo fario (called yellow trout in Scotland), which do not descend to the estuary.

Fly fishing for small pollack and coal fish round the rocks is a favourite pursuit on the west coast of Scotland and elsewhere. The cuddies, as they are called, run small, but many dozens can be taken on a whitebait fly, or a still more simple lure made by winding a little white worsted round the shank of an eyed hook, and tying on two strips from the wing feather of a swan, or other white bird, to represent wings. It is pretty fishing enough if the tackle is fine, and a light fly rod is used. The fly is simply pitched near the rocks, allowed to sink a little, and then drawn slowly through the water. In sea fishing, the fly is most frequently taken under water. There may be no perceptible break of the surface - no rise as we understand it in freshwater fishing. The angler should, therefore, keep a very keen eye on his line as he draws the fly towards him or lets it play in the tidal current. On noticing the slightest tendency of the line to straighten he should at once strike. For bass fishing the fly is best worked in a series of short jerks, very much the same as one often does when fishing for salmon. The effect of this jerk is to close, and then open, the fibres of the feathers, which gives a very lifelike appearance to the fly, making it represent a marine creature of some kind struggling to escape from the pursuing fish. When merely trailing a fly after a boat there is less occasion to watch the line which, being fully extended, will cause the bite to be felt on the rod almost the instant a fish takes the fly.

There are instances of a grey mullet taking a fly - more particularly at night - and a gentleman living at Orkney recommended a fly dressed in the following manner for the purpose: The body was to be wrapped round with wool to make it fat, and covered with tinsel; wing a white owl's feather; and a white hackle. A small piece of kid or wash-leather was added to form a sort of tail. Another angler caught mullet in the Clyde on a white fly, adding to it a piece of the bivalve spout-fish. Mr Hearder, of Plymouth, caught mullet with a red bodied fly smeared with shrimp paste. Mr R.Walker tells me he had good sport with mullet on the estuary of the Cuckmere, Sussex, using a scarlet bodied Heckham Peckham fly on a No. 7 hook.

The shad must certainly be classed among fly taking sea fish, at least during its annual visits up certain of our rivers in the spring of the year.

At evening, sunrise, and during some hours of the night, herrings will take a fly greedily enough. In fact, they are a most voracious fish. So ravenous, indeed, are they that at Peterhead it was the custom in spring to catch them for bait on bare hooks. A paternoster with a number of booms and hooks was, and, may be, still is used. The hooks were bright and shining, and the whole apparatus after being let down to the bottom was jerked up and down, the fish flying at the hooks as they moved through the water. ("Sarcelle" has described in the Field similar methods employed to catch herrings in Calais harbour. Most of the fish are foul hooked.). Quantities of herrings have been caught with the fly in Dublin Bay, Strangeford loch; in the Sutherland lochs, off Shetland; and on the east coast of England. I have not much doubt myself that wherever the angler can find himself among shoals of herrings he will get sport; but so far as I have been able to gather information on the subject, it is not much use attempting to catch these fish in the daytime. Three anglers once caught over 800 herrings in Lerwick Harbour in little more than two hours. There the best months for this branch of fly fishing are June and July, and the best hours from 9 p.m. to 11 p.m., and from midnight to 3 a.m. Eight or ten flies are placed on a line with a lead at the end, paternoster fashion, and worked gently up and down. The herring is not so particular in the matter of flies as is the trout. Black Palmers, Red Palmers, and green-bodied flies have all been recommended, and are said to be better than the ordinary Irish herring flies, which have white wings and silver tinsel bodies.

Another fish which will take a small artificial fly is the sand eel. I have not made any attempts in that direction myself, but Mr J. W. Blakey tells me that on the coast of Northumberland and Durham when the sand eels came inshore in large shoals, and were to be seen at the mouths of harbours, round rocks, &c., he used to cast for them with the piece of gurnard skin, cut to represent a small fish. One day, finding the sand eels were ignoring this skin bait, and showed a preference for a frayed knot on his line, he cut off an inch of line, frayed out all its fibres, attached them to a hook, and caught a number of fish with this singular bait. As an advance on this primitive fly, he dressed some small Palmers, rather long and thin in the body, and caught a number of sand eels with them.

Before concluding my remarks on this subject, I may, perhaps, with advantage add a word on good generalship. A man may have the best possible baits and tackle, and there may be fish in abundance, but he will catch few if his men let the boat go right over the shoal of fish when a big one is hooked, or if he wastes time, as, for instance, by fiddling about with his tackle, or insisting on stopping for lunch when the fish are feeding most ravenously. Bass lie with head up stream, and the boat should be kept rather at the side and above, than immediately above them. As soon as a fish is hooked, the boat should be rowed away from the bass, and allowed to go down with the tide a little below the shoal, where the fish may be played without disturbing the rest. After the fish has been brought into the boat, then the men row against the tide and get ahead of the shoal, but still at the side of them. On another fish being hooked the same operation is repeated. Much the same remarks apply to billet, but these fish travel more than do bass, and are not nearly so shy. With bass and large sea trout we cannot be too cautious.

From Practical letters to young sea-fishers.
John Bickerdyke, 1898.

4

FISHING BEGINNINGS

Paul Morgan

I was born, and lived throughout my childhood, at the most central point of England. Nowhere in Britain could one be further away from the sea. My angling tutors came home with me from the public library; Maurice Wiggin, Kenneth Mansfield, Bernard Venables. Well-educated, vastly experienced in angling and the ways of fish, and old, they lived in a different world to me, brought just a little closer to home by the fact that Wiggin was also from Bloxwich, and wrote of waters which I knew, or knew of. (To my regret I never met him. By this time he was literary editor of The Times, in London; remote and unimaginable to me except when writing of his fishing exploits). My mentors, through their books, told me that, whilst fishing with a worm was good, fishing with an artificial lure was better, and fishing with a fly was better still. I believed them, and I believe them still. I could see that lure-fishing was within my grasp. Lures were, after all, used for fishing for the same perch and pike that I knew. At the wonderful and mysterious fishing tackle shop, my requests for fly-spoons and plugs, after much delving into dark corners and dusty packets, met with success. Immediately I was freed from sitting on my basket. Indeed I have hardly ever sat on one since! With a few lures in my pocket I found, and still find, much more enjoyment and success than I ever found still-fishing. Flyfishing, however, was a different matter. I did not even know anyone who had ever caught a trout. Salmon and grayling were as remote from me as the dorado of the Amazon jungle, or the almost mythical monster Nile perch. With no access to these things, they would have to wait.

Orcadian interlude

The mid 1970's saw me, not following the hippy-trail to Kathmandu, but married and living on an island in Orkney. Again, books had swayed my life. In particular John and Sally Seymour's *Self sufficiency* had tempted me there with stories of fat cottager's pigs, of home-grown vegetables and home-smoked fish. And, of course, they were right. In Britain, if given the space, one can live well on the fruits of the garden and the sea-shore, and of the rod and the gun.

Sea-fishing in Orkney was both labour and recreation. Were the sea-trout as numerous in those days? We heard little of them on Shapinsay. The fish we caught were cuithes, lythe and sillocks. Cuithes are young coalfish, fish of many names; saithe, cuddies, billet, podleys and more. Pollack are called lythe throughout the North, and the very young of both species are sillocks. Cuithes in particular, coalfish between half a pound and a pound in weight, were a staple food in Orkney, being eaten fresh, salted and wind-dried, or "sour", dried without salting.

Shapinsay cuithe-fishing was, and is, carried out using "wands" and "flees", from the stern of a clinker-built rowing boat. Three bamboo canes, each with a fixed line and three white cuithe-flies are used. While one person rows along the shore-line, the other works the wands. Sitting facing the stern, on the ends of the wands, one between his legs, and one sticking out on each side, he allows the unweighted flies to trail behind the boat, quickly swinging any fish caught to hand. Occasionally a good lythe will take a fly, often smashing the crude tackle. The catch of cuithes is often counted in scores. If lythe are sought, the wands are replaced by two hand-lines trailing rubber-eels. Still rowing along the rocky shore-line, lythe aplenty are caught. My best weighed exactly 10lb.

The cuithe-flies were made by my friend, Margaret Hamblin, who tied them for sale to the shops in Kirkwall. Alas, the last of them are long gone, chewed up by fish and by moths. I would write to Margaret for more, but she stopped making them twenty-five years ago, when she gave me her fly-tying vice; the one I still use. From memory, the flies were tied on spade-end hooks, whipped to nylon snoods with red silk, which also formed the body. The wings were slips of white goose-feather.

More frequently I fished from the shore. Choosing a rocky promontory giving access to fairly deep water I would fish with spinning-tackle and a redgill eel, with a couple of cuithe-flies as droppers. Catches were not as great as from the boat, but were still very good, with plenty of nice lythe for smoking, and bags of sillocks for a fry-up. This same basic tackle, with a weighted lure (Toby spoon, German sprat etc), with flies as droppers, has served me well for fishing all around the coast of Britain for mackerel, coalfish and pollack. Working on Scottish lighthouses, often on remote islands, it frequently provided a welcome change from tinned food, as well as bait for the home-made lobster-creels I would set from the rocks.

Whilst conventional flyfishing was still unknown to me, all of this fishing was done in shallow weedy water, close to the surface, and to the shore, and with artificials small enough to cast with a fly-rod. Coalfish and pollack are real hard-fighting fish. I can't wait to get back!

With a fly-rod to Wales

Leaving the North, and provoked by memories of surface-slurping trout in moorland lochs, and leaping sea-trout in Shetland voes, I learned first to tie flies, and then to fish with a fly-rod. Frying-pan sized trout and grayling satisfied me for the first season or two, but the English and Welsh reservoirs were beginning to be stocked with trout, and opened for fishing. Also I was working as a water-bailiff on one of the best sea-trout rivers in Wales, so my flyfishing experience grew apace. Through reading Bickerdyke and Aflalo, I had long been aware that saltwater flyfishing could be successful, but it still took twenty years to progress from Black Country canal to casting a fly in the surf. Few writers explained the subject well, and most modern sea-angling writers were still dismissive of flyfishing as a method. Ever fish-hungry, for years I took the easy, and efficient way with the spinning-rod. It took a particular experience to teach me the truth about flyfishing in saltwater. That in many circumstances it is the most enjoyable and exciting method of fishing in the sea, and in certain cases it can also be the most successful.

On the Welsh coast the spring is a lean time. There are few fish to be caught between mid-winter and early summer. Then, in May, the bass move inshore, following the prawns, and the sea-trout start congregating around the river mouths. In July, if the weather is settled, mackerel move inshore chasing the shoals of whitebait, and from then until the first hard frosts fishing can be excellent.

High-water on a July evening in the late 1970's, Henry and I were chasing the mackerel shoals up and down the beach, hurling spoons and feathers out to sea. I was thrilled because I had caught a sewin, a small sea-trout, on the small chrome spoon which I had been using for mackerel fishing. Further along the beach, across the mouth of a small estuary, a tall figure in breast-waders was casting a long line into the ebbing tide using a double-handed flyrod. Our minds were full of sea-trout so when, in the darkening night, we saw him playing and beaching several fish, we were sure that he was catching sewin.

Twelve hours later, at the same stage of the ebb, we were back, armed with our flyrods. Now, in the day-time, the place swarmed with holiday-makers, several of them listlessly bottom-fishing in the river mouth. I waded into the river a hundred yards upstream from the mouth. Putting on a large double-hooked teal, blue and silver sea-trout fly I cast across the receding tide in the river channel. There were swirls, and flashes in the deeper places, and now and then a sea-trout would throw itself clear of the water. Within a few minutes I had a heavy take from a fish which headed downstream at running speed. Thinking that I had hooked a huge sea-trout, maybe even a salmon, on my inadequate tackle, I chased after it. Henry, and the holiday-anglers, made way for me while I played the fish down the river and into the sea, and eventually beached it. It was a mullet, about 4lb in weight, and foul-hooked near the dorsal fin. Back to my starting point, and I quickly hooked another. Again, I had no chance of holding the strong fish against the current, and had to follow it down to the sea. While I was playing this fish I heard a shout from Henry. He too was playing a fish which, while it fought well on trout tackle, did not force him to move from his casting position. A bass of just under a pound was brought to hand and released. So this was what the mysterious night-fisherman had been catching! Henry and I went on to catch twenty or thirty small bass between us in a couple of hours. No more mullet, and no sea-trout!

Thereafter I spent many summer nights flyfishing in the salt, and frequently met the man with the big rod. He was an elderly gentleman who had been flyfishing in the sea for over sixty years. He had many tales of large bags of bass, and of individual fish of twelve pounds and more. His flies were simple, and very effective. Half a dozen white hackles from a cock's neck were lashed, fairly crudely, to a treble-hook. This caught plenty of bass, and, although he did not admit it, I suspect that it also put an occasional bonus foul-hooked mullet into the bag.

Bass suffered a sad decline during the 1980's, and for a while my saltwater fishing was reduced to one or two evenings a year. However, the mid 1990's have been better, with large numbers of small bass present from mid-summer right through until November. The last few years have provided some interesting fishing, with mixed bags of bass, mackerel, horse-mackerel and garfish. Mullet and sea-trout, flounders and garfish, are almost always present on this coast during the summer, and while bass and mackerel provide the bulk of the flyfishing sport here, these other species provide a great challenge.

PART II
SEA -TROUT

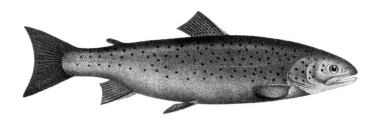

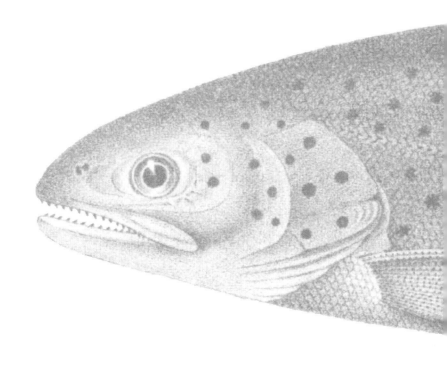

5

SEA-TROUT IN ORKNEY

Stan Headley

The fish and its environment

In Great Britain, the art of hunting (I use both words advisedly) sea-trout in the sea is very localised, being practised almost exclusively in Orkney and Shetland. Both these counties, in the far north of Scotland, are archipelagos with wide shallow bays - perfect habitats for inter-tidal roaming sea-trout shoals. With virtually nothing closely approximating a river, fish can be taken from freshwater lochs with sea-burns at the back-end of the season. But for the best and most predictable (if one can use such a word to describe anything connected with sea-trout) sport one most look for the fish where it hunts and feeds, namely in the sea. If an angler from either of these counties plans sea-trout fishing, rest assured he will be thinking of the sea.

Sea-trout love shallow water, and the bays of Orkney and Shetland are wide and shallow, where the ebbing tides reveal vast expanses of rich feeding ground, and the flowing tides race in to reclaim them. Shallow water supports most of the preferred food of the fish - gammarid shrimp, sand-eels and many other forms of crustaceans and inter-tidal fish - and where the feeding is good the fish will stay, and be exploitable by the wading angler. In other, more southern, areas where fish must move off-shore to feed, sea-trout fishing in the sea is largely a waste of time and effort. The one drawback to this scenario is that fish which are almost totally inter-tidal feeders do not attain great size. A five pound fish from such environments can be considered big, although specimens of much greater size do occur from time to time. Shallow-water feeding may not supply the means to achieve great size, but the living is easy, and security from predators, a major factor in habitat selection, is greater.

From August to April, shoals of fish inhabit the bays and are, to a greater or lesser extent, readily available to the flyfisherman. Out-with this period, little fishing is done in the sea. Fish may still be found, but blank trips will greatly out-number successful ones, and the increased growth of saltwater weed in the shallow waters can make fly fishing a nightmare. I also suspect that, due to higher summer temperatures, inter-tidal waters often attain temperatures unacceptable to the fish, forcing them to hold to cooler, deeper reaches.

Sea-trout are migratory brown trout which go to sea for one reason and one reason only. In the rich feeding grounds of the inter-tidal marine environment the ability to attain quick weight-gain is greater than in the alternative freshwater habitats. In simpler terms, the fish are there to feed, and feed hard. On their return to freshwater sea-trout are rarely, if ever, to be found in a feeding mode and can be hard to tempt. In the sea the job is simpler. The hard task is locating the fish. Great expanses of shoreline may hold a few well-defined shoals of fish, and the successful angler will be one whose skills are not in casting or lure selection, but in recognising areas where success is assured. The angler who can spot fish holding areas at varying tidal states, approach very timid and flighty fish without betraying his presence, and then practice flyfishing skills over the unsuspecting, feeding fish will do well. But the highly competent caster with all the best gear will invariably fail, and fail miserably, if he cannot locate the one area in miles of shoreline which holds his quarry.

Locating the fish

No two good holding-areas are identical but they will contain enough points of similarity to betray themselves to the hunter of sea-trout. Gradually shelving beaches of shingle giving way to sand with variable amounts of sheltering weed are the norm. Bare sand beaches rarely provide good sport because, although they may support large quantities of food in the form of gammarid shrimp and sand-eels, they totally lack cover for the fish, and they are open to attack from above and below. Shoal fish of modest size can sometimes be found patrolling these areas, but the larger more solitary fish prefer to hunt from cover. They are most often to be found lying on the edges of weed-beds or beside rocky outcrops waiting for their prey to come to them. The larger the fish, the fewer make up the shoal. Indeed they are often solitary in their habits.

Many anglers look for streams of freshwater entering the sea as indicators of fish location. (There is no argument that freshwater streams do attract fish) but such locations are better for back-end sport, when fish are undergoing acclimatisation prior to spawning runs. At other times small or modestly sized fish can be found in such areas, but bigger than average fish are frequently found in areas miles from any substantial freshwater influx. Big fish are also often found in micro-environments which usually have all the features of the big, open bays, but are microscopic in comparison and commonly hedged in by great tracts of fore-shore which are definitely not holding ground. These micro-environments are difficult to find and require many hours and miles of diligent searching to locate.

Only the most detailed maps identify them and it will take a trained eye to 'pick the wheat from the chaff'. But the effort contains its own rewards.

My favoured method of locating new ground and finding fish is to select a five or six kilometre stretch of shoreline, and walk and fish every inch of it. The success rate of this method is high, but then so is the time, energy and sweat lost.

Of course, because sea-trout are so highly mobile, drifting along the coast-line as the tide ebbs and flows, one may continually be in the right place at the wrong time, and I suspect that only resting, feeding fish will 'take'. Fish on the move from point A to point B will pass unnoticed by the angler. Waiting for fish to arrive in a known resting place has never been a ploy of mine, but it does have its adherents who undoubtedly have a greater degree of patience than I.

Once a location is selected, step-and-cast is the favoured way to search for the fish. Try to avoid repeatedly casting into areas where no response is forthcoming, but keep on the move. It is a prospecting style of fishing - if the fish are there, they will show some response to the fly, so keep walking, casting and looking. Open water over sand, or lacking any form of cover, is worthy of only cursory attention, but the edges of weed-beds, rocky outcrops, or promontories jutting out into the water, require attentive inspection. Any area that shows dark through the water is a likely holding place.

It is important to stress that sea-trout are addicted to shallow water. It is, in my experience, most unusual to find them in water above 2 metres in depth. If the angler is wading in knee-depth water with a parallel-to or on-shore wind his quarry will likely lie between him and the shoreline. And very often in water which is only just capable of covering their backs. With an off-shore wind, fish may lie 'well off', and be spooky and difficult to seduce.

Precise location, at all times, is largely governed by security from aquatic predators, availability of food, and topographic features such as rock ridges, weed-beds or troughs. Over a flat, even, beach (sometimes referred to as a 'clean' beach) I tend to fan-cast, searching for a holding depth - the first cast dropping the fly within centimetres of the dry stones, the next to cover water of about calf-depth, the last out over water which is verging on being too deep. Once the holding depth has been identified, I narrow my angle of coverage dramatically, and will expect all fish to lie within a very narrow band along the identified depth. On 'clean' beaches fish are often well-distributed. However, when fishing a beach which has a multitude of significant holding features (such as isolated weed-beds, rock formations, or troughs - a 'dirty' beach) it is better to approach each one and fish as though expecting a fish to lie anywhere in or around the feature. 'Dirty' beach fish tend to hold to such features and be extremely localised.

A useful rule-of-thumb in the art of sea-trout location is that they tend to be found in the centre of a bay at high tide levels and out on the extremities at low tide. Putting it more simply, if one assumes that a typical bay is U-shaped, then fish will be on the curve of the U at high tide, and at one or other ends of the straight uprights when the tide is low. To identify which side of the bay the fish are most likely inhabiting at low water, select the one which has the wind on-shore. Put in words this may appear confusing, but in practice it quickly becomes obvious.

Tide, wind and wave

Once a likely holding area has been located the observance of some simple rules will improve success rates. Wind direction is critical. Even when fish are present, an off-shore wind will make their capture unlikely. On-shore winds, or winds blowing parallel to the shore, are essential. Ignore the bay where a large expanse of glassy-calm extends out from the beach. Remember that sea-trout are amongst nature's 'spookiest' creatures, and some degree of wave-action and noise will cover the approach of feet and flyline. Fish will also tend to lie head into the wind/wave, and tend to be found towards the tail of the wind, where the wave action is most extreme. Presumably some degree of cover is provided by wave-action, which also tends to uncover food-items. Fish lying in wave disturbance will swim up to the anglers immersed legs, whilst fish in calm water will not be approached at all.

Always start at the up-wind side of a stretch of water to be fished. Sea-trout are unlikely to be lying in this region, but:

1) It gives the angler the opportunity to enter the water without scaring fish.
2) By the time the fish are within range the angler will be fishing well, have developed a rhythm to suit the wind and wave-action, and will be in tune with the whole environment.
3) Any noise associated with the wading process will have developed slowly and will, hopefully, be ignored by the fish.
4) Fish lying head into the wind/wave are best approached from an up-wind direction. To blunder into a shoal from behind will guarantee their speedy departure from the scene.
5) Casting down the wind allows first contact to made on a long line, denying the fish any hint of danger.

Although it is usual to advise inexperienced anglers never to step into water that they haven't yet fished, I have such a strong liking for on-shore winds that I habitually ignore this rule. That is why I always try to enter the water at least 50 metres up-wind of where I expect to find fish.

Tidal flow is a lesser feature than wind effect, but can be important. Again fish tend to lie head-into the flow, and a decent turmoil caused by tidal flow may compensate for lack of wind. In Orkney there are only a few places where tidal stream of such proportions exist, but these rare features are excellent places to locate feeding fish, particularly when tide and wind direction are opposed.

Day-to-day state of tide is more important to the fish but difficult for the angler to understand or turn to his advantage. On the full and new moons the biggest tidal movements take place, commonly known as 'spring' tides. During the waxing and waning moons occur the 'neap' tides, times of slack tides. Tidal movement during 'springs' is dramatic, with great tracks of inter-tidal ground affected. During 'neaps' the tidal range may be minimal. Sea-trout tend to be very active during 'springs', but continually on the move and difficult to 'nail down'. During 'neaps' they move more slowly and, when found, can be relied on to hang about for some time, all things being equal. The ranks of sea-trout-in-the-sea anglers are split between 'spring-tiders' and 'neap-tiders'.

I am of the latter persuasion, probably because my tendency to walk and fish long stretches of coastline responds better to times of 'neaps'. Those who like to fish known areas and await the arrival of their prey tend to prefer 'springs'.

Techniques and tackle

The actual fishing technique is very basic fly fishing. Single fly is preferred due to the ubiquitous weed, which is a vital component of sea-trout marks. Powerful leaders capable of controlling or 'bullying' heavy fish amongst wrack-beds are essential, and short steeply-tapered rods with an AFTM 7 rating are advisable for similar reasons, although longer rods do provide the ability to 'get above' the fish and steer it away from obstructions.

I normally prefer to use intermediate or slow-sinking lines because saltwater is very buoyant and flies skating on the surface will not normally be accepted. Flies tied on heavy, corrosion-resistant hooks are recommended for obvious reasons. Big flies tend to catch big fish and, although small fish will chase and bump them, one rarely has the unwelcome task of removing such unwanted fish from a suitably-sized iron.

Reel choice is subjective, and should you wish to purchase a hi-tech, state of the art, kings-ransom type of saltwater reel, then feel free. I tend to use cheap, nasty, 'line reservoirs' which gradually fade away, unmourned, under the influence of salt and hard rock. A good sea-trout may, occasionally, run 40 metres, but this is the exception rather than the rule, so drag-free systems are not essential.

My preferred hook sizes are longshank 8's and 6's. Pattern isn't particularly important, although lately I have found that fur-strip patterns are remarkably effective, probably due to their mobility factor. Colour choices include orange, black, white, red and , to a lesser extent, blue. Bodies of tinsel are 'de rigeur'. The simple factor inherent in pattern choice is visibility - stark or bright flies are almost always best. Orange, black and red work best in poor light conditions whilst white and blue are often very successful in bright sunshine.

I like to fish a fast fly as this tends to make fish show their presence. But the down-side of this technique is that the fish may sometimes be suspicious of a fast fly and though they will 'show', may not 'take'. But big flies are usually best fished with a degree of pace and when big fish decide to take an interest they almost always 'follow through' to the satisfaction of the angler.

Best times

Sea-trout are present as feeding fish in the sea right through the year. But, unfortunately, during the period 1st November - 24th February, inclusive, we are restrained from pursuing the fish by law. This law was designed to protect spawning fish in freshwater, but it (perhaps unintentionally) also covers 'maiden' fish in saltwater, which will not spawn until the following winter, and fish which have successfully spawned and have returned to the salt (often erroneously referred to as 'kelts'). The protection of 'maidens' during mid-winter months is unfortunate from a fishing point of view, but perhaps advisable from a conservation perspective.

The most productive months for sport are March, April, September and October. Spring fish are hard-feeding fish, and co-operate well with the flyfisherman during this period. Fish are also well distributed at this time of year, and weed isn't so much of a problem, the winter gales having decimated the inter-tidal growth.

In Autumn, weed growth is a problem and the fish don't help by being more concerned with reproduction than feeding. Large gatherings of fish can be found now, but they can be the very devil to tempt. A Spring fish found is usually a fish caught but in the 'back-end' it is not uncommon to have a very low catch rate whilst being amongst fish all day.

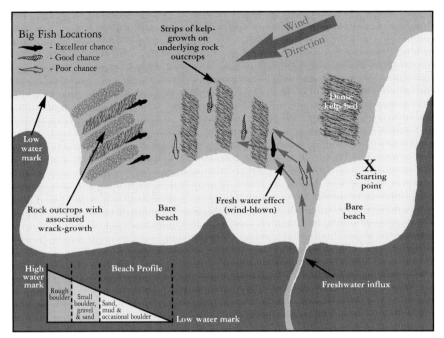

Sea trout bay at low-water

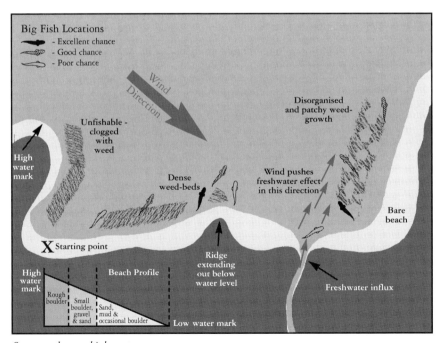

Sea trout bay at high-water

During the best months, as identified above, daylight work is most productive. The tendency shown by river sea-trout to be more catchable in the darkness hours is not applicable in the sea. Most gamefish are put-off by bright sunshine but, in my experience, this again does not seem applicable to saltwater trout. Of course this could be due to the low angle of the sun in the late and early months of the year when this sport is most often successful.

And in conclusion . . .

Don't for a moment assume that sea-trout fishing in the sea is an easy method by which to catch this most beautiful of gamefish. Admittedly, odd occasions can occur when hordes of quality fish compete aggressively for the honour of impaling themselves on the fly. But more often than not the other side of the coin can see the angler disappointed, disillusioned, and totally bewildered. Day after day passes without sign of fish, and all the 'fail-never' spots are unaccountably deserted. Whether in salt or fresh, the sea-trout has ever been a fish of mystery, its coming and goings beyond the 'ken' of common man. But when a specimen sized sea-trout is taken from a remote wilderness mark, from the vast expanses of the sea, the sense of achievement, the feeling of having overcome almost impossible odds, is second to no other.

If you are the type of angler who demands a return commensurate with effort and expenditure, manicured lawns leading to the waterside, and the proximity of civilisation as a convenient bolt-hole - stay away from the sea, it is not for you. But if you revel in solitude, love to walk the wild places, and have an element of the explorer/trail-blazer in your make-up you may find that salty sea-trout are the stuff of dreams.

6

SEA-TROUT IN THE BALTIC

Martin Jørgensen

The key to success in the pursuit of sea-trout in saltwater on the coasts of the Baltic Sea is understanding some important aspects of the trout's behaviour in respect to the seasonal changes. The sea-trout in saltwater cannot be fished for in the same way all through the year. Some key factors here are water temperature, sea-currents, the wind and the trout's migratory patterns.

A brief (natural) history

This text will discuss fishing in the Baltic area - which includes the coasts of Denmark, Germany and part of Sweden. It also covers Poland, the Eastern Baltic countries and Finland although sea-trout fishing in the salt is rarely heard of in these countries. Of the countries mentioned, Denmark has the longest tradition of flyfishing for saltwater trout, and many of the ideas and tactics used in the whole area come from Denmark. Sea-trout fishing in other parts of Europe will probably differ from this in several important areas, although much of the advice given here will be applicable in other waters.

The brown trout, Salmo trutta, has several different life-patterns. Perhaps the commonest is the well-known stream-dwelling type, where the fish will reside in a stream or river for its whole life, only moving short distances to spawn. Other types make longer spawning migrations into running water, but are significantly different because the fish live most of their lives in either a lake - becoming a lake-trout - or in the sea - becoming a sea-trout. Genetically there is no difference between the three types.

The sea-trout begins its life as other trout, in a stream, but will migrate to sea after its first year. The trout will typically stay in the sea for a couple of years before, one autumn, returning to its stream of birth to spawn. It will then stay in the stream, or the estuary, during the winter, and return to the sea in the early spring to feed during the summer and early autumn.

In this period the majority of the sea-trout will stay close to the shore-line in shallow areas, making them suitable game for the flyfisher. Changes in their environment will make them move on, or stay in certain areas, but generally they will be close enough to catch on a fly.

Mature fish will occasionally skip spawning, and stay in the sea to eat all winter. Because of physiological circumstances, the fish cannot stay on the open coasts when the water gets too cold, but have to find either warmer water or water with less salinity.

Like trout elsewhere in the world, the Baltic sea-trout have too few quality streams in which to spawn, and probably would not be able to maintain their high populations naturally. However, thanks to extensive stocking in streams and in the ocean, these fish are quite abundant. The larger and older fish are rare, though, mostly because they stay longer in the streams and then migrate into the deeper parts of the ocean to feed on pelagic fish.

Fish caught near the coast will typically range from 1 kilo (1-2 lb) up to 5 kilos (10 lb). The sea-trout will grow to 10-15 kilos and even more, but catching such a fish on fly in the sea is very unlikely - albeit not impossible. Notice that many countries have size-limits. In Denmark it is 40 cm (16”) and in Sweden 50 cm (20”).

What and how sea-trout eat

The trout that live close to the coast feed on large numbers of quite small animals. Their diet is a combination of small crustaceans like gammarid shrimps, shrimps, fry, small fish like sculpins, sticklebacks, sand-eels, and different worms.

Sea-trout are fierce and avid hunters that move swiftly in the water and have very keen senses: smell, sight and pressure, sensed with the lateral-line.

They will also sometimes browse the vegetation, stirring out small animals, or they may rest near the bottom in still or moving water, and attack prey passing by. Like trout in running water, sea-trout are more alert and cautious in calm quiet water, and more reckless and aggressive in turbulent water. This can be used to the advantage of the angler in his choice of tactics and tackle.

What tackle to use

7-8 weight, 9 or 9 1/2’ single-handed tackle is considered ideal by most sea-trout fishers. You can easily do with lighter tackle on calm days as most fish are fairly small, but in order to overcome wind and other tough conditions it can be necessary to go up in weight. The typical American salt-water tackle, encompassing 10-12 wt. single-handed rods, is a vast overkill, both in regard to conditions and to the size of the fish.

The line of choice is a floating line - either a weight-forward or a shoot-

ing-head combination. Some conditions may call for a sink-tip or intermediate line, but if you are limited to one line it should be a floater.

Contrary to what most people think, casting distance isn't crucial here.
But, if you use a shooting head set-up you can expand your range and -
not least - feel that you are covering enough water.

Leaders can be anything from 2-6 metres (6-18'), depending on conditions. The tippet could be anything from 0.18 mm (4X) to 0.28 (0X)
again depending on the fly, tackle and conditions. Normally a 0.20-0.23
mm (2X or 3X) tippet would suffice.

No matter what type of rod and reel you use you should bear in mind
that you are fishing in salt-water and that the salt will eventually ruin all
of your tackle - even the salt-resistant gear - if you do not take care.

What flies to use

If you have the choice of one single fly, choose a black or grey Woolly
Bugger, size 6. This fly represents the stem of many of the most successful flies for sea-trout in salt-water.

The variations in flies are of course endless. Most patterns are fairly simple and robust, and almost any shrimp, fry or streamer-pattern in the size
range 2-12 will be a potential salt-water sea-trout fly.

Again, do not be led astray by the American way of doing things. Their
large, colourful flies are meant for a totally different kind of fishing, for
different species and sizes of fish. A few patterns will be useful in scaled-
down versions, but on the average these flies are both too large and too
flashy. A better choice will be traditional sea-trout flies meant for stream
use. But have them tied in smaller sizes and on single hooks. The best
advice is to buy your flies locally and heed the advice - and generosity - of
local flyfishers. If you are a fly-tyer, try to get your hands on some patterns
to copy.

All flies, no matter what source, should be tied on stainless or salt-
water-resistant hooks, as a single day in - or even near - salt-water will
stain and eventually ruin any fly tied on a normal fresh-water hook.

The seasons and the tactics

As in other kinds of fishing, the hunt for sea-trout varies greatly through
the year. But unlike many other kinds of fishing, there is no low-season or
high-season. The fishing can be almost equally good all year round except,
maybe, for the hottest weeks of the summer and the coldest weeks of cold
winters. In the winter the fish will be most active in sunshine, and in the
summer most active at night. Spring and autumn fishing is best in the
mornings and evenings.

Spring: - March, April, May

In spring the fish are beginning to eat again. The spawned fish return to the sea, and all fish leave the fjords. The fish are hungry at this time, and very willing to eat large bait, such as sand eels and small herring. They will eat everything as long as it's big enough. These large food-items are most easily imitated with lures and spinning-baits. So flies aren't always the best, even though larger lures, shrimps and streamers of different kinds can lure many fish. For those not fishing flies, the spring is probably the best season. Fly-fishing gets better as the water warms, and can be good on sunny days, even in January. In the early spring fishing can be at its best in the middle of the day, but later on, in April and May, the action is early morning and evening. You can start out fishing the fjord and estuary areas in January and March, and then move out to the open coasts as the water gets warmer. Fish will go for large flies; zonkers, streamers, silvery flies etc.

In early spring it is best to fish shallow waters with a dark bottom As temperatures rise, deeper water with a sandy bottom will also fish well. The fish are very fast, taking the fly with a bang. They almost always hook themselves, and fight very hard. A large proportion of sea-trout caught at this time must be released because of their poor, post-spawning, condition. If you want to keep fish, keep only those that are pure silver with loose scales.

Summer: - June, July, August

Summer fishing can be more difficult, and late evenings and nights, when the water cools off, are best. The fish do not move around so much now, but often stay in small areas. You have to fish these areas, which typically have deep water close to the shore and plenty of circulation. In the high summer in years when water temperatures are extremely high, the fish won't even come close enough to the shore to reach by wading.

Fish can be very active in the surface and muddlers are an old-time favourite, but other bushy, highly profiled flies will also catch. For the darkest night a bit of flash can make many patterns more efficient.

Water movement is the key. In the summer, coastal points and reefs below the surface are the places to seek. Fish in the "back water" meaning behind the reef that you'll often see below points on the shore. If the current goes right, fish on the right side and vice versa.

The fish are more shy now than in the spring. They will often nibble the flies and follow without taking. However, they offer excellent sport, and drilling a large trout in the dark night can really get your heart pounding. Summer is the skilled and patient fisherman's season.

Autumn: - September, October, November

Autumn is the ideal time for catching top-condition fish; mornings, days and evenings. The fish are typically stuffed with the smallest animals, and small brown/gray flies are therefore best. If the fish do not react to these small flies a good wildcard can be to switch to a huge, colourful fly like a large Mickey Finn. You will occasionally run into large schools of fish, which you either see, or notice by catching several trout in a row. Try to stay with them while they are moving.

Autumn fish can be picky and difficult, but sport is even better than in the summer, and the beautiful, silvery, well-conditioned sea-trout are the best table-fish of the year. But note that all coloured fish should be released as they are on their spawning-run.

Temperatures are dropping, and when the water is between 6-12 degrees Centigrade, fishing is at its best. Fish will swim very close to the shore, and you should always fish before you wade. Fish can typically be everywhere, not only in fjords or places with good currents, but also on open, sandy beaches because they are migrating towards their spawning streams.

Winter: - December, January, February.

In the real cold winter, the trout has to seek freshwater because it can't tolerate salt due to difficulties with osmotic regulation. Hence the fish are found in streams, estuaries and brackish fjords. For the salt-water fisher, the fjords and shallow waters can offer good fishing in the winter.

The fish don't eat much and move very slowly, but even with ice on the shore, the fish often go for flashy, happy-coloured (red/orange/purple), deeply-fished, slowly retrieved flies. This is the time of year to use a sink-tip or sinking line. The fishing is best on mild and sunny days in shallow water over a dark bottom.

It can be a good idea to observe where there are fresh-water currents from streams or other outlets. At the same time be aware that fishing for trout may be prohibited in and near estuaries, and in some countries on the whole coast, in the winter.

Wind

The wind has a strong influence on the behaviour of the water, its temperature and the activity of food-organisms and trout. The following illustrations all show the situation when a wind is blowing off-shore in the four seasons, and show how water will be moved and affect the temperature.

On-shore wind will rarely have the same influence as offshore wind because the wind will only stir the waters close to the shore, and not move it very much. Stronger winds might move in surface-water from further out, but as this surface-water will often be the same temperature as the inshore surface-water, the overall effect on temperature is relatively small.

But... and there's a big but, onshore wind will stir the shallow water and bring lots of food and debris in suspension. This makes the water unclear and full of food, and can mean ideal conditions for hunting fish.

Most fishers will prefer offshore winds, with the wind at their back, but some people routinely choose onshore wind - and catch a lot of fish.

7

SEA-TROUT IN NORWAY

Jan Hansen

On Thursday, 30th September, 1993, the following article was posted to the flyfishing discussion list known to the internet community as simply @flyfish. (This was back in the old days when there was only some twenty messages here a day).

Subject: Silver and black
"Last night the full moon light made my path to where the river runs easy trod. There, a few good casts of line from where the river meets the sea, a thiny whinkcle on the silent moving water tells whoever listens that there, a few inches down in the dark, one of the beauties of nature might very well reside.

One cast, then another - the dark and silvery waters explodes as the beauty fights for life. Ten minutes later the sea-trout of my life are in my hands shivering.

Never being easy, I kill it for bringing home to eat together with someone I love, (but who I dont kill and eat).

Jan?.."

The cold facts were these; the sea-trout weighed 4.4 lb, the fly was a Montana with a half-inch black marabou tail, on a Partridge double low-water hook (size 8, or was it 10).

Another article - 1st June, 1994:
"A few days ago I went fishing for sea-trout in the tidal waters of a local river-outlet. Fishing had started bad this spring, very few offers - in fact only one fish pr. third trip, no one big. I fished all evening without a stroke. Before going home I felt the need to try a "hole" of mine although a bit tired and unconsentrated. All darkness or at least the kind of darkness you can achieve in Norway in early summer. A serious drag followed by strong splashing immediately followed the fly meeting the currents. A short fight after, the fly let loose as the fish was safe in my net. The fish was a beautiful sea-trout, they are all beautiful, at a weight of 5 lb."

Although there is something very special about fishing in the dark, both in the sea and in the countryside, this is not necessarily the most productive way for the sea-trout all year round. During the cold winter the fish can be considerably more active on sunny days. Also, it does not seem to have as much of its famous spookiness at this time as when actually entering the rivers later in the autumn.

The histories above have taken place at the same spot. Some of the best-known places for sea-trout fishing are in more-or-less brackish areas. The sea-trout seem to wander between brackish estuaries and more salty areas continuously through the year. At temperatures below 10 degrees C. the sea-trout is often found near the beach, whilst it tends to move out as temperatures rise in the spring.

Finding the right place to fish is really not too difficult. Any place with a good current, often provided by a combination of changing tides and the everlasting coastal currents, will do. If these places are not too deep and provide a combination of sand bottom, with huge stones and patches of underwater vegetation, you have got it.

In the southern parts of Norway the best spots are often where a narrow strait leads from the sea to a wide fjord. On changing tides the sea-trout take a stand in the currents in these places.

While fishing during the winter it is necessary to observe the water temperature to decide whether to fish the surface or put on a sinking line to go deeper. If water temperature falls below 6 degrees C. the fish tends to be moving down. With regard to the colours of flies, Asgeir has done consistent research over a few years and has found reliable connections between colour and success for many species.

This is the key regarding sea-trout flies and temperature:

Below 6 degrees C. white flies work best.
Between 6 and 9 degrees C. use a combination of orange, yellow and green.
Around 10 degrees the colour should be red.
When temperatures rise over 10-12 degrees more natural colours matching the imitation should be used.
Night fishing starts as the sea temperature rise above 14-15 degrees, and with it follows the use of black flies.
At scarce light conditions/cloudy weather, a bit of silver will bring more attraction.
Asgeir makes much use of his own 'Dog Nobbler' whilst I make much use of my own 'Silvers fancy'.

The origin of the flyfishing in the sea tradition is from the areas of south of Norway including Oslofjorden, right outside the capital city of Norway. Oslofjorden is a magnificent area, with several reports of fish above 5 kilos caught on a fly during the last few years. Other species commonly caught here are cod, pollack and coalfish and now and then a garfish, mackerel, or herring.

The sea-trout will, contrary to the salmon, enter tiny streams to spawn, and almost any stream can give life to a small stock of sea-trout. This is probably one of the reasons that sea-trout are so widespread, and so popular with Norwegian saltwater flyfishers.

8

SEA-TROUT ON SKYE - 1960

Stephen Johnson

Every experienced fisherman has one particular place which means more to him than any other; he has one kind of fish which he prefers to fish for. My place is the island of Skye, my fish the sea-trout.

You fish for them with trout tackle, and you may hook one of any weight from ¹/₂lb. to 12lb. The uncertainty is much of the fascination. But whatever their size they play better for it than a salmon. When you hook one he is off with a tremendous rush, usually ending with a jump. You then see the prize, perhaps the most beautiful silvery fish there is, and the thrill is on. He will fight to the very dregs of endurance, and at the last moment the hook may come away if you pull too hard in your excitement, for his mouth is soft.

Sea-trout on the west coast of Scotland only go to the sea for a short time each year. During the winter, after spawning, they hibernate, as do brown trout in northern rivers where there is no food to be found. In the spring, when natural food in the water increases, they are stimulated to go and look for more in the sea. It is then that spates are needed so they can reach the sea and start getting in condition. The annual growth rate in Skye is about one pound per year. If there is no rain in the late spring you may still catch kelts in the lochs in July, and others at the river mouth where they are feeding like mad trying to make up for lost time; but this seldom happens, for there is usually plenty of rain in Skye.

When they get to the sea they don't go far away from their rivers. They are not caught in the bag nets off the coast of Skye and they suffer no dangers from the Greenland coastal fishermen or the deep-water drift netters, and so they will survive in quantity when salmon become scarce.

When they make back towards their rivers and lochs they continue to feed in the estuary while waiting for a spate, and they feed also throughout the autumn in fresh water. This means that by observation it is possible to predict their taking habits - and catch them.

Sea-trout run up every river and burn round the coast of Britain where there is free access to and from the sea and no pollution. While practically every salmon river has been developed as a fishery, there are still many sea-trout burns which are seldom if ever fished. People will travel to

Norway and pay hundreds of pounds to catch one salmon, and although salmon fishing is less expensive in Britain than in any other country - if you can get hold of it - by comparison sea-trout fishing is still quite ridiculously cheap.

And what of the places where one goes to fish for sea-trout? In pursuit of our sport we see many lovely views, but usually one holds our particular affection and we can recollect every detail of it, smelling the clean fresh air, the scent of bog-myrtle in the sun, the distant tang of the sea. We can hear the absolute silence broken only occasionally by the sound of distant falling water brought on the warm wind, the cry of an oystercatcher or the breaking of a calm sea on a beach. We can walk in imagination on the path to the river and remember every rock, every boggy place and how the scene changes with each step. We can take friends with us, be children again with our parents, or walk with our own children.

Every one of us can find this, his own special place, but nobody has an exclusive right to it. Each place can be shared and hold the yearnings of countless people. I like to think that Camasunary in Skye means much to the many folk who have stayed there in the last 50 years, and I believe this to be so.

But there are many such places to be found by the eager young fishermen of today. There are few roads in the Western Highlands, but many small rivers and burns running through little valleys into the Atlantic. Years ago people lived in these valleys and you will see the ruins of their scattered crofts. Now many of the streams are miles from the nearest road, and if you visit them you will see only sheep and deer and sometimes a shepherd. Rivers by roads are all heavily fished, but many of the remote burns are never visited by a fisherman. Don't expect to be allowed to fish where other people are already doing so, but get a map and explore. Find some remote burn, where it appears that nobody ever goes. You may not have to go very far because as a nation we are losing the use of our legs. Nowadays few people leave a road, and only a tiny percentage of the visitors to the Highlands are interested in fishing.

When you have discovered a possible place, find out to whom the fishing belongs, and after shaving off your beard, if you have one, ask politely for permission to fish there. Also remember that you must always ask permission to camp if you wish to do so.

The older generation like good manners and cleanliness, if they are giving lifts or granting a favour. If you remember this more than likely you will be lucky and receive permission. This may be the last generation with these opportunities; very soon even the lonely Highland valleys may become crowded and developed.

Walking in the Highlands, if you like remoteness and beauty, is a joy in itself. But if you are a fisherman and carry a rod, with a purpose, it adds a spring to the step which eats up the miles tirelessly. The first visit to a new stream is perhaps the most exciting, but there is great pleasure in revisiting a known place. You will get to know it under all weather conditions and at different heights of water. Gradually your knowledge of where and how to fish will increase, and with it your chances of success.

Perhaps you will leave your car on a remote track and walk some way before the sea comes into sight. A tiny burn will join you on your journey, trickling among its pebbles. As you continue on your way other little burns will add their waters to it, the valley will widen and the heather beneath your feet will give way to green grass and rushes.

As you get nearer the sea there will be a few small, deep pools joined by trickles of water in fine weather, or by rushing torrents in a spate. When the river is low the surface of the pools will be calm but for the ruffle of the wind, and even under these conditions, if there are sea-trout, they can be caught there. If nobody else has fished for them, the chance of success is much better.

In fine weather and low water there is a place you should investigate before you start fishing the river: go right down to the mouth of your burn, and look at the sea. If you have had a long hot walk you will need a rest, so sit down for five or ten minutes and do the same as the thousands of holiday makers on England's crowded beaches, gaze out to sea. The only difference is that you will be looking for something.

If the tide is out there will be a stretch of shingle and a fringe of floating seaweed between you and the water. At first the sea is confined by rocks, cliffs and headlands, then it escapes and stretches away to distant blue islands and the infinite horizon. Let all this unspoilt and beautiful scene, which the old inhabitants must have loved so well, flood over you, but just keep an eye on the sea immediately beyond the fringe of seaweed. Quite soon you may see a sea-trout, and another jump within casting distance. For a while the scenery must become a background to your conscious thoughts.

You really need waders, but on your first visit you won't have any, Take off all your clothes below the waist, roll up your shirt tails and under your woolly, put your shoes back on your bare feet, and get after those fish. The sea will be much colder than you expect and it will take your breath away as you wade out and it inches its way up over your warm white skin. You will have to wade up to your waist, and as you gradually get deeper there is one moment which is worse than the others. The seaweed feels coarse and rough against the skin; but soon you will be within casting distance of a jumping fish and all else will be forgotten as you get the line out.

Whatever you do, don't try this at the mouth of a prolific and protected river. The owner of the fishery has the exclusive rights of fishing for migratory fish for one mile out to sea. But if you have permission to fish a burn or river this will include fishing in the sea. Quite a few people fish for sea-trout in estuaries, but not many fish actually in the open sea. It can be the most exciting and rewarding place to fish, but here sea-trout are unpredictable in their feeding habits, and they alter from year to year. This is because the food pattern in the sea constantly changes. To become successful, observation on many occasions over the years is of the greatest assistance. You also need much practical experience of success and failure with various lures and baits under many different conditions before you can make the most of your opportunities. I hope you are lucky on the first occasion, for this will encourage you to continue.

At Camasunary, in Skye, the shoals of sea-trout congregate at the river mouth from the end of June onwards. If there are frequent spates you don't see very many as they run up the river at once, but after a week's dry weather you see them jumping in large numbers. At first most of the fish are big ones and you seldom see finnocks in any quantity until after July 20th; from then on the majority of fish which collect in the bay are finnocks, although there are a few larger fish as well. They keep in shoals during the day. The average weight of the fish varies from shoal to shoal, the bigger fish seeming to keep together as do the rather smaller ones. They are most likely to take when they have newly arrived in the bay and are still feeding hungrily on the small fry which often come close in shore in their millions when the weather is warm and settled. The longer they have to hang about waiting for a spate, the less easy they are to catch. Nor will they wait about indefinitely. After a while the whole lot can leave the bay for several days but they will probably reappear on the next spring tide and certainly if there is a spate.

At high tide they will often penetrate as far up the tidal part of a river as they can swim. They are most likely to do this in the evening on a spring tide when they have newly arrived. Here they will be very concentrated, and easily covered from the bank, but although you cast a fly over a great many fish they can be disappointing takers. They are thinking of running, not feeding, when the enter the river mouth.

At high tide the fish move very little and you seldom rise anything. When it starts to ebb strongly the fish will drop back and others may even appear. If you cast over them they may follow the fly, and occasionally one will take, but it is usually a small one.

Once they get out to sea again they will think of feeding, and start taking. I prefer to fish the flood from about an hour after low tide for the next two hours, or the ebb at about half tide. But fish are always unpredictable in the sea, and you must keep an eye on the water at all times. If you spot them jumping, go and fish for them at once; they may hang around for an hour or so, but are unlikely to do so for much longer.

I remember one evening, just after high tide, when great numbers of fish appeared practically in the surf off a sandy beach. Some were quite red from waiting to run up, when normally they are bad takers. Many were within easy cast from the shoe without wading, and they took a fly surprisingly well. Sport was fast and furious for a while.

If you keep watching a bay you will notice after a while that there are one or two places where fish seem to appear most frequently. These are the places you should fish. Don't try to pursue a shoal if it is jumping out of reach. Wade out into position within cast of where they most often jump, and wait for them to come to you. Try a cast from time to time even if nothing is showing, but don't tire yourself by fishing all the time. A shoal of sea-trout practically always gives away its presence by one or two jumping, if it is near enough to the surface to be interested in a fly.

During the day at Camasunary the fish usually congregate over the shingle off the mouth of the main river, and off the mouth of a burn at the other side of the bay. These two spits of shingle are joined by a crescent of sand some three hundred yards long. If you wade out as far as you can, fish often come within reach. You need long waders and you mustn't forget the tide.

I lent Michael a rather doubtful looking pair of waders last summer, which had been left behind by Bobby. He waded boldly out into the sea and started fishing. About half an hour later there was an awful yell: 'Stevie, these bloody waders of your leak'. I thought it strange that they should start leaking so suddenly and said so. A minute later rather a contrite voice said, 'Oh, hell, the tide has come in over the top'. He had done a Canute.

It is probably better to fish from a boat, if you can get hold of one. You don't then have the feeling that the fish are always just out of reach, which all fishermen know so well. If you are alone, anchor yourself in about 5 or 6 feet of water and in the centre of the spot where the fish show most frequently. It is terribly exciting when you are in position and see a shoal coming towards you. You can tell which way they are going by the way they are facing when they jump.

Now comes the question, how and with what should you fish?

It is always great fun experimenting when fishing, and I never cease to do so. Over the years when fishing for sea-trout in the sea I have tried practically every spinning bait, lure and fly that has ever been invented. The spinning baits I like best are a blue and silver minnow and a small Mepps spoon, but the latter is very light and consequently difficult to cast into a wind. When you fish for sea-trout with a spinning bait, you seem to hook a smaller percentage of the offers you get than when fishing with a fly or non-spinning lure. You also lose more of the fish that you do manage to hook.

I now believe that the best thing to fish with, from the point of view of catching the most fish, is a fly rod, a floating line and a three hooked silver lure. But if you cover a number of fish and none take the least notice it is well worth trying a spinner; it does sometimes catch a fish when a fly won't. Half the secret of success is to get whatever you are fishing with over a shoal of fish without delay, because they don't stay in reach for long. In this respect a spinning rod is a disadvantage. If a large fish jumps within reach, but in another direction from you last cast, it takes some time to reel right in and cast again. In the excitement of the moment I am usually hopelessly inaccurate when casting a light bait with a spinning rod. With a fly you can whip it off the water and smack it down on the fish's nose in a second.

Any silver-bodied fly like a Butcher or a Teal and Silver will catch fish. A sole-skin lure was very effective at one time. When the fish have been particularly tiresome, I have even tried tying a piece of the skin from a sea-trout's stomach to hooks, thinking that perhaps if it smelt of fish the sea-trout might take, rather than just follow it. It didn't make the smallest difference and was difficult to attach securely to a hook with tying silk.

The lure I now use is very simple and effective. It consists of three fairly small and very sharp sea-trout-size hooks whipped one behind the other to nylon; the overall length is about 1in. The hooks are covered with silver tinsel. On the front hook I tie three hackles as a wing; a scarlet one in the centre, flanked by two creamy white ones. Any other combination of hackles or wings can be effective, but I do like a combination of silver with some scarlet. The fly I have described is simple, quickly made, and it looks quite like a small fish in the water.

It helps if you can cast at least 20 yards and keep the fly moving for as long as possible by recovering it to within 5 yards of you. The line has to float in coils on the surface of the sea, or lie on the bottom of the boat, until you shoot it again with the next cast.

If a fish jumps within reach it is almost certainly one member of a shoal of anything between twenty and a hundred sea-trout, so absolute accuracy of casting is unimportant. But try to land the fly just in front of them.

I used to recover the fly very fast, so it would look like a small startled fish trying to escape. This usually evokes a response, and bow waves appear from several directions and converge on your fly. There may follow a savage wrench and a flurry of foam as a fish turns and jumps. But very often there is only a tweak, or the fish follow along a foot or so behind the fly making no attempt to overtake it. You can see them in the clear water when they get close; then they see you and turn away. The next time you cast over that particular lot of fish one or two may show some interest, but they quickly get bored and pay no more attention.

When to strike is a problem if fish are tweaking and turning at your fly. If one misses and you strike you may snatch it out of the mouth of the next one waiting to have a go. One method is to keep the rod top pointing at the fish and go on pulling in the line until one hooks itself. This is all right up to a point, and you will hook more fish up to 2lb. by this method than by keeping the rod high and striking. But one day a 6lb. fish will take and break your 10lb. nylon with a savage tug.

Recently I have been pulling the fly in rather more slowly and steadily, and I believe you hook more fish this way. You don't see those exciting bow waves as the fish chase the fly, yet quite suddenly and unexpectedly there comes a tremendous tug. Fish seem to stalk up on the lure and take it much more firmly. The first time I tried this method was when anchored in a boat by myself off the burn mouth. Not a great many fish were about, although the first one that took; quite unexpectedly there came a wrench at he line and I was into a 4lb. sea-trout. I managed to land him and ten minutes later I hooked one of 6lb. Fortunately he went round and round the boat about 50 yards away, instead of going straight in any one direction. I could never have pulled the anchor up and followed him if he had. Both fish went over the top of lots of seaweed, but sea-trout never go into it deliberately to try to escape. In due course the 6-pounder joined his pal in the bottom of the boat, and a very bonny pair of fish they were. It is always such fun having success all on one's own and returning triumphant to the rest of the party.

I suppose food in the sea is so plentiful for sea-trout that they never need to feed for long to satisfy their hunger, and when they do start feeding your lure may be outnumbered many times by the natural food available. I have often seen a shoal start feeding some distance from the boat, chasing fry all over the surface. It may take two or three minutes to get within casting distance, and by then they have usually stopped. Then quite unexpectedly a day will come when you will be lucky.

One day there was quite a strong off-shore breeze. The sea was the brightest of blue under a clear sky, and the little waves sparkled in the sunshine. We were on our way by boat to Coruisk, but when we saw some fish jumping at the river mouth Michael and I began fishing for them. For once, every fish we cast over meant to have it. On three occasions we were both playing a fish of about 2lb. at the same time. We lost quite a number, but still ended up with eight fish in the boat, which we caught in the half hour before the tide got too low and the fish moved away.

I also like an onshore wind and a bit of a wave. Fish seem to take better, although they are not so easy to spot in a rough sea, also if there is a big sea or swell running they don't seem to come close in - and even if they did I shouldn't be there to fish for them. Never a good sailor, I find that sitting still in a rough sea is quite fatal.

When it is flat calm you can sometimes see a riffle on the surface when a shoal swims close beneath it. You see them dimpling the surface, and this is particularly noticeable in the evening when the light begins to fade. You often see monster fish jump, usually rather far out to sea, but just sometimes within easy reach. Then the excitement is terrific, yet you nearly always seem to hook a smaller one.

I have always felt that sooner or later someone would hook one of the really big ones and eventually Edward did. He wandered down to the shore by himself one evening between tea and supper, while I was chasing rabbits in the park with the dogs. There were a few fish showing so he waded out, cast a fly towards them and immediately hooked a monster. It went off at great speed. He had no control whatever over it, and twice it appeared to be making for the island of Rhum, some 15 miles away. But each time it stopped and turned parallel to the coast when he could see the drum of his reel through the backing. Eventually he had it played and walked it back to the shore. There it lay among the gently breaking little waves, and he pushed it on to dry land with a foot. He appeared at the sitting-room window, highly delighted with himself, carrying a sea-trout which weighed exactly 10lb. - 6lb.was the previous biggest. Shall we one day catch a 12-pounder?

Fishing for sea-trout in the sea is rather a specialised form of angling; nobody should imagine that it is easy. You must be able to cast a long line with speed and accuracy, into a wind if necessary, and strip it in smooth-ly and quickly right up to you. Then you must be able to shoot it all, or let it run when you hook a fish, without standing on it or getting it caught round a projection on the boat. But it is the best possible training for casting for a novice. He will soon be galvanised into becoming an adequate caster by the sheer necessity of the moment.

There is also quite an art in rowing a boat for other people to fish from. if there are two rods, only one must fish at a time. If they both try to cast long lines in any direction, they will become hopelessly entangled behind the boat. If this happens, be sure enormous sea-trout will start jumping all round you. They will be gone by the time the muddle is sorted out, and tempers - even friendships - will be temporarily, if not permanently strained. I like to be at the oars on these occasions. I try to get the fishermen just within reach of a shoal and then row away from it as the fish pursue the fly towards the boat. If one rod hooks a fish the other can come into action and try to catch another fish from the same lot. Sometimes if the boat is close to a large shoal you can come into action and try to catch another fish from the same lot. Sometimes if the boat is close to a large shoal you can order a 'broadside', and both anglers can cast, but they must remember to cast parallel to one another, or give warning if they see a fish jump off the end of the boat, and wish to cast for it. Then the other rod must stop fishing for a moment. The number of fish caught is no measure of the fun and excitement.

Now I find the sea so exciting, and so do Edward and Bob, that we seldom go to the lochs in the evenings if there is any concentration of fish in the bay. We find at Camasunary that the best place to fish in the evenings is off the sandy beach between the river and the burn. There are never any midges when you wade out into the sea even on the calmest evenings.

After a good dinner you put on waders and walk the 200 yards to the sea-shore. The sun is getting low and the islands are pale in the distance. The dogs are happily hunting rabbits in the bracken, fish are jumping all across the bay, and someone else is doing the washing-up. Could anything be more perfect.

Two or three of you can wade out over the firm sand, 50 or 60 yards apart. On a calm evening the fish generally come within easy reach, in fact quite often they appear between you and the shore. At first they still swim about in shoals, but when the light begins to go they disperse and become spread out right across the bay. As it becomes dark you often see them dimpling the smooth surface of the sea all round you.

Some of the fish you cast over take, others don't; but you all share in the excitement when anyone hooks a fish. A reel screams in the quiet evening, and there are mutters of suspense from the lucky fisherman. If all goes well he backs ashore to land the fish. You congratulate him if he is successful, and condone if his gentle words turn to wrath. You also warn one another when a shoal is moving along the shore, or a particularly big fish appears close inshore. If you are lucky each fisherman may catch four or five fish during the evening. There should be several of over 2 lb.

Gradually the light dims. Features on the mountains fade in darkness, leaving only the jagged black outlines. The islands disappear for the night, and the horizon out to sea blends with the sky. Hinds and their calves come down to eat the grass just beyond the high tide mark, and watch you without alarm. The seabirds drift in on silent wings and settle on the shore to roost. They make quiet, comfortable noises as they go to sleep. The air turns cold after the heat of the day. You don't realise how cold your hands have become until you put one in the sea, and the water feels quite warm.

In July you can see to fish until well after midnight , then quite suddenly you feel cold and rather tired. You can think of nothing nicer than a final whisky and a warm bed, so you wade ashore for the last time, gather up your catch and return to the welcoming light which shines from the window of the house. Soon you are all back in the snug little sitting-room, reliving the recent excitements and discussing plans for the following day.

From *Fishing with a Purpose*, 1969.

9

HEBRIDEAN SALTWATER SEA-TROUT TODAY

Richard Davies

Sea-trout and finnock (young sea-trout) can be caught around the coast of the Hebrides throughout the early summer (May to July), and even as late as September if they haven't run the rivers. You can catch them using fairly traditional loch-style flyfishing techniques. You could, however, catch many more by speeding everything up and using larger flies or by slowing everything down and using smaller flies. I hope the following passages explain why this is the case.

Sea-trout around Lewis and Harris are often feeding on small crustaceans, young sea fish (pollack, coalfish, etc.), and during the summer, sand-eels which come close inshore. Depending on the time of year, tide patterns, state of tide, weather conditions and on the breeding success of their prey, the sea-trout, if in a feeding mood, will usually be taking on one or two of these food-species. Many marrow-spooned fish have confirmed this.

Brown trout which are feeding selectively on insect species are fished for using close imitations of those insects. In the same way sea-trout respond best to flies that represent whatever they are eating at that particular moment. I say moment because they can start to take sand-eels after spending hours feeding on tiny shrimps. The trick is to vary your tactics until you hit upon the one that works best. Sometimes at low tide they will not co-operate at all, and of course there are times when they are not feeding and will not look at anything. I am afraid I have no answers as to what to do at such times.

My approach on any saltwater fishing trip for sea-trout is basically the same. To start with I will make up an 8lb leader of around 12 feet and tie on a single sand-eel imitation, such as a long-winged silver stoat or a slimly dressed tube. Then I will locate a group of fish and cast the fly into the middle of it, being careful not to line any of them, and strip in at about a hundred miles an hour. If they are taking sand-eels, there should be a flurry of white water, out of which will dart a silver sea-trout, traveling at about two hundred miles an hour. The fly and the chasing fish, concealed by a large bow-wave, come closer, and sometimes there will be a heart-stopping take which can almost wrench the rod out of your hands. A lot of the time, there is just a boil and nothing is felt. If this happens a lot, I alter the speed of retrieve slightly, either faster or slower. This usually does the trick and more firm takes can be had. Using this fast stripped sandeel type of fishing to begin with is an efficient move because the results are immediate. Either a fish follows or it does not. After a dozen casts it is clear whether you are going to be successful or not. Fishing a small fly slowly is not as dramatic, and it can be difficult to detect takes so more time could be wasted.

When the fish do not respond to the stripped sandeel I move on to my second string, the small pollack imitation. The method of fishing is similar to that used for sandeeling, but generally the retrieve is slightly slower (but still much quicker than in normal fishing) and a different fly is used. My favourite fly for this is a size twelve treble dressed with a gold body and a red calf hair wing with a few strands of orange surrounding the body. This simple pattern reflects the colour and size of the prey moving at speed. Because the prey is fleeing and moving quickly, I do not believe it is necessary to spend too long trying to tie exact imitations. We only need the illusion of a fish for a fraction of a second. That's all it takes to entice a fish to attack.

If the fish are feeding on shrimp or other such food types, they can completely ignore the large stripped flies described above. Although I have had little success in bright daylight with small flies, once darkness falls, small fuzzy flies fished very slowly have proved irresistible. I was using a single small black fly in the dark when I had my most memorable sea-trout fishing experience.

I had anchored a small dinghy in the centre of a small estuary where sea-trout had been showing all day. My quick retrieve techniques had not been very successful so I had changed to the slow approach. I did not feel any takes until after a while, as I lifted off for the back cast, everything went solid. A good fish of around 2lbs was duly netted and returned. This was the beginning of a great evening's sport. The fish were not taking as sea-trout often do, with a crash bang wallop, but were gently sucking in the fly. I can only assume they had been doing so and rejecting it without my knowledge until this accidental hooking. With my senses tuned in to the much more gentle, almost undetectable take, I managed to land fourteen fish averaging 2lbs plus a handful of finnock. I kept one sea-trout for breakfast, the rest were all carefully unhooked and returned unharmed to the sea. These techniques are known to work at other places in the Hebrides. Whether or not they work elsewhere is for you to discover.

10

ORKNEY SEA-TROUT 1940's - TWO HOURS IN SPRING

R.N. Lochhead

March 194-. Wind, gale force, moderating later, occasional snow or sleet. Tide. 11 feet, 1310 hours.

Ideal sea-trout conditions. Wind and snow of no vital moment. Tide all important. The first high tide of the spring run, at least, so I hoped, and by missing my lunch I could just catch the tide.

With this short expedition in view I made all my preparations well in advance, put up my rod so as to save time, attached cast and fly - a blue and white Terror - laid out gumboots, oilskin and net, packet of biscuits and two bars of chocolate, and blew up bicycle tyres.

Twelve-twenty found me on my cycle, gale astern, and oilskin making an excellent spinnaker, covering the ground like a Derby winner. A very few minutes brought me to my destination, and one more minute and I was fishing.

Picture to yourself a rough expanse of sea, waves running before the gale, low cliffs at my back and jutting out to wind-ward, a small bay with a gravel beach, shelving gently into comparatively calm water. Tide rising fast to high water mark and making quite a perceptible current where it rounded the point on my right.

I started fishing just where this rocky point merged into the gravel of the bay, wading in knee deep and casting along shore just clear of some floating seaweed. The first few casts each produced a tiny splashy rise, probably a school of baby saithe, taking shelter from the storm outside. Ignoring such trash I continued casting, working slowly round my little bay till I came to the extreme end where the tide had now reached the base of the cliff. I could go no further, so I returned to my starting point, for the sea-trout, when they come on a rising tide, like to nose about in the seaweed close inshore. At about my second or third cast I heard a splash just behind me.

Here they come! that must have been a good fish and he will be travelling in my direction. Now I stand very still and cast a short and delicate line, just where the rough water merges into the calmer water of the bay, and there! a touch! No, not a fish, just a piece of seaweed which is quickly detached and casting resumed.

Splash! another fish, or perhaps the same one, right in the middle of my bay. Two false casts to get out line and I am over where he was, and as the fly touches the water he comes out of the side of a wave, jaws gaping, and seizes the fly with a wicked jolt. No fear of him not being well hooked for he has seized the lure and in the same swift rush is making tracks for America.

Thirty yards out he leaps from the water, falling back with a mighty splash, then he turns and makes for the rocks and breakers on my right. A few palpitating seconds of heavy pressure and I have him travelling towards me, when suddenly he slows up and I feel as if I had a 30 pound salmon on my line instead of a good sea-trout. He has run into weed.

Luck is with me, for the weed pulls free and hangs on the line, tiring the fish far more effectively than I could ever hope to do, and inside four minutes of hooking he is safely in the net. Looks like 30 pounds or over and very shapely.

Is he alone or one of a shoal? There is not time to dally over speculation and admiration. Here comes one of the snow showers; how glad I am that I have my back to the wind and am partially sheltered by the cliff behind.

Without moving I started casting again, but after a dozen casts, decided to follow the tide, and move up to the other end of my little haven. As the snow passed the sun broke through and I disencumbered myself of my oilskin, and started casting with renewed vigour, for in twenty minutes I must be off.

A longish cast towards the deeper water at the base of the cliff produced a strong underwater pull, and, I was in another!

Is this a kelt? He is not behaving like a fresh fish, for he is coming in to my very feet, and the rod hardly bent. I take a step or two to one side to clear a bunch of weeds, and, hi! presto! my movement has given him a fright, and no kelt is he. As if insulted at my mere thought, he departs at high speed round the shores of the bay, leaping every few yards, and tearing off line in angry jerks. He is big, and he is very fresh, and he is going in the right direction and keeping clear of rocks and weeds. He is a Gentleman, a Prince. The battle was fought out in clear water, and ended in my favour, with a lovely fresh five-pounder in the net.

Fish in bag, rod in hand, I mounted my bicycle and pressed off against the wind, and was at my desk, one hour and forty minutes after I started out, lungs filled with good fresh air, mentally refreshed and exhilarated, and with one more fishing memory to store up, exaggerate, and retell in the smoke-room, and two 'silver beauties' of 5 pounds 3ozs, and 4 pounds 1oz., to bring to table, swimming in parsley butter. Yes, real butter, for we are in Orkney.

From *With Rod Well Bent*, 1951.

11

SEA-TROUT ON THE INTERNET

Eur-flyfish@

This typical exchange on the Internet newsgroup 'eur-flyfish@' illustrates the exchange of information, and the cameradie between, saltwater flyfishers on the 'net - as an introduction to Scandinavian sea-trout angling develops into a specialised discussion on the spawning migration of Nereis rag-worms - the 'worm-hatch'.

At each stage quotations from previous letters are in square brackets.

On 18th April Jan Gunnar Furuly wrote:

First: I was totally unexperienced on flyfishing for sea-trout in salt-water, until last night. (Even night-fishing with a flyrod - Where I usually fish during summer we have midnight sun . . .) OK. Last night I went out to a place nearby, along the Oslofjord.

Even if the water still was very cold, lots of nice sea-trouts were jumping high in the air during this beautiful evening on the Eastern side of the fjord. Hard to imagine that couple of weeks ago parts of the fjord in this area were covered with ice. One sea-trout hit my fly very intensively, but I was not lucky enough to catch it. I was fishing with flies in size 4 and 6. Mostly dark patterns, after the dark came. The flies were well below the surface, and I kept rather good speed on the line while handing the line in. I used a floating line.

A fellow 8-10 metres to the left of me fished with flies that cruised the water surface. He had three sea-trouts on his rod. Two of them were landed. The fishing was best after the dark came. Just 4-5 metres from the shore, we could glimpse and hear sea-trouts hunting for food.

My question to the sea-trout experts on the list:

1. Is it best to fish with floating flies during night fishing for seatrout?
2. Would you prefer to fish this high, rather than to let the flies go a little bit deeper?

4. What size of flies would be best?
5. This guy had flies with calf-tail hair-wings. According to him the calf-tail helped the flies to float. According to a Norwegian book about sea-trout fishing, other hair materials than calf is recommended. Calf hair is said to be too stiff and 'dead'. The author prefers more soft hair material. Any views on this?
6. Please give me other advices on how to catch sea-trout, if you have any good hints!
7. Any good sea-trout fly patterns for salt water are appreciated!

Regards, Jan Gunnar Furuly, Ski, Norway.

The same day Wolfgang Küter replied from Germany:

Welcome in the group of saltwater sea-trout anglers...

[. . . lots of nice sea-trouts was jumping high in the air during this beautiful evening on the Eastern side of the fjord.]

You can call yourself lucky that you started in a night like that, it does happen that sea-trout break the surface and jump high in the air but you'll not always have the fish showing themselves.

[I was fishing with flies in size 4 and 6. Mostly dark patterns, after the dark came.]

Dark patterns are generally a good choice in the night.

[Is it best to fish with floating flies during night fishing for sea-trout?]

Usually the tactic for night fly fishing is to fish flies on or just below the surface.

[Would you prefer to fish this high, rather than to let the flies go a little bit deeper?]

You should not fish the flies deep.

[What size of flies would be best? This guy had flies with calf-tail hair-wings. According to him the calf-tail helped the flies to float.]

My first choice for night flyfishing is a deer-hair muddler, perhaps with a bright body, and a wing and tail made of black marabou. This pattern will float high in the water, give a good silhouette against the sky and has caught many a sea-trout in the Baltic waters.

[According to a Norwegian book about sea-trout fishing, other hair materials than calf is recommended.]

Have a look at the book by Jan Grünwald, about sea-trout saltwater fishing, it was originally written and published in Denmark but was translated into Norwegian.

[Calf hair is said to be to stiff and 'dead'. The author prefers more soft hair material. Any views on this?]

Personally I don't use calf tail. My hair wings mostly use polar fox. Some are zonkers with rabbit strips as a wing. I'd recommend rather soft material. You'll get a good overview about flies from the Grünwald book.

[Please give me other advice on how to catch sea-trout, if you have any good hints!]

If the water is very cold, fish flies in shocking colours rather deep and slowly. Under normal conditions, especially in spring-time when sea-trout are chasing fish use rather big streamers (size 2-6) imitating fry. As the water gets warmer use smaller flies imitating small food items like shrimp and other small animals.

Make some special grey brownish shrimp flies in size 6-8.

Hackle flies in size 8-10 like the Red Tag are good models.

For night fishing use muddlers.

Use flashy material on most models but don't use too much of it. Some 4-6 strands are enough.

Best wishes, Wolfgang. wolfgang@zaphod.allcon.com

Arvid Bjerkan replied:

[Have a look at the book by Jan Grünwald, about sea-trout saltwater fishing.]

Jan Gunnar, I second that. Jan Grünwald's book about saltwater fishing for sea-trout is very good. The fly patterns at the end of the book work very well in Norwegian waters, specifically the innermost part of the Oslo fjord (trust me, I know. I flyfish for sea-trout in the sea around Oslo from November to May, if it's not covered in ice).

Martin Jørgensen then joined in:

Jan and other potential sea-trouters,

[Is it best to fish with floating flies during night fishing for sea-trout?]

I would definitely recommend a floating line. Most of the fish will search for food that moves high in the water and will use the sky as a background when looking for moving food items.

[Would you prefer to fish this high, rather than to let the flies go a little bit deeper?]

Certainly. Actually the best fishing will sometimes be "in" the surface, using patterns that float, stream and create a few waves. I personally prefer small muddlers for this fishing and try to keep them dry and change fairly often.

[What size of flies would be best?]

I have a size 10 as my base fly. But sometimes I use flies as large as 2 and 4 on long-shank streamer hooks. The small flies will generally set much better. Just be sure to use a light and sharp, wide-gape hook like the Partridge John Holden.

[According to a Norwegian book about sea-trout fishing, other hair materials than calf is recommended. Calf hair is said to be to stiff and "dead". The author prefers softer hair material. Any views on this?]

Sure. When it comes to night fishing, I'd say that you can fish with a piece of cork on a hook. The fish see movement and profile - not a more or less undefined thing called 'life'. One of the most successful Danish night patterns is called 'The Cigar' and is actually just a hook with a spun deer-hair body covering the whole shank. Absolutely no 'life'. I prefer visually more pleasing flies, and a good material for that is polar fox or Icelandic sheep. Both should be readily available in Norway.

[Please give me other advice on how to catch sea-trout, if you have any good hints!]

Fish your fly in varying tempo. Sometimes you can jerk the line creating a small splash and sometimes you can take it in with figure-of-eight retrieve. Don't strike before you feel the fish in the rod/line. Night fishing is good for learning that, because you tend to strike early when the fish and fly are visible in the surface. Watching the fly and that revealing wave behind it can be more than a good man can take...

[Any good sea-trout fly patterns for salt water are appreciated!]

You probably know the address: http://www.idg.dk/mj/flies.

For specific night patterns try:

http://www.idg.dk/mj/flies/smallmud.htm,
http://www.idg.dk/mj/flies/blackfrede.htm or
http://www.idg.dk/mj/flies/nutriamd.htm

Skitt fiske, Martin. martinj@login.dknet.dk

And the next day:

The pattern Martin described; 'The Cigar', is very good for night fishing. Specially if you tie it with some deer-hair pointing to the front. This can be glued and modelled so it becomes stiff and upstanding like this \\|//. The pattern is known as 'The skater'. Quickly stripping it, it skates on the water and makes a splashing sound. The glue I use is a cyanacrylat that is quickly drying and water-resistant. A company in Germany called K+S Industiebedarf from Schonbrunn makes it and brings it on the market as K+S-Vielzweck-kleber.

Karel H. Das. kareldas@globalxs.nl

Then Waldemar Pfrengle:

Hi Jan,
  Good to hear somebody encountering and catching sea-trout on flies. Here are my experiences on the matter:

[I was fishing with flies in size 4 and 6. Mostly dark patterns, after the dark came.]
  I think you did ok with this. I usually fish black flies at night.

[The flies were well below water.]
  I like to fish high, especially at night. Imagine the fish sees your fly against the nightly sky. So if the fly is below the fish in the water column it is hard for them to detect. That's roughly my imagination on this matter. So if you fish high chances are better for your fly to be detected by a fish.

[And I kept rather good speed on the line while handing the line in. I used a floating line.]
  A floater is good, although you might want to try a slow intermediate, especially under very calm weather conditions (no wind, flat dead surface). I recommend a slow retrieve with traditional flies. Although I

had also responses with a fast two-handed retrieve using big sand-eel and herring patterns. However, the classical approach is a slooow retrieve, give the trout some time to turn before setting the hook.

[A fellow 8-10 metres to the left of me fished with flies that cruised the water surface.

He had 3 Sea Trouts on his rod. Two of them was landed. Using a greased black muddler at night is a good tactic to lure fish going after spawning worms. A black muddler is the night fly of choice for many fishermen.

[The fishing was best after the dark came. Just 4-5 metres from the shore, we could glimpse and hear sea-trouts hunting for food.]

That's right, although night fishing is common in summer I do not know of many people doing it in winter or spring. Fish (not only sea-trout and not only in salt water) come close to shore at night.

[Is it best to fish with floating flies during night fishing for sea-trout?]

Take a floater as your bread and butter line. I would also carry a clear intermediate or exchangeable tips of the latter for special occasions.

[What size of flies would be best?]

Depending on conditions. Calm and warm weather I tend to use smaller: 6 to 8. Rough water requires larger and heavier patterns: 2 to 2/0.

[This guy had flies with calf tail hair wings.]

I like this material too. I use it on classical wet fly style flies.

[According to him the calf tail helped the flies to float.]

Mine dive. I have never dressed them to float. I would use a muddler instead.

[According to a Norwegian book about sea-trout fishing, other hair materials than calf is recommended.]

Dyed fox hair is a great material. I go to a furrier / fur shop and ask for their waste. Black fox makes great night flies for summer. Lots of movement, very durable.

[Calf hair is said to be to stiff and "dead".]

Makes great flies too. I use those (sparsely dressed, bright colors) in spring.

Hope these comments are of help. Keep up going. It should be the right time now.

Tight lines. Waldemar Pfrengle. pfrenglew@pt.cyanamid.com

Jan Hansen from Norway joins in:

Wow, I jump right into this one and expect Martin and Mr X Vihovde at last to join: Jan Gunnar writes about the sea-trout in the sea and I claim myself as quite into this sport:

[Is it best to fish with floating flies during night fishing for sea-trout?]
  Yes.

[Would you prefer to fish this high, rather than to let the flies go a little bit deeper?]
  Yes.

[What size of flies would be best?]
  Large, in fact they can be very large.

[This guy had flies with calf tail hair wings. According to him the calf tail helped the flies to float. Calf hair is said to be to stiff and "dead". Any views on this?]
  Indeed. Tie a black Montana on a Partridge size 6 low-water double salmon hook and add to it an inch of black marabou pretty thick tail. I for myself don't use much muddlers or floating things in the sea. My Black Magick (version of Montana) goes right under the surface, cause as Jan Gunnar claims; "when the sea get warm enough for night/surface action you can safely pull the fly in very fast".
  If you fish shallow waters (2-3 feet) you will soon experience the excitement of seeing the sea-trout coming like a shark fin stripping the surface, believe me - try to keep calm at such glorious moments

[Please give me other advices on how to catch sea-trout, if you have any good hints! Any good sea-trout fly patterns for salt water are appreciated!]
  Well, I have never been much modest, look it up at the fly section in http://www.flyshop.no Jan Hansen's sea-trout selection.
  In the section on flyfishing in the sea (which is newly moderated thanks to Paul M. (swff book) look up that sea-trout taken on this fly. In fact, some of the flies that Martin J of Denmark and Asgeir Alvestad use in the

sea are there as well. Pass along some real good stories. My God you really did it, I am going out now, Friday 18/04, 19.15hrs

I shall tell my wife that you did this.

Jan. Jan.Hansen@flyshop.no

And Jan again:

Speaking about sea-trout, I sometimes fish very shallow waters; two to three feet in the dark hours.

Fish can suddenly come rushing against the fly from ten to twelve feet away, making WAVES as it moves. This is . . . well yes . . . to keep the speed up at this moments and get ready for just the right moment to set the hook is very challenging.

Seeing fish attacking the fly from such distances where it is simply impossible for the fish to get a silhouette I have started wondering if it is sensing the movement of the fly. Do you Oslofjord or Baltic sea fishermen experience this? Take a look at a trout that was caught this way: http://www.flyshop.no/guide/saltwat/bginfo/sea-trout2.htm.   This picture is rather large so get a cup of coffee while waiting, I promise its worth it. The fly is there as well.

Regards, Jan. Jan.Hansen@flyshop.no

Wolfgang again:

Paul Marriner wrote:

[Hey fellows, do you know if Grünwald's book was translated into English? I'm interested in sea-trout fishing in the salt. Paul Marriner]

I don't think that the book was translated into English. The reason why it was translated into Norwegian might be that Jan Grünwald goes to Norway for salmon fishing every year (at least his reports of salmon mostly in the lower stretches of the Stjordalselv can be seen in the window of the Saxhaug tackle shop in the town of Stjørdal almost every year).

So he's rather closely related to Norway and as salmon fishing was bad one year he tried his proven tactics for saltwater sea-trout fishing successfully in Norwegian waters. Since there was a change in the Norwegian law some years ago that allowed saltwater sea-trout fishing all year round (it was forbidden for most time of the year so far) there was a demand for a good book available in Norway. Danish and Norwegian are very similar, so the translation was rather easy.

IMHO (though I can hardly read or speak Danish, I, as a German, have to guess the sense more than read the book) the Grünwald book really gives a good overview about all aspects of saltwater sea-trout fishing.

By the way the title of the Grünwald book is *Havørred: Spin og flü in saltvand*. In English that is: *Sea-trout: Spinning and flyfishing in saltwater*.

Best wishes, Wolfgang.

And again:

[I will run back to the tying bench directly from work, and try the sea-trout again tonight.]

On your next way to the tying bench stop at a tackle shop and perhaps get yourself some saltwater hooks. I'd recommend the following models:
For streamers: Partridge Sea Streamer, Code CS 11, either in Grey
Shadow finish or (new) in stainless steel, very sharp, almost rust-free.
Available in sizes 2-8
For shrimps: Partridge Saltwater shrimp hook, Code CS 54, Grey
shadow finish. Available in sizes 4-8

These hooks might be difficult to obtain in Norway but IMHO they are the best hooks for saltwater sea-trout flies.

Best wishes, Wolfgang.

A quick reply from Arvid:

[Wolfgang wrote: These hooks might be difficult to obtain in Norway...]
Not difficult at all, I'd guess most well-stocked flyshops in Norway carry them. I use them myself, bought them in a flyshop in Oslo called RS Flür, where I do most of my ff-related shopping.

Arvid Bjerkan. arvid.bjerkan@mbs.no

Next day Lennart Widmark wrote:

Hi listers, seems like most of you prefer mighty big hooks for the sea-trout. I suggest that you try smaller ones, size 12-16.

More about the coast-technique and preferable hooks at

http://www.ts.umu.se/~widmark/lwdobb.html   especially   the   FAQ
section.

Best wishes. Lennart W. widmark@ts.umu.se

Wolfgang replied:

Small flies are a good idea, sometimes (!!!). In general I'd say that the
warmer the water, the smaller the fly. I know that on the Swedish East
coast small hackle flies (10 -14) are widely used. I'd use them for mainly
for summer fishing.Perhaps these small flies are more successful compared
to big flies (4-8) in the very brackish water along the Swedish east coast,
because in that brackish water sea-trout feed mainly on small crustaceans,
this is only my theory. I may be wrong, there may be many sea-trout being
caught along the German and Danish coasts of the Baltic sea on very small
flies. I've not seen many. Why not try small flies? Big sea-trout might
take them.

Best wishes. Wolfgang

On 20th April Ole Wisler contributed:

Hi List-members
   In continuation of Wolfgang Küter's latest reply I would like to con-
tribute to the discussion about sea-trout-techniques and hook-sizes.
Mainly because I've often seen that different flyfishers have different views
on what is best regarding sea-trout fishing at sea. Many FFishers conclude
that smaller flies that imitates smaller crustaceas is the best way of
gaining success.
   This conclusion is normally correct because it provides them with success at their specific geographical part of the sea-trout-continent. But it
does not necessarily apply to other parts.
   The feeding sea-trout is an opportunist and will therefore eat what is
available. This doesn't mean that the sea-trout can't become selective on
specific items at certain times of the year - especially during summer and
early autumn when there is plenty of food. But it means more or less that
the trout will be more focused on sandeels in areas with lot of sandeels
   ASO. Autumn fishing for coloured migrating sea-trout is another discussion. I have the pleasure of living in a place where both inner fjords ond
outer coastlines are in range of a short driving distance. Sometimes I've
been taking friends - who normally fish the fjords for sea-trout - out to the

outer coast. Here they experience a lack of flies in the box, because they only carry smaller imitations of crustaceas and not that great a variety of larger fry-imitations.

So on behalf of my humble experience I can only agree with Wolfgang: There is a tendency towards better success with smaller flies in brackish waters and larger flies in waters with higher salinity. It's not a rule as it's sometimes vice versa but it's an observation which is worth remembering.

The rule is to find the food-items for the sea-trout and then sort of 'match the hatch'. Mostly it works but sometimes something absolutely different from the original works much better e.g. Steen Ulnit's 'Christmas Tree' or the 'Mickey Finn'. Sometimes the ways of the sea-trout are mysterious.

Back to the hook-sizes. It is quite difficult to tie a sandeel-imitation on a #14 hook. Therefore larger sizes are legitimate and as Martin Jørgensen recommend the 'John Holden' hooks (#1, 2) from Partridge with a large gape are great hooks for the largest imitations. For smaller fry imitations the "Jens Staal" Sea trout hooks (#4,6,8,10) from Partridge are recommended.

The 'Dutch' way of tying larger imitations such as sandeels is a way of reducing the weight of the fly. By the 'Dutch' way I mean using a braided nylon (make a loop-eye) as shank and then tie a small treble-hook in at the end of it. Also Hugh Falkus had some sandeel-imitations tied on tandem-hooks in his book 'Seatrout-fishing'. I normally use the tandem-flies to imitate different species of the Neries worms (e.g. Neries virens and Neries diversicolor) which can be quite effective especially from March to April, sometimes sooner.

I liked to add another thing: Larger flies are more easily spotted when night-fishing. ("Small flies - small fish * big flies - big fish" :-) just a snappy conclusion.)

Tight loops and lines. Ole Wisler. olewj@imv.aau.dk

Arvid replied:

Traditional wisdom often has it that you should use large flies in winter/early spring and smaller flies as the water heats up towards and during summer/early autumn. I don't know, I've not found this to be true all the time. I've often done the exact opposite, and fished small flies in mid-January with good results. In the beginning of January this year I fished a small (#12, for sea-trout, at least in my eyes, that's small) white SLF/fox-hair creation of mine and both sea-trout and cod absolutely hammered the fly. I must've caught about a dozen fish in an hour and half or so. By then my hands and feet (stocking-type waders is not the best solution in freezing water) were totally without feeling from the cold so I had to quit. Now, for me to catch that many fish is NOT the norm, whatever season/size of fly, so there must've been something else that day that drove the fish crazy, but it just goes to show that with flyfishing nothing is ever certain and "acknowledged truths" are nothing of the kind.

Arvid Bjerkan. arvid.bjerkan@mbs.no

Wolfgang came back:

[Ole Wisler wrote: I normally use the tandem-flies to imitate different species of the Neries worms (e.g. *Neries virens* and *Neries diversicolor*) which can be quite effective especially from March to April, sometimes sooner.]

This leads me to the following question:

On some occasions in springtime I was fishing when there were many Neries worms around, normally they live in the ground or under stones but in springtime when they spawn they swim around. Seagulls picked them up in large numbers and they were swimming around my waders. As they were plentiful I think that under these circumstances every sea-trout around had only those worms in mind.

Tying an imitation is not too difficult, which is what I did.

It has to be rather long, hackled and brownish. However I never caught a sea-trout when the worms were swimming around. Maybe my worm imitations are not good but I believe because there were so many worms around that the trout simply were packed with the worms and hardly interested in imitations.

To the fellow sea-trout anglers:

What are your experiences when fishing while the worms were around?

Did you catch any or did you come home without fish?

Literature says that the fishing is good but my experience shows that it is bad under these circumstances.

What do you say? Best wishes. Wolfgang.

Martin Jørgensen:

I have seen the swarming a few times, but never caught a trout on a worm imitation. I know no fishers who have had consistent success with this fishing. But... the Danish magazines are full of stories about this famed fishing which is said to take place each spring when certain circumstances meet.

I think it is highly over-estimated - use a gammarus imitation instead. The fish are filled with hundreds of these almost all year round.

Martin. martinj@login.dknet.dk

And Wolfgang Küter:

Which is just the same as I experienced. Though the press says that fishing with worm imitations during the "worm hatch" is very productive, I'd say that the opposite is correct. To me all this seems to be some sort of fairy tale.

I've never tried small Gammarus type flies during the 'worm hatch'. Either I fished normal to rather big flies or simply went home. Maybe small flies are productive, who knows, nevertheless I do believe that the trout feed on the worms when they are swarming. Normally sea-trout will eat what is available and if there are many worms, why not eat them? Them worms are rather slow and to me they seem to be an easy prey for a sea-trout. But catching sea-trout during 'worm hatches', no, I must admit that I failed in those situations.

Wolfgang.

Arvid:

When you say Neries worms, do you mean bristleworms, Latin: polychaeta? 10-25cm long worms that live in sand/mud bottom, with small "feet" sticking out along their body? I think we mean the same creature, they swarm in the spring when the water warms to about 6-8 degrees, which usually means sometime in April (around here, at least). They swim around in shallow water in a sexual craze, driving the sea-trout and cod even crazier. Not always easy catching fish then because, just as you say, your fly is one among hundreds (of naturals, that is). Around here these worms can be several colors, at least brown, green and grayish black.

A Woolly Bugger style fly on a #6 6X long hook (e.g. Tiemco TC300) will work just fine, but even better is a tandem hook style imitation, e.g. two #10 Partridge J.S. Sea streamer hooks with 10cm of monofilament (or use dacron fly-line backing if you've got some left over) connecting them, with chenille wrapped along from the hook eye of the first hook to the bend of the last hook, hackle palmered along the front hook and "rubber legs" tied in along the rest, and finally (not necessary) a tail of marabou.

Arvid Bjerkan. arvid.bjerkan@mbs.no

25.04.97 Ole Wisler wrote:

Sea-trout often stuff themselves with Neries when they are spawning - almost until they puke. I've experienced poor-conditioned trout early spring which actually had a nice belly although they just recently arrived in the sea from the spawning areas in the streams - but a nice stuffed belly is not necessarily an indication of good meat-quality.

Another explanation is that there's plenty of worms but no sea-trout on that spot . . .

Concerning the imitations I don't think they have to be that accurate to animate the trout to strike. Some of my fellow fishermen have achieved good catches while spinfishing with long lures that used to imitate sandeels - they just painted them black during the Neries spawnings.

I believe that a slow wiggling/jiggling movement of the imitation is very important - perhaps even essential.

[Literature says that the fishing is good but my experience shows that it is bad under these circumstances.]

I've experienced the same. Lots of Neries worms but no fish. The explanation might be that there's simply no sea-trout in that area at that moment. In early spring sea-trout move around seeking food and there's not much compared to late spring and summer. Therefore places that fished well one day might be empty the next and vice versa. If it's a place where you normally find sea-trout at that time of year and there's lots of Neries I would recommend trying the place the next day - then the trout might be back.

I'd also experienced some of the wildest fishing - with catches from 20-30 sea-trout in 4-5 hours of fishing when Neries was spawning. At those 'crazy-Neries-days' everything seems to work. For instance last year, early April - in the bottom of the "Århus Bay" there were about 10 fishermen on a stretch of 7-800 metres. Some spin-fishing with bubble-floats and flies, some with lures, some with wobblers and some flyfishing. Everyone got fish and it was hard to tell which technique and imitation was the best as sometimes the guys to the left got fish, then after a while we got fish and then the ones to the right got fish. I believe it was depending on where the schools of trout were in the area and not as much depending on what was at the end of the line. I think it's fair to say that fishing is good when the Neries are spawning, but there has to be trout around.

There's many species of the Neries and they have their specific life-cycles and spawning times. Not much is to be found in scientific papers regarding spawning of the worms. A scientific report from the 'Limfjorden' in North Jutland by Kaare M. Ebert showed that different species of Neries are found in sea-trout stomachs all year round - and also in large quantities. So it's not necessarily spawning-periods which are interesting for the imitator.

One has to be aware that this may vary from place to place, but as the trout is an opportunist it'll surely eat the worms available. The worms also expose themselves when leaving their shelter to feed in e.g mussel-banks. Also, I believe that there is a migration from deeper water towards the lower shore in early spring and then again out to deeper and warmer water in late autumn. Here the worms expose themselves again. That is just a subjective civil thesis based on my observations of stomach contents in late autumn sea-trout - not a conclusion based on scientific research.

This year we haven't seen that many Neries (N. virens and N. diversi-color) spawning in this area although there was a bit of activity in late March before cold weather and storms put an end to it.

The spawning time depends on day-length, water-temperature and moon-phase. Normally the right factors are to be found in late-March and early-April - depending on the water-temperature. If it is very warm (around 8-10 degrees) at that time the spawning is normally done within a week. This year we have had frost at night and water-temperatures averaging 6-7 degrees from late March until now and not much has happened. Hopefully we'll get some real spring soon.

Although the Neries season is nearly finished and has never really started this year, it might be nice to know THE NERIES TANDEMFLY or "the real børsteorm" as it is named here in Denmark.

A very dedicated and innovative flyfisher - Claus Richness from the FF-shop, "Go Fishing" in Dense, Fen - invented/created the nice goldhead tandemfly imitation of the Neries with a body of cactus-chenille (diff. colours to imitate diff. species e.g black/purple, dark greenish, brown/reddish) The tying technique of the fly is great, but I don't like the flashy cactus-chenille when fishing at bright daylight, but at night the main factors are the contour and movement. For fishing at daytime I use hackled imitations (the Hoffmann saddles provide very long hackles which is great when tying a 10 cm. Neries - which is actually just a small Neries) with a body of wool-yarn/thread in dark green, black or brown. As tail a bunch of marabou fibres 1.5-2 cm long in coherent colours. Using soft Kevlar-thread when connecting the hooks (Partridge J.S.Seastreamer #8 front

#10 rear) for the tandem-fly makes the body wiggle a bit when the fly is retrieved. The goldhead also supplies life in the imitation when retrieved.

Tight loops and lines. Ole.

Then Waldemar wrote:

During a summer holiday in southern Denmark end of June 1995 my Danish friend told me about an outing he had the night before in his boat in a fjord on the island of Als. The worms were all over the place that night and he could see the small tracks they made on the mirror-like calm water surface. There were also many trout around. In fact he had never seen so many, and so big trout in one place before. The fish were sipping the worms from the surface right near his boat. However, as many of you have experienced, he did not even get a strike.

I tied up a bunch of worm patterns that day and the following evening saw two flyfishermen in his boat. The action came again that night although it was not as intense as the night before. And again no strikes, not even on my deadly and surely unresistable worm pattern. My guess is that too many worms were around. I had also the impression that the sometimes-intense circling and wiggling action of the worms could be an important aspect considering the triggering of strikes. We could perfectly study the worm behaviour from the boat and my guess is that the motion of the worms is hard to imitate. Having read about you guys' similar experiences I really doubt if I want to encounter the worm hatch again, although it is spectacular to see in the water.

Tight lines. Waldemar. pfrenglew@pt.cyanamid.com

Our flyfishing group has also had the pleasure to fish during a 'worm hatch'. In the beginning we had the same experience as described earlier by others. So we decided that each of the eight of us would fish a different pattern.

The best was the one Menno van Dam used: the String Leech.

Body: Just an 8 cm strip of red rabbit fur. In front a gold head. A kevlar string (7 cm) with a #12 hook one end and at the other end a loop. Here we attach the head and the rabbit strip. Thus the strip and the string are not one part they can move freely.

(See page 453 of Trey Comb's *Steelhead Fly fishing*).

Tight lines. Dick Bollemeijer. e-mail : dbollemy@worldaccess.nl

I am overwhelmed by all the instructive replies to my request on the best techniques for flyfishing for sea-trout in salt water! All the responses have been to great help for me. This has been a solid inspiration on my new path as a salt water flyfisherman!

Thanks to Wolfgang Küter, Lennart Widmark, Jan Hansen, Paal Gisle, Waldemar Pfrengle, Arvid Bjerkan, Marius Hildebrandt, Martin Jørgensen, Stig Idsal, Sven Ostermann, Ole Wisler Johansen, Karel H. Das and others for all hints and advices. Thanks also for a whole bunch of tying instructions for salty flies!

This is something that makes eur-flyfish@ a great place to be!

Regards and skitt fiske from
Jan Gunnar Furuly,
Ski, Norway.
jan.gunnar.furuly@aftenposten.no

PART III
BASS

12

BASS IN SOUTH-EASTERN ESTUARIES

Peter James

It was September 17th, 1990, late into the night. I'd given up on the plugs and livebait to catch a few tiny schoolies on the fly. These fish were the early bonanza provided by the exceptional spawning of 1987. The night was still, the water calm, the air damp, the jetty deserted; one of those lovely autumn nights that always seem to promise something, even if in the end they fail to deliver. Maybe the expectancy is enhanced by the anxiety that comes with awareness of how close is the season's end.

Further inshore, under one of the lights, I heard a swirl. It sounded more substantial than those of the little fish I could see chasing whitebait in front of me. Time to check it out. Perhaps it was a rare better fish. Careful does it, stay clear of the light, transfer the weight gradually from one foot to the other, no heavy footfalls. Yes! As I'd hoped, occasionally a dark shape would glide through, or turn at the edge of the lit area. Size? 4lb? Whatever, it's bigger than anything else I've had flyfishing. I'm getting very excited now. What chance of catching it? What should I do? Return to the plugs which over previous years had produced the odd good fish? Stick with the fly? A positive action; stick with the fly. Having edged closer to the lit area I cast uptide and across so the fly would land beyond the light, giving it time to sink before retrieving through the lit area in front of the jetty. Twice I watched the tiny silhouette return through the fry with no interruption. A third cast. Out from the shadows to my left came the fish. 'Take it. Take it!', I shouted inside my head. The bloody thing appeared to look at the fly before turning once more for the shadows. 'Damn it'. A little disappointed, but not surprised, I looked for the inch-long lure. Not a sign. Then, wallop, a wrist-wrenching jerk as the rod-tip was unceremoniously dragged into the water, most of the rest of the rod following right down to the alarmingly arced butt. I quickly cleared the loose line and let the fish have its head. For the next ten to fifteen minutes the fish dived, ran and sulked, whilst I stripped-in or released line, turning the rod to left or right in the hope of keeping both fish and line clear of the various piles and obstructions all covered with line-chaffing barnacles. Unusually, I managed to stay with the patient approach, despite the intense excitement. Gently does it. Eventually the fish began to tire, just holding in the tide, occasionally shaking its head. By now I could see most of the rod, a bit of pumping and there was the fish. A few last-gasp dives, a failed netting attempt, a little panic, then in the net it went. A beautiful, plump, silver jewel of a bass. 6lb 9oz. I couldn't have been more pleased. A moment of achievement to be savoured. My first proper bass on a fly. It was deceived by a Missionary - size 8.

The above mark no longer exists, which is a shame, but others do provide worthwhile fishing if approached with an open mind and realistic expectations. Since the memorable night described above I've had a fair number of bass using fly-rods, the great majority under 2lb with a sprinkling of fish in the 2lb-4lb class. Fish above this weight are quite exceptional. This is in part a consequence of the estuary environment of sand/mud and the scarcity of mature fish (netting etc.), but I think it also indicates the limitations of the method. Its great fun but not generally the most effective method of catching big bass unless they are preoccupied with tiny baitfish. The more-than-adequate compensation is that on balanced tackle a two-pound fish feels huge.

Locations and technique

Whatever the method used, it should always be remembered that by far the most important factor in catching bass is to find the fish. In the southeastern estuaries I fish, there is little point in trying to fish deep. The water is too dirty and the tides are usually too strong. The fish have to be near the top or in shallow water (less than 7ft). Water clarity is greatest (3ft) during periods of settled weather, during small tides, or at the bottom of very big tides. What I look for in trying to locate fish are all the obvious things; creases (fig 1), funnels (fig 2), structure, anything that might focus or hold bait. Piers, points on to which the tide runs, patches of rocky-ground or shallow races. Crabs being the dominant food-item of local bass, it is usually worth exploring the weed-covered rocks that make up the sea-wall, there being few other rocky areas to be found. For preference, choose an area where the wall reaches below the low-tide mark. The walls slope quite steeply so the fishing is very close, a few feet beyond the weed. Cast out, then allow the lure to swing round. Retrieve almost parallel with the shore (figs 3 & 4). Where the tide runs onto some sort of structure the fish are likely to be uptide, except during exceptional flows. Thus, the lure must be fished uptide of and parallel to the structure, preferably head to tide. In this situation a dinghy would really be the ideal solution (fig 5). If you have to fish the structure itself then tackle loss and stress are pretty much inevitable, but it is the best way. This often requires short casts, up and across, then a fast retrieve with the rod

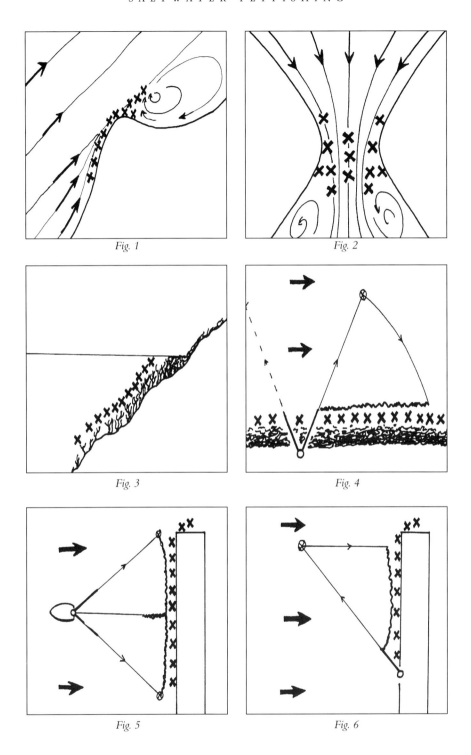

Fig. 1

Fig. 2

Fig. 3

Fig. 4

Fig. 5

Fig. 6

pointing directly into the tide, possibly submerged (fig 6). Alternatively, in some cases a cast directly into the tide followed by rapid retrieval of the slack generated by the line sinking and drifting back can produce a fish. The effective fishing time with this technique is only a few seconds. when the lure turns then lifts as the line tightens before being lifted off. Marks where there are lights are worth a look, though I've found to my intense frustration that fish usually melt away. On the rare occasions when they don't I've usually found them contemptuous of my offerings.

Tackle

On the subject of tackle I have little to say. There is more than enough information and advice available already.

Rods: I use a Daiwa CF98 105H #7/9, reduced to 10ft by accident. It cost £62. The rings have been changed for the largest snakes I could get, plus two butt-rings from a spinning rod.

Reels: 4" Graflite, Leeda LC100, System 2 #8/9. The latter is pure self-indulgence. Any decent-sized reel will do.

Lines: Nine-weight shooting-heads, intermediate and DI6. A slow-sinker might be handy but for now I make do with the intermediate, plus a split-shot or pinch of heavy metal attached to the leader - 4-8 feet of Berkley Big-Game clear; 15/20lb butt, 10lb tippet.

Flies: Missionary, Polystickles, Tadpoles, Dog-nobblers, Deltas, Glass-head Fry and Balsa/Marabou Sliders, none very large. Really big flies require heavy gear. In such situations I would turn to spinning. It is more sensitive, more fun and more effective. I'm not a fly-only fanatic, nor an expert. I fish for fun.

Wielding heavy gear doesn't interest me; whether its a cod pole or heavy-weight flyrod. One last word on tackle. If you can't catch fish with one of the many reasonably-priced lure-rods currently available, you will not improve your chances by spending more money (unless its on a fish finder).

p.s. Don't forget a line-tray.

13

BASS FROM THE LLEYN PENINSULA

Gary Coxon

Mullet, mackerel, bass and pollock are the most common fly-rod quarry along the stretch of the Welsh coast where I fish. The Lleyn Peninsula, from Nefyn on the northern side around to Criccieth in the south is a wild, unspoilt corner of North Wales, where choughs and peregrines still make their homes on the cliff-faces.

Bass are, for me, the epitome of saltwater flyfishing in the UK. Their fighting qualities are equal to any other fish I have ever caught. As juveniles, or "school-bass", fish of up to two or three pounds, they tend to shoal, and it is quite likely that, having found a shoal, you may catch several Having passed this size they become "loners" and can grow well into double-figures. In this area the bass seem to move in from deeper water towards the end of May. Although July, August and September have proved the best months for me, I have taken odd fish as late as mid-October. In other locations these times will vary as research has shown that their feeding-habits and movements depend largely on water-temperature and climate.

I have had most success on the South-west side of the peninsula, from Aberdaron to Abersoch. This stretch includes two or three large storm-beaches and endless rocky coves, overlooked by daunting cliffs, many of which are far too difficult and dangerous to attempt climbing. In this part of the world, the best places to flyfish for bass are nearly always the most difficult to reach. Bass being a relatively shy species, they will seek the sanctuary that such terrain has to offer, especially during daylight hours, when the beaches and coves attract the attention of holidaymakers.

Bass eat almost anything that crawls or swims and, although a most voracious predator, they are also opportunists and scavengers. Small mackerel, crabs, shrimps, prawns, and sand-eels seem to be their staple diet around the Lleyn, as they forage into the sandy bays and estuaries or run the surf of the more exposed storm-beaches

Being able to adapt and survive in such a wide range of habitats, bass are not always easy to locate and consequently blanks are not uncommon. However, as in most forms of flyfishing, the odds can be lessened with observation, awareness and a little experience. It is always worth watching where terns or other sea-birds are diving into the shoals of baitfish, as sometimes bass will cause these shoals to push up close to the surface. Often, when the tide turns, a tide race is formed just off a headland, this is also an ideal place to locate bass as they will often be in the less turbulent parts of the race waiting for food items to be washed past them - and so it goes on!

Although daytime fishing can be productive, if I had a choice I would always choose to fish an incoming tide on a dull, warm evening. Bass are far less timid when approaching shallower water at this time of the day and will feed far more confidently only a few metres from the shoreline. Long casting is not necessary and a stealthy approach with good presentation is far more important and productive . 'Presentation' may seem a rather elaborate description when you visualise the vast expanse of waves in front of you, but bass fishing in a situation such as I have described is not just a case of "chuck it and chance it". It is more on a par with stalking in clear water. Techniques may vary depending on factors such as the state of the tide, the time of day, the species we are fishing for and the imitation we are using. One method which I particularly enjoy is to fish a crab or prawn imitation in a "dead-drift" style. I cast as close to the rocks or cliff-face as possible and allow the swell of the waves to move the pattern naturally, without any retrieve at all, but simply keeping the line quite tight in order to register a take. Inevitably the swell will nearly always move the belly of the line away from the cliff and cause a gentle drag to occur as it pulls the pattern slowly seawards. When using this method takes can be sudden and aggressive, or may merely feel like a slow draw, as the fish moves off. The success of this method seems to depend mainly on restraint from any form of retrieve, but to be able to leave the swell of the sea to its own devices in making the pattern appear natural. Its true to say that you do not always catch the species you are hoping for no matter what technique is employed.

I remember a perfect evening a few years ago when I set up to fish the 'dead-drift' method. The depth of water was barely 12" as the tide had only just turned and I was casting in hope rather than anticipation as it was still a little early. My fly had hardly had time to settle when the rod was almost wrenched from my hand as a strong fish headed for deeper water. After a couple of decent runs it was brought to the side of the rocks and I was amazed to find it was not the expected bar of silver but a colourful wrasse of about two and a half pounds. A pleasant and acceptable beginning to what I anticipated as being a good session. Of course, I did not catch another fish that evening despite conditions appearing perfect, but that's bass fishing. I have only ever caught one other wrasse on a fly, and that was a few nights later whilst stripping a sandeel pattern through a weedy gully. Although I know that there are many wrasse taken by bait-anglers around the peninsula, it seems strange that more do not come to the fly.

There are occasions where long casting is required, particularly if the fish are chasing sandeels or whitebait, and long pulls are needed to make the imitation appear natural. Even then, however, casting along the waves or rocks, rather than out towards the horizon is often the most effective technique. Once the bass are close into shore they will feed and swim along the beach.

The northern side of the Lleyn is pollack-territory. They are normally found in slightly deeper water with a rock-strewn sea-bed interlaced with sweeping kelp-thongs. The area from Nefyn to Aberdaron is ideal, with many small bays and inlets between rocky outcrops. These rocky outcrops can make excellent platforms from which to make the long casts often needed to reach the deeper troughs amongst the kelp beds.

Flies and tackle

There has been very little written about saltwater flyfishing around our coastline and even less about the fly patterns we can use. Consequently, the fly-tyer has "carte blanche" when imitating the vast food chain which the sea has to offer. Sandeel and baitfish patterns can be tied by using the techniques we are familiar with from tying trout-flies and lures. Shrimps, prawns, and crabs offer greater scope for experiment. With the materials now available, excellent lifelike imitations are not difficult to create. This is a further fascinating side to saltwater flyfishing.

For those who do not tie their own flies, all is not lost! Crystal River, who are based near Rhyl in North Wales, distribute an excellent range of saltwater patterns. I have personally fished with many of their range and can vouch that they do catch fish and are exceptionally well-tied.

Flyfishing for bass around the Lleyn will take you to some of the most scenic areas in Britain, but take heed! Some of the favoured spots described require a reasonable climb, or at the very least a good scramble, in order to reach them. The right equipment is essential. By this, I do not mean ropes and crampons - I am certainly no mountaineer - but good footwear. Do not wear wellington-boots or canvas beach-shoes as the rocks can be both sharp and slippery. Wear warm, light clothing and carry the minimum of fishing equipment.

Over the years, through trial and a lot of error, I have discarded many of the accessories which we flyfishermen have come to believe are necessary. Climbing around rocks all day with large tackle-bags is uncomfortable and awkward. If it does not fit into a pocket on my chestpack, it is left behind. A 9', 4-piece travel-rod, rated #6 to #8, is ideal for my purpose. This can be pushed down inside the back of my shirt leaving my hands free whilst climbing. One reel, loaded with a floating or intermediate line, a few braided leaders of varying sinking-rates, a few spare spools of leader-material in 6, 8 and 10lb breaking-strain, a box of assorted fly-patterns, a good pair of polaroids to stop the glare and to protect eyes, and a collapsible line-tray as the rocks are very sharp and soon ruin lines. This is the basic tackle I carry for a day on the rocks and I would reduce it even further if I could.

One final word on tackle. We probably do not need the specialised ten-weight and heavier saltwater fly-rods which are now available in the UK, as we are very unlikely to encounter the types of fish these were designed for. However, the same style of rods rated #6 and #7 are ideal tools. They are fast-actioned and have the necessary backbone needed to cast a good line into the head-on winds which prevail on our coasts. Reels are also an important item; a good drag-system is important when controlling the long runs that a sizeable bass is capable of.

No matter what tackle is used, we must always clean and wash the gear at the end of the day. The corrosive action of salt and sand will ruin the best tackle unless this is done.

BOATCASTING FOR BASS - A NEW APPROACH

14

EVOLUTION OF A BASS ANGLER

Nick Cosford

1977 - I have never been lucky enough to live near the sea, but went as a teenager on holiday to the west of Ireland. I loved the country and the fishing, and have returned almost every year since. Unfortunately the books of the day said that to catch bass you needed to wade out in a big surf with a beachcaster capable of casting a heavy weight beyond the breakers. Lacking the equipment and the knowledge to tackle bass I headed inland to spin for sea-trout. I fished rock marks for pollack and mackerel, but caught no bass.

1983 - Visiting a girlfriend near Southampton I whiled away an hour floatfishing a piece of mackerel. Despite unpromising conditions I was rewarded with my first bass - a monster of over ten pounds! It was the first bass I had ever seen.

Over the next couple of years I returned several times but all I caught were mackerel and garfish - no more bass. These early experiences re-inforced in my mind the idea that bass were difficult to catch, enigmatic; an almost mystical fish.

1989 - Now married, back on holiday in Ireland and desperate to catch a bass! Equipped with a beachcaster, I was plagued with tropical weather conditions. Where were the great Atlantic swells and beautiful creaming surfs full of bass that Clive Gammon and Des Brennan described so vividly?

One evening a bit of a surf built up, and together with two other anglers I fished a night tide. I was lucky enough to take the only fish of the session - a three pound bass.

The surf dropped away the next day and the hot settled weather resumed. As I approached the end of my holiday I was getting anxious. A radical approach was called for.

Rising at 6 a.m. I explored a nearby bay. I had half a dozen floating plugs but the terrain was so shallow and bouldery that I feared that I would lose them all in six casts. I tied on a skirted spinnerbait; good for pike so why not bass? Virtually weedless, I was fairly sure that I would not lose it. Second cast and everything went solid - the bottom I thought. Then, as it does in these situations, the 'bottom' began to move - rapidly! After a hard fight in the shallow water I landed my third bass. At eight and a half pounds I was very contented and satisfied that I had worked this out for myself.

I had learnt several important lessons: bass do not need a surf to be catchable; they will feed in very shallow water; and even in hot, settled weather they can be caught on plugs or spinners.

On the following two mornings I caught four more bass, the largest seven pounds. That was it, I was, as in the title of Mike Ladle and Alan Vaughan's book which I had recently read, *Hooked on Bass !*

On my return, one of the first things I did was join the B.A.S.S. society. Over the next few years I learnt a great deal and caught plenty of bass, on a light beachcaster if there was a surf, and on plugs if conditions were quieter. However, during this time I became interested in the idea of catching bass on the fly. Although it had enormous appeal I was most concerned about being able to cast a large fly far enough to put it in front of a bass. I spent time improving my fly-casting, had a few lessons and learnt to double-haul. I even built myself a ten foot, #9/10 flyrod, especially for bass fishing.

Like many other anglers, I suffered rather a problem of confidence in a new untried method. However I was greatly helped and influenced at this time by reading Lou Tabory's book, *Inshore flyfishing*. I learnt that there was already a flourishing coldwater flyfishery for bass - for striped bass on the north-east coast of North America. I read how American anglers were pioneering methods and tackle which were sure to influence British anglers. I hoped that this would influence the way anglers saw our own sea bass, and that this would help bass to gain the status and recognition they deserved.

1995 - (This account of an Irish fishing trip with fellow-enthusiast Mike Oliver, was previously published in the B.A.S.S. magazine.) The intention was to travel around and use the fly gear as soon as we got a chance. Upon our arrival the weather became hot and sultry; Ireland felt more like the Mediterranean coast. Our first session started at 4.30a.m. at a mark we fancied with a flyrod. Mike was happy to do the hard work with the flyrod whilst I decided to go prospecting with a spinning rod. As we walked down I could see another angler there already. He hadn't caught anything nor had he done well during the last few days. As he was a very experienced bass angler who I'd always expect to out-fish me I was not optimistic for my chances. However, we were not about to give up yet.

After a while he sensibly left us to it. It was very bright and hot but there was enough wind to give an 18" wave.

Out of the blue Mike was into a fish. He pointed to where the fish were and I then spotted the odd swirl in the waves. After a good scrap Mike landed a 2lb 4oz schoolie. Having photographed it I ran to the car and assembled the new #9 10 foot flyrod I had recently finished. I was all fingers and thumbs. I stripped off some line and cast to where the fish had been; I'd hardly started to retrieve and Bang! My first bass on a fly rod. I remember being surprised at the ferocity of the take and the doggedness of the fight. Eventually I was holding a 2lb 4oz bar of silver, with a fly hanging out of its mouth. We were over the first obstacle: the method worked! In the next couple of hours we caught and released 14 bass. At one stage my shooting head and fly were totally static on the bottom while I was sorting out a different head. Suddenly line was streaming seawards as a bass picked up the static fly. The fish was hooked and landed.

That evening we returned to fish the mark with two other anglers. Mike had six and I had seven; again all between two and three pounds. The fly seemed every bit as productive as the plugs and freelined baits used by the others. These bass were feeding on small sand-eels, and our four inch long, 1/0 and 2/0 white Deceivers were a good imitation.

At 8.30am the following morning it was bright, hot and flat calm; we blanked. That night I had three. The next day we blanked again in the morning but in the evening Mike had eight and I had seven - all on the fly. By now we had found that the most productive way to fish a beach was to move around until we located fish then we would move together and both catch a few until they moved on. Then we'd have to find them again. While doing this Mike hooked a fish, I moved next to him and also hooked a fish. To our astonishment, when Mike landed it, both of our flies were in its mouth!

We also learnt to use constant hand-over-hand retrieves and good solid strikes to set the hooks. Hooks were carefully honed to maximum sharpness. Mike also squashed down the barbs on his flies. When we had the opportunity of fishing in a current we found that casting across and letting the fly sweep around was very effective. It was also easy to fish over shallow snaggy ground using a 'bend back' style of fly and a floating flyline. Most of the time I used shooting heads. On the whole these made casting easier and meant I could carry several line densities in a small packet, rather than carrying several bulky reels. Their main disadvantage is that they are awkward to fish into a wind.

The weather was abnormally bright, hot and settled but fish could be caught in blazing sunshine if a bit of wind broke the surface up. If it was flat calm we had to wait until evening.

Really we spent too much time fishing. By the end of the week we were shattered, but contented. On the last evening we agreed to postpone some of the packing and have only a few hours sleep. The intention was to gain a last couple of hours after the bass. We took the minimum of gear and left the camera, which was awkward to carry, behind.

We soon found the fish concentrated in one area. Over a couple of hours we each caught several schoolies. As darkness fell and we were thinking of leaving I started to hear the odd big splash. I cast further, trying smaller flies in case the splashes were made by sea trout. Still nothing. I went back to a bigger fly. Suddenly I got the most vicious take I'd had all week. This was a better fish, taking line off the reel very quickly, but within seconds it was off. The atmosphere was so exciting I didn't have time to be disappointed and carried on casting. I was beginning to wonder if bigger fish had come in to feed and were pushing the smaller ones out of the area.

Mike came out to join me and we agreed to fish on and go without sleep for the journey back. Soon Mike had a better fish of about 4lb. As I reeled my line out of the way I discovered I had spent the last twenty minutes fishing without a fly. The fish I'd hooked earlier couldn't have been just pricked but had broken the leader where I'd probably weakened the line with a wind knot. I surmised, disappointedly, that it must have been a good fish; 16lb leader doesn't normally break easily even with a couple of wind knots. I tied on a new leader and fly - promptly pricking a fish. Again it was soon off. I could still hear the odd big splash in the darkness. It seemed obvious that something out of the ordinary was bound to happen. Twenty yards away Mike's reel started screaming. This fish was fighting harder but neither of us paid much attention as we wanted to get on and catch some more. Annoyingly Mike seemed to take ages to play it, but I still stood next to him with the net. Eventually it slid into the mesh and I slipped my thumb down the line. My thumb went into its mouth and I gripped it by the bottom jaw pulling it towards me into the beam of the headlight. Astonished, I was looking not at the expected 3 - 4lb fish, but one of around 7lb. We have both caught bigger fish but this was the most silver, most beautifully conditioned bass I had ever seen. Both of us were a bit stunned by its beauty and size. I can still picture it in my mind now. The sight of that fish would have convinced any sceptical game fisherman that the bass is every bit as much a worthy quarry as any salmon or sea-trout. I knew Mike wouldn't want to kill it just for a photo and although I have no qualms about taking the odd fish it somehow didn't seem fair to take this one when we had been granted so many.

We measured it against the landing net handle - it was 26". Mike and I admired it for a while. This was the fish we had come for. A good bass on a flyrod! Mike slipped it out of his hands and back into the darkness.

Back at the bungalow we threw the rest of our packing into the back of the car, in the process of which we were virtually eaten by huge clouds of midges. The alarm clock was set (in the car!) for thirty minutes time. I drove first. After twenty five minutes I was feeling very drowsy and had to stop and wake Mike. Thirty minutes later Mike woke me. It was an unpleasant journey, but by doing short stints at the wheel I don't think it was too dangerous. However I will never get that tired on holiday again.

When we got to the ferry we hired a cabin, to get into a bed was bliss. I shut my eyes and all I could see was dark shimmering water disturbed only by the swirls of feeding bass.

1995-96 - The birth of a daughter prevented me going to Ireland the following summer. However I now had confidence in the method and my ability. In May 1995 my work took me to the Welsh coast for a few days. Rising at 5 a.m. I managed to get a hour's fishing and be back at work for seven o'clock. The first morning, in an area I had never fished before, I was delighted to catch and return three bass to two and a half pounds.

The following day at 2 p.m. I was on my way home when I decided to stop for a last quick cast. By the time I got to the water's edge I was regretting having worn my neoprene chest-waders. It was sweltering hot and very bright. Good conditions to fish at dawn or dusk, but not during the middle of the day.

The water was shallow and very weedy so I tied on a bend-back fly. As I waded carefully among the rocks I had several casts without result. Moving slightly further out I cast and waited a moment for the fly to sink. The fly slowly swept around in the current, then, on the first pull of the retrieve I had a solid take. This was not what I had expected! After a strong fight I landed a fine bass of over five pounds.

On three subsequent sessions in the same area I only managed one bass - hooked and lost. Sometimes, for no apparent reason, the fish are just not there. Since then, although I feel that I have only scratched the surface of the potential of fly-rodding for bass, I have had tremendous fun with the method. I have even caught a few bass in surprisingly bad weather conditions.

I have just heard from John Quinlan in Ireland that he caught a four-pound bass on the fly on 4th February! I still feel that the ability to cast a long line is an important asset to this kind of fishing. If you learn to do this you have the versatility and ability to cast big lures, and to cope with difficult headwinds. You can now tackle conditions and locations where previously you would have had to resort to plug or spinner. I find this a great challenge - and very effective!

Tackle - After my rod, reel and flies, my most essential item is a line-tray to keep retrieved line out of the water. I use a washing-up bowl lined with synthetic grass, strapped around my waist with nylon webbing and a quick release buckle. Safety should always be considered when flyfishing in the sea. I always wear sun glasses during the day, and clear protective glasses at night. A bass-sized fly in your eye could cause a horrifying injury. I have a halter-type, CO_2 powered, life-jacket. When fishing alone at night, or in unknown waters, it is very reassuring. I would recommend one to anyone wading, especially in estuaries, or fishing potentially dangerous rock marks. I always carry a waterproof camera. Although I do like to eat an occasional bass, I don't want to kill a big bass just for the sake of a photograph.

Careless talk costs bass! - Bass populations can be quite localised and are extremely vulnerable to commercial pressure. If you come upon a good mark do not be too quick to tell all and sundry. In the past, populations of bass have been netted to extinction after anglers have advertised their success. Even unscrupulous rod fisherman can decimate a small local population.

Having said that, one of the pleasures of angling is making new discoveries and exchanging information with other anglers. But do be careful about this, especially if there is a risk of commercial netting in the area.

The majority of the bass I have been catching in recent years have been from the abundant 1989 year-class. They are now three to four pounds in weight, and should be six pounds plus in two years' time. As long as the ban on commercial bass fishing in Ireland is maintained, there should be some fantastic fishing over the next few years.

As much as I love fishing in Ireland, I have to make the best of whatever weather conditions prevail during my visits. The experience I have now gained enables me to cope with a range of conditions and methods. Even though the weather might be atrocious for flyfishing, I always carry a made-up flyrod in the car. Conditions can change faster than you might think and eventually, I am going to be in the right place at the right time and get the fishing experience of a life-time!

I hope that reading this book will encourage you to take the opportunity of fishing for this beautiful but largely unappreciated gamefish.

15

BASS IN MORECAMBE BAY

Martin James

Some of my most exciting fly fishing experiences in Britain have been when chasing bass. Whenever a friend suggests I join him for a day's boat fishing for bass I jump at the chance. Not for me an uptide casting-outfit but a ten-weight flyrod and a selection of flies. Summer flyfishing for bass is as exciting as any form of flyfishing in the world.

Last year after a few days of hot weather Stewart invited me out for a days fishing in Morecambe Bay. The conditions were excellent; bright sunshine, clear water, the sea flat calm. I was dressed in shorts, tee-shirt, neoprene booties - these latter are perfect when boat fishing. Stewart was going to bottom-fish until we spotted the diving sea-birds which would then lead us to the bass. Then he would spin for them while I chucked the fluffy things.

As I sat reading the *Daily Telegraph*, Stewart caught a succession of dabs and small whiting. Some eight hundred yards away on the horizon, I spotted diving gulls.

"Lets go, Stewart. The bass are over there". In with the tackle, up-anchor, then off skimming across the smooth glassy surface. As we got within a hundred yards the motor was throttled back. I was ready to shoot line, gulls were screaming and diving, and from below I imagined the bass slashing and tearing into the frightened swirling baitfish.

My chosen fly was a Polar pattern which had proved so successful for bass and many other fish. Barracuda and kingfish just love them. As we drifted within casting distance I shot some twenty yards of floating line, letting the fly lie on the surface among the mass of bait fish for a few seconds then I twitched the rod tip. As the fly came to life a bass pounced, I tightened and a nice fish was hooked.

Minutes later it was close to hand. Bending down I slipped the barbless fly from the fish. Two false casts and the fly was back among the bait-fish. Once more a bass struck, a second fish was bought to the boat, and unhooked. Nine casts and eight fish later the bass had gone. Brian spinning with a silver sprat had two fish. Spinning ensured the lure was in the area for only a few seconds, whereas the fly could be kept among the bait-fish for as long as needed. We followed the shoal around, and after an interval of some thirty minutes or so we were back among the bass for a few more hectic minutes of catching, playing and releasing. Then the shoal would move on again. We moved with them. It was exciting fishing - equal to anything in the world.

Editor's note:

This is the kind of saltwater flyfishing which is available wherever shoaling predators occur. Whilst the use of a boat enables the angler to chase the shoals of feeding fish, similar tactics can be employed from the shore. Mackerel are the most likely catch in these circumstances, but bass, pollack, sea-trout and other predators all feed in this way. I have caught small bluefish and striped bass when fishing in exactly this way in Chesapeake Bay.

Many anglers would disagree with Martin about the tackle needed on such occasions. For casting into a wind from the shore, or for playing heavy fish, the ten-weight outfit is most useful. However, when casting from a boat to shoaling school-fish, you can fish much lighter and improve both presentation and sport. In Chesapeake Bay I used an eight-foot, 4/5 weight travel-rod which coped adequately.

16

B.A.S.S. AND BASS CONSERVATION

Roger Baker

Like many other species, bass have good and bad years for reproduction. Over the last fifty years scientists and angler-naturalists have been surveying and recording populations of immature bass. Scale readings and length measurements, have been used to confirm the strong year classes produced by good spawning years or high survival rates. This work also identified those estuaries and harbours which were most important for young bass, and was the basis for the legislation which designated protected Bass Nursery Areas in 1990. Angler and naturalist Donovan Kelley was awarded the M.B.E. in recognition of his pioneering work in this field.

Between 1947 and 1987 there were only three really good years when large numbers of bass fry were produced or survived long enough to become adult fish. These were the fry which hatched in 1949, 1959 and 1976.

The bass is a very slow growing fish. However, in 1968 the average bass caught from the shore along the Essex coast was five pounds, and 'catch per unit effort' by shore-anglers was one fish for every two sessions. By 1977 boat anglers were catching fish from offshore sand-banks like the Kentish Knock, and the average bass was over six and a half pounds. The fishing was outstanding compared to today. As an example, one boat trip, skippered by my friend and fellow campaigner Bob Cox, concluded with eleven anglers catching ninety-nine bass over 8lbs in less than three hours! Most of these fish were returned alive.

The bulk of the bass caught during an eight year 'golden period' around the Thames estuary were from the successful spawning of 1959. This was the last good year-class of bass prior to the arrival of monofilament gill nets and the commercial onslaught.

In the late 1970s came the development and widespread use of mono-filament gill nets which were to decimate our inshore fish stocks, especially bass and sea-trout. The 1976 year-class of bass was exploited by nets from the time they became sizeable (32cm), at 4 to 5 years old (1980/81). The east-coast anglers never saw the 1976 year-class as mature fish, in any numbers. By the time they reached

4lb in weight they had been wiped-out by the commercials!

Some great bass fishing was still to be had in the south-west in the early 1980s. Unfortunately before I moved down there! One notable catch was taken by my friend Malcolm Gilbert. Twenty-eight bass averaging over eleven pounds each (best 13.12) in a single day! Although Malcolm would see this as a biological phenonemon, rather than a great angling feat.

Since 1987 a succession of mild winters and warmer sea temperatures, possibly due to global warming, has done the bass a lot of good. 1987 was a good year-class, 1988 was even better, while 1989 was a massive 4.5 times better than the 1976 year-class, the best in the previous forty years! The 1987, 1988 and 1989 bass fry were also the first to benefit from the introduction of a new size limit of 36cm and the thirty-four newly pro-tected nursery areas around our southern coastline.

In the last 10 years we have had eight of the best year-classes in the last fifty years! Every year since 1987 has been good and collectively the result is that there are now record numbers of juvenile bass in the sea. Most of these fish are still undersized but with the right protection, within a few years we could see great changes in the fortunes of our sport, reversing the trends of the last twenty years. By the year 2005 the survivors of the 1989 year-class could weigh 7 to 8lb. Year-classes 1995 and 1997 may be as good as 1989. Combined, all these year-classes mean that we could have a fantastic bass fishery by 2010, if only adequate protection and enforce-ment is put in place!

Imagine, a world-class wild sport-fishery, enjoyed and harvested in a sustainable and controlled manner. The sort of fishery you have to travel to the Florida Keys to experience today.

The fish from year-classes 1987 to 1989 should now range from 3 to 5 pounds and we could be experiencing the calibre of bass fishing we believed the nursery areas would deliver. Unfortunately we are not! The bass from these strong year classes have been cleaned out, not only by gill nets, but also by British and French pair-trawling teams fishing out the huge shoals of bass as they move along the English Channel from the win-tering grounds off the south Cornish coast.

In late January and early February these fish start to move eastward up the channel, spawning as summer approaches. The pair teams run through them with specialist mid-water trawls, day and night. Last year's catch by this method was estimated at between 5,000 and 6,000 tonnes, but there is no Total Allowable Catch for bass anyway, and therefore no limit to what the trawlers can take! Ironically, the bulk of these fish are from the 1989 year class, the first to benefit from the nursery legislation!

The 1987 year-class of bass has now been hammered by trawlers for four

Robert Lai's ragworm flies.

Barry Ord Clarke

Above: Flyfishing in the snow in the south of Funen. *Rudy van Duijnhoven*

Left: Irish sea-trout with sand-eels. *Rudy van Duijnhoven*

Fat 42cm Danish sea-trout that took a shrimp imitation.   *Rudy van Duijnhoven*

Estuary school bass caught on a slider. *Peter James*

Bass streamer. *Rudy van Duijnhoven*

Shannon bass. *Rudy van Duijnhoven*

Dutch fly-caught sea bass.   *Rudy van Duijnhoven*

Tommy Rowlands nets a mullet caught by Paul Morgan. *Rod Calbrade*

5lb mullet caught by Andrew James. *Rod Calbrade*

Mackerel taken on a streamer meant for bass.   *Rudy van Duijnhoven*

Fly-caught Irish pollack.   *Rudy van Duijnhoven*

Coalfish.   *Rudy van Duijnhoven*

Small cod taken on a sea-trout fly. *Rudy van Duijnhoven*

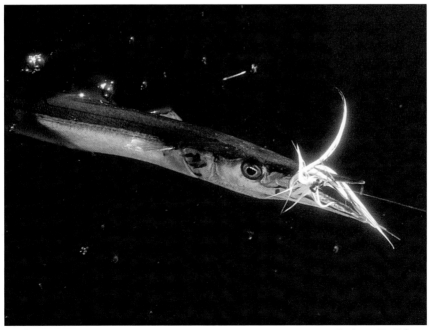

Garfish hanging on to a streamer. *Rudy van Duijnhoven*

René Flohil and skipper John Brittain admire an Irish blue-shark. *Rudy van Duijnhoven*

Rudy's blue shark fly. *Rudy van Duijnhoven*

René Flohil and a box full of sea-streamers.   *Rudy van Duijnhoven*

Changing flies at an Irish rock mark. *Rudy van Duijnhoven*

Fat 45cm sea-run rainbow (steelhead) caught at Funen. *Rudy van Duijnhoven*

A shower of scales from a twaite shad.   *Rudy van Duijnhoven*

Candy Eel

Pearl Bass

Ultra Shrimp

Darters

Crab Patterns

Fire Edge Shrimp

Bonefish Slider

Needle Fish

Flies from Crystal River.

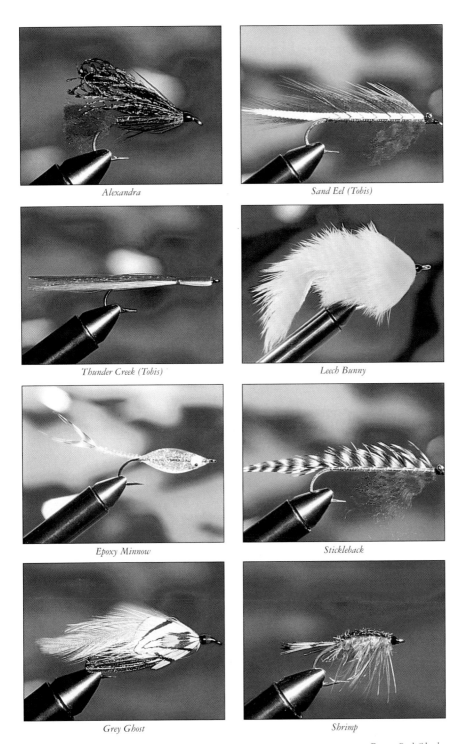

Alexandra

Sand Eel (Tobis)

Thunder Creek (Tobis)

Leech Bunny

Epoxy Minnow

Stickleback

Grey Ghost

Shrimp

Saltwater flies.

Barry Ord Clarke

Robert Lai shrimp pattern. *Barry Ord Clarke*

Small version of the famous Scandinavian sea-trout surface lure 'The Cigar'. *Barry Ord Clarke*

consecutive years. The numbers of individual 1987 fish alone, now missing from our beaches, is a staggering 7,000 five-pound bass per mile, for 1000 miles of coastline!

Did we expect investors and shareholders in commercial fishing machines to become the major beneficiaries of Donovan Kelley's lifetime work for conservation and angling? No we did not!

Commercial interest in bass only came about because stocks of cod and sole had already been decimated, and eating bass has become popular in fashionable restaurants. The British commercial industry contributed only £500million pounds gross to the economy in 1996, and yet for that it received £76million in grants and subsidy! Our taxes have been used to destroy our sport!

Mediterranean fish farms produced 25,000 tonnes of bass for the table in 1996. We are led to believe that bass under the minimum landing size (36cm) openly displayed for sale in Britain originate from European fish farms. Commercial fishing of wild bass is a wasteful use of a resource capable of yielding much higher returns in incomes and jobs by managed recreational exploitation. The future for some forms of netting is in jeopardy and transition to the more secure gainful activity of recreation and tourism would be in the interests of some netsmen and their communities, socially and economically.

B.A.S.S.

In 1973 a small group of bass anglers formed the Bass Angler's Sportfishing Society, dedicated to exchanging information on bass and angling methods, but especially to conservation and to research into the species. B.A.S.S. members has been actively involved in assisting research by Donovan Kelley and M.A.F.F. scientists through scale samples and surveys.

B.A.S.S. Objectives

1. We are committed to raising the status of bass to that of the first European Saltwater Game Fish. This would involve licensing for commercial bass fisherman and for anglers. The requirement for a licence to retain bass would reduce the black economy fishery; raise the status of, and permit some regulation of the sport fishery; and provide funds for better management.

2. We want precautionary restrictions on trawling for overwintering stocks of bass between December and April, primarily in the Western Approaches where they shoal up prior to spawning.

This unregulated fishery allows stocks from specific geographical populations to be heavily depleted.

B.A.S.S. Strategy

Recently a group of members have been actively working to raise funds to employ a political lobbyist to promote the interests of the bass angler. However this has been overtaken by the appointment of Gabriella Bianca by the European Anglers Alliance and the European Fishing Tackle Trade Association to represent the interests of anglers in Europe. We are currently working with our national bodies to make use of this lobbyist, one of whose principal concerns is overfishing of stocks by commercial fisheries at sea. The National Federation of Sea Anglers, whose chairman, Jack Reece, is a strong campaigner on behalf of conservation, now fully support our aims.

It is time for politicians to give sportsmen a fair hearing and where it can be shown that a specific resource can generate and sustain more of an economic and social base as a sportfish than as a commercial species, then that species should be managed for recreational exploitation. Such management needs to be ongoing and it requires stock assessments, mortality, recruitment etc., to be monitored so that controls in the form of bag limits, size limits and closed seasons could be implemented on a precautionary basis, if necessary. This could result in a massive growth in healthy recreational outdoor fishing activity and would be sustainable!

Membership of B.A.S.S. is open to all anglers. Minimum membership is £13 for adults, £18 for families and organisations, and £6 for old age pensioners and juniors.

Further details are available from: Steve Pitts, 18 Highfields Close, Stoke Gifford, Bristol BS12 6YA or at http://www.ukbass.com, the B.A.S.S. internet web-site.

Current Legislation

No bass of less than 36 cm may be retained. The nursery areas designated by M.A.F.F. are closed to commercial fishing. Angling from boats is also prohibited here, but shore angling is permitted.

PART IV

MULLET

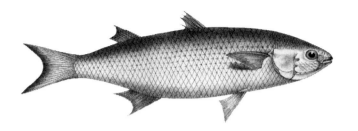

17

FLYFISHING FOR MULLET
ON THE DORSET COAST

Mike Ladle

I am not a 'fly-angler'. In fact I object to being labelled as any particular kind of fisherman. I am just as happy float-fishing a maggot for dace as I am wobbling a dead-bait for pike, and I get as much satisfaction from catching a salmon on a prawn as from hooking a bass on a plug, or a conger on a lump of mackerel. The truth is that I try to use the method which will give me the best chance of catching the biggest fish which are available. When I fish with a fly-rod, a fly-reel and an artificial fly it is because I think it is the most effective method, not because I think there is anything superior about fly-fishing. The flies which I use are rarely exotic creations of coloured silks, fluorescent flosses or fancy feathers, but they are the closest imitations of natural fish-food that I can create. In other words I try to "match the hatch", whether it is sand-eels, herring-fry, woodlice or maggots. Having got that off my chest I don't need to make any more excuses and the remainder of what I have to say will hopefully be clear to all.

In the months of April and May each year, when the sun begins to heat up the water in shallow sheltered bays along the Dorset coast, thick-lipped grey mullet can be seen, on calm sunny days, basking near the surface with the occasional fish leaping clear of the water.

As the tide begins to flood they get their heads down on the flat rock surfaces from which they graze the green filaments of algae or brown diatom-films. In these situations, where tough fronds of bladderwrack and other brown weeds prevent easy fishing, light float-tackle is usually the only option open. This is the conventional method which can be used to catch thick-lipped mullet and it is very effective at times. Coastal mullet, however, have several different methods of feeding and one of these provides the opportunity for fantastic sport with fly-tackle. Yes! Mullet often feed at the water surface.

Surface-feeding mullet employ several different and distinct feeding-tactics which present scope for real initiative and originality on the part of the angler. Coarse anglers know that different species of fish taking floating food use different approaches, and the 'rise-forms' of trout provide game-fishermen with a constant topic of conversation. We have all seen the pet goldfish with it's lips breaking the surface as it gobbles up the ants' eggs. By slowly swimming forward and, at the same time, pumping water into its mouth and out through the gills, "old Gilbert" manages to create a constant stream of drifting fish-food into his regularly pulsing lips. Carp and tench often break the silence of the lake-side with loud sucking noises as they take snail-eggs or insects from among the lily-pads. Fish such as trout, chub, dace and grayling use a wide range of sipping or sucking movements to take trapped or emerging insects. All of these fish are susceptible to angling methods designed to present a bait at the water-surface.

It is no coincidence that so many species feed 'on the top'. The so-called surface-tension of the water creates a sort of invisible skin which acts as a trap for small animals. The buoyancy of the water also forces many of the lighter fragments of plant and animal remains to the surface. This natural larder of floating particles (properly called neuston) provides a concentration of food too good to miss.

The edge of the sea is no different to most fresh-waters with regard to it's rich supply of surface-food, and several species take advantage of it. Sand-smelt, bass, pollack, garfish, sea-trout and particularly grey mullet, are all quick to seize their chance of an easy meal. Mullet are quite capable of sucking in individual food items from the surface just like any of the species mentioned above. Accounts of such surface-feeding have appeared in the press from time to time and Des Brennan gives a stimulating description of landing a large thick-lip from an Irish harbour by using free-lined, floating, bread-crust.

Grey mullet have a second method of taking surface-food which is more akin to that used by basking sharks and whales. With their large mouths wide open and their keen eyes focused along the surface-film, they swim steadily about, like living plankton nets, sieving the surface-film for floating scraps.

Just as in any other form of surface-angling, it is first necessary to decide what the fish are taking and to "match the hatch. Seaweed fly larvae, pupae, mosquitoes (buzzers), fragments of eel-grass, kitchen-waste or sea-weed beetles are all gobbled up from time to time.

Having decided on a suitable bait, we are then faced with the problem of how it can be presented to the fish. Over the years a variety of methods have been applied to catching surface-feeders, mainly in fresh-waters. A number of techniques enable surface-feeders to be caught by anglers using light and fragile baits on tackle designed for more conventional methods, but dry-fly gear is a complete system just for the presentation of surface baits.

The lure used on fly-tackle must be sufficiently tough to withstand the stress of casting and this generally restricts the method to the use of artificial flies. This restriction does not seem to be too serious in the pursuit of trout, grayling or chub but the eagle-eyed mullet is more critical of fur, feather and nylon.

Mullet are wary, not only of the looming figure of the angler and the carelessly presented fly, but of the fly-line on the water-surface, the nylon cast floating in the surface-film and the fly itself, if it does not look and move exactly like the genuine article. The reasons for this fastidious behaviour are not difficult to determine. The eyes of the fish are focused right at the water surface and are perfectly positioned to see items on or above the water. This is logical because surface-sifting mullet need to distinguish carefully between the living (food) and the dead (rubbish) (of which there is a great deal) to avoid wasted feeding activity.

As an example of how to catch surface-feeding thick-lips which are using the "scoop and select" feeding approach, I shall describe a situation which I know very well, but first a few words about their main prey. On many of the world's coasts, kelp flies or seaweed flies are almost unbelievably abundant. For example, on the beaches of California it was estimated that a million tonnes of kelp were washed ashore each year and on a warm summer's day there could be as many as ten million kelp flies on every kilometre of shoreline. The maggots of these flies feed on the rotting seaweed and along the South coast of England they are equally abundant. In the years 1953-4 the flies were so numerous on our southern shores that they were described, in the national press, as a plague. This annual bonanza of seaweed fly maggots is just what the mullet ordered. The biggest pile of natural groundbait in the world! As the spring tides approach their two-weekly peak the thick-lips congregate along the shore-line at each period of high water.

The following anecdote recalls a trip which I made many years ago with one or two pals and which has been repeated on hundreds of occasions since. It was a superb sunny day, sea conditions were warm, calm and clear. For ease of walking, in the sweaty conditions, I was wearing a pair of plimsolls which had seen better days, ancient, tatty jeans and a tee-shirt more brightly coloured than was sensible. After a two-mile walk we found a reasonable-sized mound of decaying weed. As the sea crept towards the high-water mark, the little, soft, white maggots of the seaweed flies floated out of the weed-mass. There was no wave-action or wind-drift and the maggots collected in white, scummy clumps close to the tide-line. Small numbers of average-sized mullet (one or two kilos in weight) were gathering to gorge themselves on the free feast. They were feeding in water only 25 cm deep and within a metre or two of the sea's edge. Swimming busily along the gentle longshore current they were scooping the maggots into their wide-opened, chubby-lipped mouths.

By keeping a low profile it was possible to approach without alarming or dispersing the shoals (a common problem). This cautious stalking had the disadvantage of requiring the angler to kneel or squat in the slimy, stinking, rotten weed. The rod was an old, eight-and-a-half-foot hollow glass fly-rod made from a cheap kit. (I now use a 3.5 m carbon rod with a number 7 tapered floating line. The reel (now defunct) was an old "Pridex" which had long been fused permanently to the reel fittings by the corrosive action of sea water on aluminium. The line was the usual cheap, plastic, double-tapered, floating number 6, needle knotted to an 8ft cast of 6lb nylon. The cast was armed with a good quality, number twelve dry-fly hook. A spindle of white ethafoam, whipped at each end to secure it on the hook-shank, and garnished with four white maggots (bought at my local tackle-shop) completed the set-up.

By casting at an oblique angle to the shoreline it was possible to place the fly beyond a group of feeding fish. A slow, progressive lift of the rod caused the fly to skate sedately through the middle of the shoal. One or two false-bites were the result of fish brushing against the cast and these were punctuated at regular intervals by more positive twitches of the line as fish mouthed the fly.

Because of the crouching stance necessary to keep out of the fishes' field of view, movement was a bit restricted and the response to a bite had to be a full swinging movement of the fly-rod. A successful strike was met by solid resistance as a decent thick-lip felt the hook, boiled on the surface and tore away out to sea. Following the typical, initial, long and powerful run the fight resolved itself into a characteristic, dogged, tug-of-war interspersed by the short fast surging runs of the fish. Gradually the line built up on the spool of the reel and after about five minutes the first fish was wallowing under the rod-tip on a short line. By now Dave had reeled in his float-gear and was by my side wielding the large landing-net. The fish plunged and made a final short run before it slid into the meshes and was drawn on to the beach.

Dave returned to his fishing and I carried the captive mullet, still in the net, away from the waters edge to be unhooked. It weighed just over 1.5 kg, about average for fly-caught thick-lips. Dave was already in to a decent fish, one of six similar specimens which we landed on float or fly-fished maggot that evening. In the course of the session we also lost about three times as many fish as we landed, mostly because the small hooks tore free. It would be foolish to pretend that surface-feeding mullet are to be found everywhere, but fish behaving in the manner described occur on many parts of the Dorset coast, the Channel Islands and the Isle of Man. It is well known that seaweed flies are widespread on British shores and it would be interesting to learn of other instances of maggot-feeding (or indeed any surface-feeding) mullet or bass (yes bass join in the feast and I have landed them up to 4 kg on the maggot-fly), so that anglers can form a picture of where and when these fish behave in this manner.

So much for thick-lipped mullet on the fly but what else can be caught in this way?. Thin-lipped mullet which haunt the tidal reaches of rivers will also, occasionally, skim food from the water surface and would surely be susceptible to the dry-fly (although they are much more consistently caught on ragworm-baited spinners). Sand-smelts, bass and less often small pollack and wrasse have also taken my surface flies in the sea.

18

MULLET IN HARBOURS AND CREEKS

Martin James

The size 16 maggot-tipped Bloody Butcher disappeared as gently as a brown trout would take a dry fly. I tightened into my first saltwater fish hooked on reservoir flyfishing tackle; a mullet of some 3 lbs.

Over the years I had caught many mullet on float-fished maggot, but was determined to catch one on the fly. I determined on the lower reaches of the Sussex Rother to try my experiment, and I chose the Bloody Butcher and maggot combination thinking the red in the fly would act as an attractor along with the maggot to give it some life. It worked. That experience happened some years ago.

Many species of sea-fish have declined dramatically because of over-fishing by British and foreign trawlers, illegal gill-netting and pollution. Not so the mullet. Visit the harbours, creeks, docks, estuaries and marshes, and there you will find the mullet. Not a fish for the faint-hearted. Sometimes they fish can be caught quite easily, but more often they prove very difficult to tempt. Mullet are a super fish for the fly fisher.

Tackle, as in all saltwater flyfishing, should be designed for the salt. I use a Greys of Alnwick Colorado, a 10 ft 3-piece rod, rated for a 7/8 line, with a fast middle-to-tip action. Designed for freshwater fishing, I had my Colorado built with corrosion-proof fittings. It's an excellent bonefish rod.

I use a Loop model 2 with a spare spool. One spool is fitted with a Scientific Anglers weight-forward floating line and the other spool is fitted with a Ryobi Masterline "Illusion" a very slow sinking line. On both types of fly-lines I have a nine-foot leader, tapering to a 6lb point. My flies are all tied on barbless hooks in small sizes - 12's and 14's.

My mullet-patterns include Bloody Butcher, Red-Tag, Baby Doll and Bread Fly. All are tipped with one or two gentles. The Bread Fly is used with great success in harbours and docks. I start off by feeding with liquidised bread or mashed rice, often adding some pilchard oil to get the fish interested and feeding.

Several of my friends in the United States use Smelly Jelly which they rub into their flies to create a smell. The stuff comes in small jars in dozens of different flavours. I feel that it could have applications in many saltwater flyfishing situations, both for mullet and for other species. It can be purchased in the UK from Harris Angling (Telephone 01692-581208).

Over the past few years we have been very lucky in getting a few weeks of very warm weather with little or no wind. The perfect conditions for mullet. Last year I found a shoal of fish alongside a dock wall. They were cruising up and down without a care in the world inspecting anything that looked like food. A dog appeared on the wall close to the waters edge. A swirl and a splash and the fish had gone.

I sat in the warm sunshine, watching the world go by. When the mullet appeared again I threw in some small pieces of bread. The fish began knocking and nudging it about. Soon pieces of bread were being taken. Time to fish. I tied on one of my Bread Flies and cast out. Luckily the fish didn't spook. Soon a fish nudged the imitation, then another. I sat with bated breath, willing a fish to take. As two or three fish knocked the bread and the imitation about, another fish, some what bigger, cruised over and without hesitation sucked in my fly. As I saw the leader moving across the surface, I tightened gently. As I did so all Hell was let loose as the fish realised it was hooked and dived for the bottom. In some two and a half hours I had seven fish and probably missed the same number.

Editors Note:
Martin raises some interesting points using ground-bait and fly-and-maggot. Chumming or ground-baiting, the use of scent or flavouring agents on flies, and the combined use of bait and flies are frowned on in almost all freshwater situations. Indeed, in most circumstances they are prohibited or even illegal. Even where not specifically banned, their use in stocked fisheries, or against wild salmonids, is rightly regarded as unsporting and unselfish.

Fishing in the salt has not attracted the same restrictive legislation. Nor does it generally have the same problems of conservation. Any legal method is legitimate, and the combination of some of these methods with flyfishing provides exciting new avenues for exploration. If the use of scent, or added bait, on artificial flies, enables the capture of otherwise difficult or impossible species of fish, it widens the scope of sporting flyfishing, and is a welcome progression.

19

KIM'S MULLET : A SAD TALE

Kim Jacek

I have a story from Tunoe, a little island outside a city called Hov about 26 km from Århus. We arrive Saturday morning and, the wind coming from the west, we fish on the east side of the island. I catch a sea-trout.

On Sunday was the wind gone. I was fishing on the west side, and the mullet were there. I use my fly rod and a fly I called Allan's Mullet Fly.

I hook one. This is a very strong fish and a very shy fish. The fish run about 100 yards with the fly in the mouth, the fish jump out of the water and the fish was gone, and the other mullet was also gone rest of the day.

I have nightmares about this fish. Kim suggests the following patterns to try for mullet:

John's Mullet Fly
      Hook: 10-14 lightweight wet.
      Thread: Green 8/0.
      Tail: 4 or 5 green peacock eye herls.
      Body: Green peacock eye herl wrapped around the hook shank.
      Hackle: Again green peacock herl to form a collar.
               Tied like a Pheasant Tail Nymph

Kim's Mullet Fly
      Hook: Kamazan B980 size 8-10.
      Thread: Black uni 8/0.
      Body: 2-3 Green peacock eye herls.
      Tag: Red.
      Hackle: Brown hackle.

Ole's Mullet Fly
      Hook: Kamazan B980 size 8-10.
      Thread: White Uni 8/0.
      Body: Dubbing mixed of hare and white SLF.
      Hackle: Grizzly tied sparse.

Kim also suggests the following patterns; Diawl Bach, Red Tag, Black Palmer, all tied on light-weight wet-fly hooks fly.

Or red or white maggots!

20

FLYFISHING FOR MULLET 1888

John Bickerdyke

Fly fishing for grey mullet in the daytime, though it is often tried, is rarely successful. The fish will follow a fly, but will rarely seize it. At night the fly fisher stands a better chance, and will now and again take a few fish on a white moth. The dressing of a night fly for mullet was described in the following letter, published in the *Fishing Gazette* of June 18, 1887:-

"Sir, - I believe there are some rivers - generally shallow ones- in which mullet will not take a bait. With regard to flies, I have taken some mullet at night with a silver-bodied moth: wing, owl's feather; hackle, white; tail, a bit of kid or wash leather. The body should be first wrapped with wool, to make it fat, and the tinsel wound over it.

In the *Gazette* of September 3, 1881, Mr J. D. Dougal says that 'a man used to take them on the Clyde with a white fly, on the hook of which he put the bivalved oval spout fish, called on the Clyde Garrocher, the scientific name being *Mya arenaria*. Part of the flesh of this - probably the spout, which is exceedingly tough - he put on his fly. He angled at low water, and took numbers, from 3lb. to 5lb. each'.

I think this plan would be worth a trial where the *Mya arenaria* can be got, and I believe it is common on the British coast".

I am, &c, E. Gosling. Aberffraw, Anglesey, June 13.

A gentle placed on a hook might be cast as a fly with success, provided a few gentles were thrown among the fish, to make them feed on that bait. I have not tried the experiment.

From *The Book of the All-round Angler.* John Bickerdyke. 1888.

The only artificial bait of any use in mullet-fishing is a fly. This may either be a tinselly 'coach-man,' or a fat white fly. The time for this fishing is sunset.

From *Sea-fishing on the English Coast.* F.G. Aflalo. 1891.

21

MULLET ON FLY : A SHORT-LIVED SUCCESS?

Paul Morgan

Tommy Rowlands is the manager of the Tyn-y-cornel Hotel on the shore of Talyllyn; one of the most beautiful lakes in Wales. While most of our countrymen single-mindedly pursue the sewin, or else spend their weekends flogging the waters of Brenig and Trawsfynydd in pursuit of a place in the Welsh team, Tommy and I share a love for wilder places. We both fish for salmon and sea-trout; and we have both fished successfully in competitions, but we also like to drift the hill-lakes in our float-tubes, casting for wild mountain trout; and even more, we love to fish, with fly, lure and bait, for the really wild fish of the salt shore.

Tommy is an expert at catching mullet by traditional means, but he also constantly experiments with new methods and techniques. He and I have frequently tried casting a fly for these difficult fish, but with little success. Mullet are almost always present when we fish for bass, but beyond an occasional "follow", they had shown no sign of being interested in taking an artificial fly.

Last summer a couple of angling journalists, Cliff Waters and Andrew James from Trout Fisherman magazine, were to visit Talyllyn to write a feature on the loch-style fishing for brown trout which the lake is so famous for. They were to be accompanied by our mutual friend Rod Calbrade, who was to take photographs for the article. Tommy was keen to show them some different, perhaps more exciting, fishing, but as the date for their arrival approached the weather grew rough and we ruled out flyfishing in the sea as an option. Then, the day before they were due, Tommy telephoned me: "I've cracked it! I've been catching mullet on the fly!"

Fishing in a brackish lagoon on a nearby estuary, Tommy had found that fishing a team of small flies brought frequent follows, and he had landed several mullet of up to four pounds. He was keen to take the journalists the following day. Now, I am not experienced at catching mullet, but I have talked to a lot of people about flyfishing for mullet and I know that, unless they are preoccupied with an imitatable food item, they can be exceedingly fickle and difficult to catch with an artificial fly. Many people have caught an odd mullet on fly, but very few of them could repeat the feat. Whilst I did not doubt Tommy's story, I had real reservations about him being able to do it again for the camera.

Next afternoon I met the others at Talyllyn. They had had a successful morning on the lake and had some good photographs 'in the bag'. We drove to the estuary where we tackled up. I set up my 10'6" loch-rod with a WF8 line and a three-fly cast on three pound nylon; a finer leader than I would usually use with a fairly heavy line. Tommy had caught his fish on dark spider-patterns, so I put a Black Pennell and a black and silver spider on the droppers and a weighted black buzzer on the point.

The lagoon, at low water, is a huge area of uniformly shallow, knee-deep, water. The water-surface was rippled by the breeze, making it difficult to spot fish, but as soon as we began fishing we began getting follows from mullet. As I retrieved my flies at quite a brisk pace in the shallow water, the following fish created a heart-stopping bow-wave. After several abortive follows eventually one took hold and I was the first to hook a mullet. In the shallow water the fish sped away, taking line. It took me several minutes to get it under control, giving Rod, the photographer, plenty of time to splash through the mud and get the pictures he needed. Tommy netted the fish for me; not a big one, perhaps a pound and a half, but an important one for us. We were all thrilled that we had managed to catch a mullet on the fly, and with a photographer present! We all went on to catch and return fish; we all lost fish during the long ensuing fights; and I think that we were all broken by large fish. The highlight was a mullet of about five pounds caught by Andrew which took forever to land, providing Rod with some wonderful action photographs.

During the afternoon I found that mullet would follow the flies even in water only four or five inches deep. The only one which I hooked in such shallow water took off in a shower of spray and broke me around the only snag within a hundred yards. It seemed that every time I was able to cover a fish with my flies it would follow, and each time I found a shoal of fish I would have a few minutes of casting to them before they drifted away. We all experimented with different flies. I used the point-fly position especially for this, trying various nymphs, buzzers, gammarus shrimps and small lures. Despite this, all of our fish were caught on small (#14) black and silver spider patterns. Only one fish was killed; my first. We checked its stomach contents but only found the mullet's usual black, muddy, algal soup. There were no obvious prey items present, and the fish were not seen to take or chase anything except our flies.

Now comes the sad part! After three or four days of wonderful fishing, the mullet stopped taking, or even following, and we have not experienced the same success since.'

And now my theory. The part of the lagoon we fished is nearly a mile upstream from the river mouth. Our successful fishing period coincided with a period of low neap tides during the summer when, even at high water, the tide did not reach as far upstream as the lagoon. In consequence the lagoon was slowly shrinking in area and, being fed by the river, becoming less saline. The end of the successful flyfishing coincided with the first new influx of salt water as the tides grew bigger, approaching "springs". I have read elsewhere of land-locked mullet becoming easier to catch after they have been denied access to the sea for a while. In this case the selectivity of the fish makes me suspect that our success was not merely due to the fish having depleted their food supply. It seems more likely that in the brackish conditions following the period of small tides the mullet had become accustomed to feeding on flies or their larvae. The major influx of sea water at next big tides could destroy the flies, as well as refreshing the mullet's sea-borne sources of food.

ALWAYS WEAR PROTECTIVE GLASSES

22

MULLET ON FLY : A SUMMARY

Paul Morgan

Since the successes detailed in the previous chapter I have fished among shoals of mullet on several occasions without success. Robert Lai's ragworm flies and shrimps, Gary Coxon's prawns and Tommy's spiders have all failed me! It seems that unless the fish are preoccupied with a food-item sufficiently large to represent with an artificial fly, they are not easily taken.

The circumstances when they can be caught seem to be as follows:

1. When they are feeding on sea-weed fly larvae as described by Mike Ladle. In Britain this seems to occur most often on the English Channel coast, but it could happen almost anywhere. Watch out for it!
2. Mullet in harbours and marinas become accustomed to feeding on scraps thrown from boats and quays. In these circumstances they are less difficult to catch. Bait-fisherman enjoy success using bread-flake or scraps of mackerel flesh for bait and flyfishing with white 'bread flies', fished dead-drift, can be successful.

This opens up the possibility of fishing with flavoured flies. I know of anglers who have taken mullet with baby-doll type wool-bodied flies, impregnated with the flavour of mackerel guts. I have not had time to pursue this myself, but expect to see progress made with absorbent flies and attractor scents. The maggot-tipped fly can succeed in these circumstances:

3. Mullet feeding on other sizeable food items can sometimes be caught on fly. My friend David Burnett has had success by drifting a long-winged green fly to mullet feeding on drifting weed. Mullet are known to feed on soft weeds and this could be tried elsewhere. I have tried it and failed miserably!
4. Mullet when land-locked or temporarily isolated from the effect of the tides seem to take flies and baits more freely. I still have no idea whether this is because they are hungrier, having thinned out the

available food supply, or because (as the last chapter would seem to suggest) they become accustomed to feeding on imitable insects in the less saline water. Either way, I look forward with keen anticipation to similar tides next summer.

Mullet are one of the most widespread and numerous seafish in southern British and European waters. They are certainly the most visible. During calm summer weather they can be seen cruising at the surface of almost every harbour, estuary or tidal creek - usually well within casting distance of the shore. They are sizeable fish, mostly between 1 lb and 5 lb in weight, and are one of the strongest fighters of the temperate seas.

I have emphasised that they can be very difficult to catch on the fly, but I believe that the time spent angling for them is seldom wasted. Mullet flyfishing presents a terrific opportunity to refine the skills of delicate presentation, and to experiment with imitative fly patterns. They are found in the most attractive, as well as the muddiest of places. For the holidaying flyfisher the mullet can provide hours of exquisite frustration - and occasional glorious success.

PART V

PART V
POLLACK & COALFISH

23

POLLACK, COALFISH & WRASSE IN DORSET

Mike Ladle

One- and two-year-old pollack and coalfish are frequently caught by shore-anglers around England and, according to the time of year, range from 15 to 40 cm in length, (usually 15 to 25 cm in Dorset). The bigger fish can be quite a handful on lightish tackle. In their third winter, when they are two-years-plus, they move offshore and are unlikely to be caught by shore-anglers again. Unlike their more northerly brothers and sisters, English channel coalfish move offshore as one-year-olds and are more or less replaced by the much more numerous pollack.

Again a description of a trip probably says it all. It was mid-April, and Harry Casey had twisted my arm into trying an early-season bass-fishing session. We tackled up with buoyant plug baits on carp rods, fixed-spool reels and 8lb lines and set out along a stretch of rocky shoreline. The beach was a mixture of cobbly stretches, ledges, lengths of boulder-strewn rock, thickets of tough weed and little shingle-backed coves. Harry stopped on a short stretch of shingle and began to cast and retrieve a six-inch, dark-green Rebel plug with a red, fluorescent belly-stripe. I continued on my way to fish a long flat ledge using a black and silver J11 Rapala. Conditions were perfect with clear water, a strong flow of tide and a steady but lively surf, but an hour of hard fishing produced no bites.

I made my way back to the spot where I had left Harry casting. As I rounded a jutting buttress of cliff I caught sight of my pal just as he swung a wriggling fish to hand. I quickened my pace and arrived at his side as he was about to free his catch. He held it out for inspection: it was unquestionably a young coalfish. During the following thirty minutes, as dusk fell over the calm sea, we managed to catch half-a-dozen coalies, all in mint condition and looking like peas in a pod. The whole exercise was more interesting than exciting because the little fish were ridiculously overmatched by the carp rods and lines. As the sky darkened the shoals of coalies begin to show on the flat surface of the water, ringing and ruffling the sea like a group of rising trout.

We killed a few of the bigger specimens to freeze down for conger and bass baits and after we had packed in I gutted a couple of fish to examine their stomach-contents, in the hope of finding what had attracted them inshore. The guts were crammed with maggots; obviously the coalies were filling the gap which is occupied later in the year by surface-feeding grey mullet. The good weather continued and two days later we were down at Coalfish Corner again, knowing that there was a good chance, because fish are creatures of habit, of a repeat performance. Harry was again fishing a big plug in the hope of catching a bass, and I was armed with a trout-fly rod, floating line and eight feet of 5lb nylon attached to the fly.

My first cast was, in fact, with a tiny, black Delta eel in place of a more conventional fly (I have also used mackerel strips with great success). The tide was only half-way in, so I was really just warming up my casting muscles. Cast and retrieve, cast and retrieve... Harry meanwhile was ten yards to my left pitching his plug well out to sea, probably about three-times my maximum range. After about five fishless minutes of near-surface-fishing I decided to try a little deeper. To judge the sinking rate of my 'fly' I flicked it out at my feet and counted as it sank through the water, eight seconds to reach the sea bed. I worked out some line, made a modest cast and waited for the fly to sink. After a count of eight I raised the rod steadily to set the "Delta" in motion, the line was already tight and a fish was on!

The battle was a short one with the fish sheering right and left in the manner of a big dace. I swung it to hand and removed the fly which was firmly lodged in the angle of the jaw. My catch was a 20 cm coalfish in prime condition but it was a flash in the pan because neither of us had another bite until the light began to fail.

By this time I had changed to a silver-bodied fry-fly and Harry was legering with a ragworm bait. In the following hour the fish went berserk and I landed 11 more and a couple of pollack for make-weights. In the course of catching the fish, at least three times as many were missed or made good their escape; an excellent evening's sport. Harry's contribution was a single coalie on worm; his only bite of the session after a couple of indeterminate pulls on the plug.

The moral of the above account is not that I am a better angler than Harry; I am not. Nor that fry-flies are more effective than Delta eels, ragworms or plugs; but simply that the right method in the right place at the right time will give the best results. Also, it must be obvious that if small coalfish can give decent sport on trout-gear, then the bigger ones which are so prolific in our northern waters are a potential source of outstanding entertainment to anyone with the nerve to wield a fly-rod or light spinning tackle from the rocks in the evening light.

My unusual experience of catching lots of small pollack and coalfish from the shore on fly-tackle was good fun. Many sea-anglers would, I am certain, think that there is little or no skill involved in catching these tiny predators on conventional beach-casting gear, and I would agree with them wholeheartedly. In the past my only real use for these 'small fry' would have been for bait but with out a doubt some recent events have totally convinced me of their potential to provide sport and excellent entertainment. Perhaps another account will reinforce the matter.

Some years ago my pal Colin Nice invited me to give a talk to the members of the Sidmouth S.A.C. I knew that Colin was an extremely good angler and the excellent turn out for my little slide-show combined with the annual prize-giving confirmed that the Sidmouth group includes many other real enthusiasts. Certainly, I did not have things all my own way and the questions and comments on my approaches to bass and mullet flowed freely, long in to the evening. Much interest was aroused by the bits and pieces of fishing tackle which I had taken along as a demonstration, and one or two of my home made bass 'fry-flies' were given away for potential use on local trout reservoirs. Now I'm no great shakes at tying flies but the little scraps of Mylar definitely bear a striking resemblance to 'young-of-the-year' sprats, herrings, sandeels, roach, rudd or what have you! To cut a long story short, a couple of weeks after the talk an envelope landed on my door-mat. It contained a little box in which was a whole swarm of beautifully tied fry-flies on stainless-steel hooks. Colin Nice clearly inherited his father's ability to tie an artificial because the imitations were works of art. I added them to my tackle box with gratitude.

The flies remained, unused, in their plastic compartment until the first week in May when, an opportunity to try them out occurred. Together with Dave Cooling I was trying (without success) to catch an early bass. We were both armed with spinning rods, fixed-spool reels and buoyant plugs as we tramped down to Chapmans Pool. The hills were shrouded in chilly, wet mist and a northerly breeze ruffled the surface of the sea with in the cove. We opted to take the rugged walk towards St Aldhelms Head, a massive rocky peninsula projecting in to the English channel.

We worked our way along the shore, casting and retrieving from each point of access to the sea's edge. Suddenly Dave gave a call and I looked up to watch him play a beautiful yellow and bronze ballan wrasse of about two-pounds. The fish fought well but was no match for Dave's eight pound Maxima. Shortly after this event my J13, black and silver Rapala was taken with a fierce pull and my senses said "Bass!" but before long my eyes contradicted my mind when a hefty ballan hove in to view. The fish was well over three-pounds and was coloured deep orange with white mottling on the belly shading to bluish grey spots on the flanks.

"Fantastic!"

I returned my incredible fish and we moved on a bit further. Dave had a follower, another wrasse, which despite its persistence refused to hook itself. The light was now beginning to fail so we made our way back towards the shingle beach of the cove to try for a pollack or possibly even a bass. We had heard of a decent bass lost there a few day's earlier.

During our spinning session I had carried my fly-rod with me, laying it carefully against a handy boulder each time I halted to have a cast. The idea, based on past experience of the place, was to test my hunch that the thickening dusk might provide a few pollack or coalfish on the fly. Sure enough, as the gloom deepened, a few ringing rises in the edge of the sea showed that something was active. I tied one of my little tubes of Mylar (armed with a tail-treble) on the eight-foot nylon cast and flicked it out to sea. As I retrieved I noticed that the hollow tube was very buoyant and even on the slowest draw it skated along the surface. Clearly the imitation was just what the pollack ordered because time and time again one of the little fish would fling itself into the air as it snatched at the fly above its head.

The odd thing was that I never managed to hook a single fish despite the three needle-sharp points at the rear of the fly. After about ten frustrating minutes I decided to try a sub-surface fly and diving in to the box I came across Colin Nice's specials. With some difficulty (and cold hands) I tied a fly on to the cast and began to fish again.

"Bingo!" Every chuck (or almost every chuck) a winner.

One after another the pollack hung themselves on the flies. Every fish ripped line off the reel in a characteristic tearing run and then gave a creditable imitation of a decent trout before it was brought to hand, unhooked and returned to the sea. During all the excitement Dave plugged away along side me with a medium-sized floater without a sniff. Obviously the lure was much to big, although we do catch a few of these fish on spinning-tackle at times. I enjoyed catching the pollack so much that, as soon as I returned home, I rang my photographer friend Ken Ayres who was keen to take pictures of sea-fish. I must have painted a glowing picture of the afternoon's sport because on the following day he was following me about on the beach, camera in hand, waiting for me to catch a fish. Right on cue, as darkness fell, the tell-tale rings appeared on the surface of the sea. This time I had tied up a cast of two identical flies and, unusually for me, the camera did not put a jinx on the fish. In fact, the pollack were so co-operative that I was able to ask Ken whether he needed me to catch another one!

On the sessions described, the fish were mostly about 0.5 kg, hardly the stuff of which wreck-fishing spectaculars are made. Nonetheless these pollack were quite the equal of similarly-sized trout or grayling which I have often caught on identical tackle. Rarely have any fish taken my fly so freely or with such enthusiasm and I can recommend the salt-water "evening rise" to anyone. Of course, this is only scratching the surface of the matter and who knows what a season or two spent by a competent reservoir-man might produce?

Mullet, pollack and coalfish are only a part of the flyfishing potential around our coasts. Bass, mackerel, sea-trout, scad, garfish, cod and whiting are all potential candidates for the fly rod. It has the big advantage over game fishing that it is free, there are no bag limits and you never know what you will catch. Above all, flyfishing in the sea provides a challenge which is almost untried, certainly there is enough interest to keep me going until I am too feeble to totter along the rocks. Believe me, your first mackerel on trout-fly-tackle will be an experience to remember. It certainly was for me.

24

FLYFISHING FOR IRISH POLLACK

Alan Hanna

To many minds, the art of flyfishing and the trout are inseparable. Virtually all flyfishers have grown up in their sport on an exclusive diet of salmonid fishing, with the result that the ubiquitous trout, or his close relatives, continue to hold centre stage in the dreams and longings of most flyfishermen. However, in recent years a growing number of 'discontents' have emerged from these ranks, and flyfishing has increasingly been adapted and developed to catch other species, some of which wouldn't have earned a second thought in years gone by.

This rapid development of interest in new freshwater and saltwater species has a very simple explanation: - it is all to do with angling preferences. Let me explain what I mean. For many years Gary Montgomery and I have hunted trout all over Ireland. The remarkable thing about our long-term fishing partnership is that our angling preferences are completely different. For him, the take is everything; the subsequent struggle and the size of the trout landed are merely incidental. Gary's preference is reflected in his favourite lake - the famous Lough Melvin - where the unique sonaghan are plentiful but small. For me, however, the strength and size of the catch are just as much a source of pleasure and satisfaction as the take itself, and size is certainly not incidental. I favour Lough Sheelin, which seems to yield five-pound-plus fish to the bob-fly just about every week of the season. I have often wondered how we get on so well, but I suppose it only goes to prove the old saying that opposites attract!

The upshot of all this is that Gary has virtually no interest in catching anything with his flyrod other than trout, whereas my angling preference gives me an appetite for anything that swims, especially if it's big. It is this simple difference in emphasis that fuels my desire to experiment with new species of fish, and over the years I have indulged this desire whenever possible. Without trying too hard, I have hooked mackerel, grey mullet, pike, perch, barracuda, bream, rudd, roach and pollack, as well as trout, sea-trout and salmon, with my flyrod. It is clearly evident that many other flyfishers share a similar urge to experiment - this book proves it! I am quite certain that we shall see many more developments and adaptations of the traditional flyfishing method in years to come. The more, the better!

It was quite by accident that I became interested in catching pollack on the fly. For many years I lived and worked in the greater London area, where my angling needs were adequately met by that faithful old friend, the rainbow trout. From time to time I would make the trip home to my native county of Fermanagh, situated in the north-west of Ireland, and then I would get in some 'real' trout fishing (between all the mandatory visits to relatives and friends). During one such visit, an old friend invited me to spend a day touring the rugged Atlantic coast of Co. Donegal. He was an occasional rock-angler, and kindly offered to help me catch my first ever fish from the shore, which, he assured me, would be a pollack. I was really looking forward to catching my first pollack and eagerly anticipated the trip. However, my heart sank on the morning of our departure when I saw the huge spinning rods and fixed spool reels he was stowing in the car, so I surreptitiously slipped my flyrod in along with his 'hardware' before we set off.

St. John's Point is a long, jutting peninsula which stirs the crystal clear waters of the gulf stream, and is flanked on both sides with sheer drops into the sea - well worth a visit just to look. We pulled up at a deep-water mark where, my friend assured me, he had once hooked and lost a blue shark. He was relating the details of the experience to me as I watched him pull a rod from the car loaded with fishing line that looked more like rope. He proceeded to fix about two tons of lead on the end.

"Going to try for another shark?" I asked.

"No, no. This one's for the pollack." He completely missed my jibe.

I thought about asking him how big the pollack would have to be before the rod would bend, but instead I reached for my flyrod.

The rocks dropped straight down into the water, which churned and tossed about ten feet beneath us. As I peered into the depths, wondering how on earth I was going to approach this with a flyrod, I had a sudden inspiration - the Queen Mother Reservoir at Datchet, in west London! We often fished hard on the bottom in fifty feet of water with boobies and fast-sink shooting-heads. The trout would chase the enormous shoals of sticklebacks which hugged the bottom, and the buoyant boobies would enable us to fish close to the bottom without snagging up. "Just the ticket for getting down deep while still avoiding all the rocks and seaweed", I thought.

After a bit of rummaging back at the car, I got tackled up and joined my friend at the edge. He was flailing away with his iron-mongery and he stopped to laugh when he saw my AFTM 8 'wand'.

I didn't tell him it was my heavy gear.

"Oh, so you're trying for that shark then?" he quipped. I couldn't help thinking that the subtlety of his second-hand humour matched that of his tackle!

I stripped off about thirty yards of backing and shot it out. I didn't really expect to catch anything, but on about the fifth cast, those doubts were firmly laid to rest. Wham! I watched my fly reel spin and once again the word shark flashed through my mind! The fish stripped off about fifteen yards before I managed to stop him and, after a struggle lasting a few minutes, I got him to the top, not knowing what to expect. It was a pollack, about ten pounds in weight, and the mixture of shock and surprise I felt at that moment was only exceeded by the look of shock and surprise on my friend's face! "It's a big one!" I yelled. "Quick, get the net!".

"What net? I don't use a net!".

I looked at him in disbelief. "I just lift them up on the rod!", he continued defensively, as he began scrambling down the rocks to the foaming water. By this time, the pollack was on its side, and I guided it to him. He made a grab for the fish and the 'net' result was that the fly and the fish parted company. We watched, helplessly, as the pollack languished on its side for a few moments before kicking itself upright and disappearing into the depths.

I was too dumbfounded and annoyed to speak, so I gathered up my line and cast again, while my friend returned sheepishly to his rod. He didn't speak for about five minutes! Nor did I - for at least ten.

About an hour later, it was time to pack up and go. I had a beautiful pollack of 6lb lying on the rocks, while my friend had caught one of about eight ounces, which he only discovered was on when he lifted his rig out to recast. It then fell off at the last minute. How I laughed!

All things considered, it was a fabulous introduction to rock-fishing for pollack, and stands out as one of my most memorable fishing experiences. It was also a real triumph for the flyrod! Since then I have spent many, many happy hours on the rocky shores of western Ireland, and I have rarely returned home without a fish.

The wonderful thing about pollack is that if you can find them, they can be caught without too much difficulty on fly-tackle. It's all a matter of knowing how. I cannot count the times that I have joined anglers with heavy rods and lures, and noted their smirks when they saw my fly-gear. They will usually wish me luck, but their general demeanour and facial expression often betrays their true opinion:- "He'll definitely not catch anything with that". Yet I would often catch three or four good fish in an hour, while they remained fishless.

A good example of this occurred when my family and I recently holidayed in Killala, Co Mayo, and we visited a well known fishing spot called The Flags, a few miles north of the village. On arriving we joined a solitary angler who had caught only one small pollack in two days fishing. He was exceedingly confident that I was wasting my time with a flyrod. On my very first cast, however, I took a 3lb pollack, virtually from under his feet. I've never seen an attitude change so quickly! Ten minutes later I caught a second fish and this convinced him it wasn't a fluke. I had 1001 questions after that!

Locating the pollack.

Catching pollack from the shore has at least as much to do with choosing the correct location as adopting the correct method. The most important question to ask in choosing the location is whether it provides access to deep water. Because fly fishers are limited in casting range, the only marks worth trying are those where a shelf or cliff face drops off steeply into deep water. The end of a pier can provide just such a feature, but rocky outcrops or shorelines are to be favoured for their variation of habitat. By deep, I mean at least ten feet, preferably fifteen or twenty, or even more.

The type of bottom is also important. In general I have found that pollack, being a dark-coloured fish, will always choose locations with a dark bottom, such as rock or kelp. They will usually avoid an area with a sandy bottom as this affords no camouflage. I have spent some time diving and spearfishing around the Irish coast, and the pollack's favourite coastal haunt appears to be patches of kelp. The fish will cruise around in a loose shoal just above the kelp, sometimes swimming among the fronds. Good sized fish are not usually found in water where there is less than eight feet of clear water between the top of the kelp and the surface.

Another point worth remembering is that pollack will often patrol along a cliff-face, or any spot where there is a sharp drop-off. These locations can be very productive, especially for bigger fish. I once remember joining three anglers who were spinning for pollack and had caught nothing. They were standing at the very end of a rocky outcrop and casting their lures as far out into open water as possible. Where the rocky outcrop joined the shore a narrow deep channel had been formed, but this was ignored. It was only about ten feet wide, but was so deep I couldn't see the bottom. I took four lovely fish from the mouth of this channel in about an hour, the biggest around four pounds. Many times I have caught my best fish by casting along the shore instead of straight out towards the horizon. Of course, this only applies where there is a sheer drop off into the water.

A good way to spot potential locations is to buy a detailed map of the coastline. Checking the contours will often reveal areas where deep water might be found along a rocky coast. Of course, the easiest way of all is to find local anglers (usually in the local tackle shop) and persuade them to divulge their secrets!

There is no special season for catching pollack from the shore. Most of my own pollack fishing has been done in the summer months as one tends to visit the coast more often in summer than in winter, but pollack are available to be caught all year round from the rocks.

The method

I almost always use the method I have previously mentioned: an ultra fast-sink shooting-head coupled with a buoyant fly. My leader is usually about six feet of 8lb. mono, and I always fish with a single fly on the cast. As the shooting-head sinks, the buoyant fly is dragged down, and once the line has settled, the fly will remain suspended six feet off the bottom. A slow retrieve will cause the fly to swim about three feet clear of the rocks, depending on the buoyancy of the fly. Increasing the speed of retrieve will cause the fly to fish closer to the bottom. In this way, it is possible to fish consistently near the bottom.

There are three golden rules which will maximise your chances of success with this method.

1. Give the line enough time to sink. It is important to get down deep, and the most common fault is starting the retrieve too early. I use a line rated to sink at six inches per second, and anything less than this can be tedious.

2. Always use a buoyant fly. A buoyant fly will survive the hazards of the sea-bed ten times better than a regular type which sinks. The only way to fish consistently close to the bottom without snagging every cast is to use a buoyant fly which sits up off the bottom during the retrieve. It is also important to get the buoyancy just right. A fly which is too buoyant will look unnatural and will keep a long length of fly line off the bottom along with the leader. On the other hand, a fly which is close to neutral density will not sit up high enough to avoid snags.

3. Do not retrieve too fast. The faster the retrieve, the closer the fly will swim to the bottom. A slow retrieve will produce far less snags and will maximise the chances of a fish taking the fly.
   Of course it is possible to vary this method. The retrieve can be commenced before the line settles on the bottom if the fish are in mid-water, or if a fast retrieve is desirable close to the bottom.

Experimentation and variation should always be part of the angler's approach to his pursuit.

Shooting heads are best

A full-length fast-sink line will do at a pinch, but there are two very significant advantages in using a shooting taper (ST), for this kind of fishing. The first is distance. Casting a full thirty yards of fly line requires a lot of false-casting, and once it is out it still looks pitifully inadequate against a vast expanse of sea. A shooting head can easily be cast forty yards with little assistance from a following breeze, and it only requires one or two false-casts. The other advantage of the ST is that only the front ten yards of line is weighted to sink. (The ST backing line is braided or solid mono, and it is close to neutral density). This means that only seven or eight yards of line are on the bottom during the retrieve, whereas a full length line will quickly settle to the bottom along its entire length. This creates a huge belly of line between the rod-tip and the fly, and this has at least three drawbacks: 1) the belly reduces direct contact with the fly; 2) the line is more likely to foul up on the bottom; 3) as the belly forms it draws the end of the fly-line back towards the shore so that the cast is significantly shortened.

I thoroughly recommend that all flyfishers learn how to use a shooting-head. It is quite easy and will considerably improve one's versatility in all flyfishing situations.

The fly

Almost any pattern will do, especially lures. Light colours do best, especially white and silver. I have developed a pattern called the Silver Sandeel, which, as its name suggests, is an imitation of a sandeel. It is absolutely deadly for pollack, (probably because they feed on sandeel a lot!), so I use it most of the time.

Hook: size 8, longshank.

Head: white plastazote cylinder. (Plastazote is a dense-cell foam, similar to that used for swimming floats).

Body: white dubbing.

Tail: Dave Tait's Glitterbody (Produced by Gordon Griffiths) or similar, tied in and separated into individual strands with a dubbing needle.

This is a very easy pattern to tie. Plastazote cylinders can be purchased from most fly-tying suppliers, or they can be cut from a block of plastazote.

Insert dubbing-needle up through the centre of the cylinder, and thread the cylinder onto the hook, either from the hook-point, or over the eye.

Glue in place behind the eye with superglue.

Tie in three or four strands of Dave Tait's Glitterbody, (or similar) and trim to required length, (usually between two and three inches). Tease out carefully with a dubbing needle, until each individual strand of tinsel is separated.

Finally, wind some white dubbing behind the head to make a continuous body between the head and the tail. Tie off between the head and the dubbed body.

Safety

Although safety consciousness in all sports and leisure activities is probably at an all time high these days, I am still surprised by people's thoughtlessness for their own safety. Rock fishing is extremely dangerous compared to most kinds of freshwater fishing, and beginners cannot be too careful. Safety is dependent largely on good choice of clothing and a judicious use of common sense.

Clothing. Footwear is the first consideration. Depending on the season, and the location, I will use trainers, walking boots or, in some cases, wellington boots. The walking boots are usually my first choice. Good ankle-support is vital, as well as a good sole. Use Dubbin regularly on leather footwear, as salt-water is very hard on it. On hot days I will wear a pair of trainers for comfort, especially if the climbing is not too demanding. I only use wellington boots where I must wade through pools which sometimes form along broken rock-strata. I use the kind with wire in the soles to add to the grip. In my experience, though, no kind of footwear can be trusted on slippery rocks. Care is the best defence against accidents. Second-best is to avoid footwear with smooth soles at all costs. Studded boots are probably the best for negotiating slippery rocks, but they can be dangerous on smooth, hard surfaces. I never wear waders.

For the rest I wear a windproof jacket and leggings. I like Goretex garments, which are light, windproof and dry, but don't suffer the drawback of sweating. Climbing over rocks is hot work, and breathable waterproofs are very comfortable compared to PVC garments. I usually take a balaclava to keep my head and ears warm if it is windy.

I will often wear a buoyancy aid, especially if there is a heavy surf, or if I am not familiar with the location.

Common sense. There are 1001 issues which could be covered under this title, but we will look at only the most important - the need to pay due respect to the sea. Every now and again, an exceptionally large wave will strike the shore. It is true that every seventh wave is larger, but sometimes a much larger 'freak' wave will hit. Almost every year people are drowned by being washed in by such a wave, so always make allowance for this when you choose your spot. Allowance must also be made for the tide, especially when it is flowing (coming in). With the distraction of fishing, it is very easy for the waves to creep closer and closer without noticing, and before you know it you are standing knee-deep in a wave. It is also easy to become stranded by a flowing tide.

Tackle requirements

The wonderful thing about flyfishing is that so little tackle is required, and this is a real boon when it needs to be lugged for half a mile over rocks! Any rod rated between AFTM 6 and 10 will do, mated to a standard or kingsize reel with fast-sinking line. Apart from these, the only other piece of tackle that is absolutely essential is a net. Choose a net with a long handle, preferably a telescopic type.

The usual bits and pieces such as sun-glasses and priest can be taken along, but the list of absolute essentials is refreshingly short: - rod, spool of mono for the leader, flies and net. The only word of warning I would give regarding trout-tackle is to always ensure that the reel has a lot of backing on it - the sea can produce very large fish indeed!

Catching pollack from the rocks is one of my favourite 'alternative' methods of flyfishing, especially when it can be combined with getting a good suntan! In fact, most of my pollack fishing has been done on those warm sunny days when the whole family visits the seaside. The kids play happily on the beach and mum usually gets lost in a book, which means I can wander along the coast at my leisure, flyrod in hand, or take the car to look for a good spot nearby. On many of these family outings the pollack have come in very handy for those summer evening barbecues on the beach which my wife and kids enjoy so much. It sort of, you know, makes things up a little bit for disappearing for hours on end!

25

POLLACK IN NORWAY

Bjørnar Vihovde

Pollack are usually easy to find in the surf zone. Where the sea lays white and seaweed waves underneath, hungry for spinning baits, are good places to try your fly. A single fly-hook usually cuts itself free, and imitates a small fish hovering in the water much better than any metal lure.

Flyfishing for pollack is enormous fun! It offers the possibility of fighting large and strong fish of up to 6 or 7kg, but even the average-sized fish of 1 to 2kg show great sport. They take a wide range of flies, and give good opportunities to experiment with new patterns and materials. As a good bonus I can mention that pollack are a great food, both roasted and boiled!

How

The pollack is a strong fish that dives into the sea-tangle or rocky crevasses when hooked. Therefore is it necessary to use a rod that has enough backbone to force the fish to the surface. I use a ten-weight rod and AFTM 8 sinking line. A long rod is preferred because it gives me more backcast, and allows me to steer the line outside the nearest waves that always want to tangle the line into the kelp-fronds .The coast is often a windy place. This means using rather heavy weight-forward lines, preferably sinking, and a rod that can give a high line-speed. A heavy line is also much more comfortable to cast big flies with. The pollack spends much its daylight-time near the seabed. This means that a sinking line is preferable.

I have a cheap non-corrosive reel with a rather poor brake. Even though the pollack is a strong fighter, does it not give long runs. The fish seeks safety by swimming towards deeper waters and into the sea-tangle. It is not necessary to use long leaders. I use a 3m leader made of 2 metres of 0.50mm and 1 metre of 0.40mm. A 0.40mm tip is necessary because of the pollack's sharp teeth - it has a nasty habit of swallowing the fly - and its usual escape-dive down into the tangle.

The most common tactic is simply to cast out, let line and fly sink to the bottom, and then retrieve with long (2 to 3 seconds) pauses, allowing the fly to sink again. Very often the fish takes during one of this pauses. I prefer light flies that are able to hover in the water. I believe that these imitate a little fish much better than a heavy fly that sinks as soon as you stop the retrieve. A light fly also fishes better over shallow waters with much sea-tangle and weed.

When

The pollack comes closer to shore in the brighter time of year, they are not fond of cold water. That means that they are easier to reach between late spring and early autumn. I usually fish during the day-time. I haven't found it necessary to try fishing at night. I prefer those days when it's hot and calm. On this kind of day look for spots were you can see what is going on under the water. It is great fun to watch your fly, and all the fish which are interested in it. With some care you won't frighten those fish - there are usually more than one - which follow the fly.

Where

Good places to fish for pollack are exposed rocky shorelines with much weed and kelp. It seems that the fish stay just outside the belt of sea-tangle, and hide in the edge. I have caught many just outside this edge on rather short casts.

Especially good is where tidal currents gather food, and food-fish. Such a place will also be a hot-spot for other predators like cod and mackerel.

To try to get those really big ones you have to get in a boat and find off-shore banks - not too deep - with steep edges that will give the fish good access to food and a quick escape to the safe deep waters. I haven't tried this due to the lack of a boat, but I will. This method would certainly require a fast-sinking shooting-head and plenty of backing.

Flies

These patterns are only suggestions. Our saltwater species seldom need an accurate imitation of anything. But they do need to convey "life". Use materials that swim in the water - soft hair, marabou, hackle-feathers and soft flashy materials. I start with one of my favourites.

Muddler:
  Hook: 6/0 and down.
  Tail: marabou, single coloured or two colours (black/orange, blue/white, black/white, green/white, etc).
  Body: the marabou from the tail and tying thread.
  Rib: I use copper-wire, mainly to strengthen the fly.
  Wing: marabou (same colours as the tail) and perhaps some flash.
  Head: muddler head (natural, red, green, etc).

A good Streamer series:

Hook: from 6/0 and down.
Tail: marabou or hair.
Body: silver or pearl braided mylar tube.
Rib: copper wire.
Wing: black hair and marabou. I also use a bright wing on the underside of bigger flies.
Eyes: ball-chains, pearls on copper wire, or similar.

Easy Streamer:

Hook: long-shank (or a braided leader with a hook at one end and a loop in the other).
Wing: some long hackles (white and blue) or hair.

Easy to tie and catch fish

I have also caught pollack on large Red-Tags, Mickeyfins and Shrimps. The patterns above are not precise. I seldom tie flies that are just alike. I use the materials to hand, and tie the flies to be light, able to hover in the water, and give an impression of being something eatable that's swimming.

There are many good patterns and tying-styles in American saltwater flytying-books. Just simplify the ones that you like.

Use strong tying-thread and plenty of varnish. I use nail-varnish because it's easy to get (leftovers from wives/girlfriends) and the brush mounted in the cap makes it easier and less time-consuming to cover the heads of bigger flies. It comes in pretty colours too!

I mostly use a nickel-plated hook from Mustad. This hook will corrode after some time but will last longer than the brown un-plated ones. They are much easier to sharpen than stainless hooks. And yes, the hook must be sharpened regularly due to corrosion, and to the slopes of naked Norwegian rock that jump up and touch your fly on the back-cast. The fact the hook will corrode also ensures a regular turnover of stock in the fly box.

And remember: Flyfishing after pollack ain't art, neither in flytying nor in casting, just good fun!

26

YORKSHIRE COAST 1895

John Bickerdyke

During the summer and early autumn months, shoals of coalfish come close to the rocky coast of Yorkshire, and elsewhere in the north, to feed on the herring fry or 'sile', as it is termed by the fishermen. This gives the fly-fisher an opportunity of enjoying his favourite sport in salt water, for, while chasing the baby herrings near the surface, the billet - as coalfish of moderate dimensions are spoken of in Yorkshire - may frequently be beguiled into taking a fly; one with a silver body and a white wing, with tail, legs and underwing of peacock harl being the best. The fly is doubt-less looked upon by the fish as a juvenile herring, for, when they are not feeding on the sile, other baits - notably the india-rubber eels - are more killing. At times, sport with the fly is very good indeed. Everything seems to depend on the sile; but though 'no sile, no billet' is a fairly accurate statement, it unfortunately by no means follows that the presence of sile necessarily indicates the presence of billet.

One morning, having armed myself with a sixteen foot grilse rod, a large wooden reel bearing eighty yards of eight-plait tannned hemp line, and a stout gut cast, to the end of which was attached one of these sile flies, I made my way along a huge reef of rocks running out a quarter of a mile or more into the German ocean. The rocks were of a curious forma-tion, presenting to the north a series of immense steps or ledges, which sloped away to the south and gradually lost their form in a confused mass of irregularly shaped boulders, many of them as large as a small cottage. On the north side I looked for the fish, but looked for some time in vain; so sat me down on a rock and smoked with the patience becoming an angler.

It was an impressive scene. Beneath were the massive ledges which for thousands of years had borne the brunt of furious seas driven by howling winds winging their way unchecked from Arctic regions. The great sea, solemn and mournful, now almost at rest, stretched far into the hazy dis-tance, while the sun setting over the land caused the cliffs to stand out dark and terrible. Here and there caves showed out blackly, and I could just make out the path, far above high-water mark, from which, during a northerly gale, when the tide was at its lowest, a great wave had washed two unfortunate persons into the raging waters at the foot of the cliff. On a marble tablet let into the rock their sad story is told and a warning given to all men passing that way. No sea birds were visible, no sound was to be heard but the plash of the water on the rocks; and sitting there, far out in the sea, with night coming on, and the story of those two poor people running through my head, a sort of uncanny feeling began to possess me.

But what a trifle will change one's humours! The ledge beneath sloped upwards to its edge, but lengthways it fell away gradually to the sea, which covered the inner portion of it, and so formed a small lagoon. Along the margin of this little lake I noted a ruffling of the water, as if coarse sand was being let fall into it, then came a silver splash, and half a dozen little bits of silver leapt right out of the water on to the rocks; not long to remain there, however, for three leaps and most of them were back in the water. The bits of silver were sile, and the splash was caused by feeding billet.

All uncanny thoughts fled; and in a very few seconds I was on a rock whence I could cast over the lagoon. Within certainly not more than three minutes from the time the sile appeared, a fish was making the rod bend, and me to wish myself on some safer ground than a round-topped rock covered with sea-weed, at the foot of which was six feet or more of water. Strong fellows are those billet, and though their staying powers are not great, the fight they make for the three minutes is redoubtable. I had no net, and this fish was a little too small to gaff and a trifle too large to lift out of the water, while any attempt to land it with the hand would assuredly have conducted the experimenter straightway into salt water. However, after two misses, the gaff took hold, and billet the first reposed in my bag. Then the fish seemed to become a little shy, for though they were still feeding on the herring fry, breaking the surface just like small trout seizing Mayflies, the most they would do was to follow my fly, and then turn tail and go down with a swirl. But among the shoal were a few fish less wise or more greedy than the rest, and one of these every now and again would seize my fly, and after fighting bravely was entombed in the bag. As it grew darker the fish lost their caution, and each cast resulted in a rise, with or without a billet to follow. By-and -by the rising tide dislodged me from the rock, and every quarter of an hour or so a retreat had to be made farther and farther from the spot where the first billet was hooked. But the fish shifted their position too, and kept within casting distance.

The billet seemed to me wonderfully sagacious in their method of feeding off shoals of herring fry. Out of the lagoon there was but one way, and this they guarded most carefully. Each time the sile attempted to escape, their pursuers swam in front of them, and drove them back into the shallow water, in a sort of cul-de-sac at the end of the little lagoon, and a mighty feast they must have made there. Every billet caught was simply choking with sile, and brought up five or six when it was gaffed.

In about an hour from the time I commenced fishing, the red glow went out of the sky, and fearful of a fall among the rocks in the dark, I hastily put up my rod and made my way to the shore. Then came a serious question. I had forgotten the tide (what a number of important things one forgets when the fish are rising! - time, tide, trains, meals, and much besides - one man forgot his wedding!), and as at high water the sea reaches the foot of the cliffs for some distance, the question was whether it was best to risk breaking my neck in the dark among the cliffs, or attempting the walk home by the shore and possibly wading up to my waist, or deeper, in water for a portion of the distance. I decided upon the wading, if necessary, and was glad I did, for on coming to the point which the water touches first, found that there was just six inches of dry sand between the sea and the cliff. The water being calm, this was enough, and in due course, bearing my uncomfortably heavy, though cheering weight of fish, I arrived at the quiet little Yorkshire town which, for the time, was my abiding-place.

From *Days of My Life,* John Bickerdyke. 1895.

27

YORKSHIRE COAST 1931

A.F. Bell

Let us consider those places on the east coast of England which are already famous for the sport. The best known are perhaps Filey Brig, Hayburn Wyke, and Cloughton Wyke in Yorkshire.

Filey Brig is a somewhat sinister reef of rocks running out perhaps half a mile into the sea, and round and about it large numbers of billet (pollack and coalfish) and mackerel are wont to feed freely near the surface throughout the late summer months. On this reef large numbers of anglers may be observed casting their flies into the ocean, whence they collect some surprisingly good baskets, and not infrequently surprisingly wet clothes into the bargain. The Brig, though normally safe enough, is not always free from danger, and there are cases of anglers finding themselves unexpectedly wallowing among their quarry either through the agency of a slippery piece of seaweed (unpleasant) or an inordinately big wave (diabolical). It is a reef that wants knowing, and the question of tides should be studied with some care.

Most anglers use a salmon rod of from 14 to 17 feet in length (either whole cane or greenheart), a checked salmon reel, and a waterproofed line. The cast is generally made of salmon gut or gut substitute with three sea flies attached.

The word 'fly', of course, is not strictly accurate, for although the monstrosities used in the sea are tied much in the same way as flies, they are, in fact, imitations of small fish. There are numerous excellent sea flies on the market, and there is not much to choose between most of them, since the sea fish, when on the feed, do not show the nice discrimination of the Test trout. Perhaps the most popular patterns for the Brig are Percy Wadham's celluloid-bodied flies in green and silver with white wings. Strips of sole or gurnard skin are often used instead of the white feather. There are also some rather primitive though killing patterns compounded chiefly of white rubber tubing or white leather.

That the sport is at times first class is shown by a letter from a friend which I have before me. He writes as follows: "At times the sport is excellent but very uncertain. Big coalfish and pollack are taken, with many mackerel and gurnard, and often a good codling. Once or twice I have known a salmon taken here, but this is a very rare occurrence. Personally I have caught 90 pounds (estimate, most of the fish being returned to the sea alive) of pollack, averaging 4 pounds each, in an afternoon, and I have seen catches of upwards of 200 mackerel taken in the same space of time. The largest fish I have killed on the fly is a pollack of 10 pounds and a cod of 9 pounds. My wife has killed a 12-pound pollack. Larger fish are frequently hooked, but seldom landed, since it is difficult to hold them out of the adjacent weed beds".

An uncle of my own who at one time fished fairly regularly from Filey Brig, and who, by the way, favoured a split-cane trout rod, used to tell the story of how, fishing with three flies, he landed simultaneously a coalfish, a mackerel, and a Skye Terrier dog (the last-named having, of course, dived in after the first two). Personally, I was always a little disappointed that he did not round off the story with a gigantic wave precipitating the whole "boiling", uncle and all, into the ocean.

Speaking of trout rods, I have always found that the most satisfactory and delightful rod to use for all types of fly-fishing in the sea is a 12-foot split-cane trout or sea-trout rod. It can be wielded with one hand (wrist strength permitting) and will assure the maximum amount of sport.

That the dividing line between fly-fishing proper and spinning is a very narrow one is shown by the methods sometimes adopted at Scarborough. Seven or eight plain white flies are attached to a long cast at intervals of a few inches apart. A light lead is fastened to the head of the cast and another smaller piece of lead to the tail. The whole contraption is lowered into the water and worked with a sink-and -draw motion close along the pier side. This method often accounts for big catches of coalfish and an occasional mackerel or cod. The fly used is a narrow white feather from a duck's wing lashed to any make of hook. How in the world the fish can mistake the formidable array for anything subaquatic, unless it be a marine flag day, will always remain a mystery.

While on the subject of Scarborough it might be of interest to mention that sport can be had at 'The Lady's Dock', a rocky place at the north end of the Marine Drive, and at the first point on the south (about 1 mile from the town) where two little bays formed by the quarrying of stone for pier building provide inlets into which the billet and mackerel pursue their prey.

At Cloughton Wyke and Hayburn Wyke the methods of angling are crude and primitive, and the anglers are chiefly farm-hands and labourers. These worthies use long bamboos with a short tight line attached to the top and a white fly of the rough-and-ready type previously mentioned. Considering that even on this tackle plenty of fish are caught, what a wonderful opportunity for the expert fly-fisher!

The fact that a great deal of fly-fishing is done on the east coast does not mean that there are no other places equally good. For instance, some of the sea lochs on the west of Scotland are wonderful places for coalfish.

I had an amusing experience once when salmon fishing near Loch Inchard (top north-west corner of Scotland). One evening I happened to notice a lot of fish "boiling" in the sea loch and promptly rushed for a sea-trout rod. In the absence of sea flies I put up a Durham Ranger and started casting among the fish, which on closer inspection proved to be coalfish. They were not in the least shy, and in half an hour I had beached eight or nine fish up to about 4 pounds, and an excellent fight the bigger ones put up. The conclusion of the sport coincided with the appearance of a fat seal, whose intrusion the coalfish seemed to resent; anyway, they departed with great promptitude.

From *The Book of the Fly Rod*, edited by
Hugh Sheringham and John Moore. 1931.

Editor's Note:
Does our north-eastern coast still fish as well as this? Mr Bell refers to six different species of fish caught on the fly at Filey Brigg; including the only references that I can recall of gurnard and cod caught on the fly on the coast of England.

And a nine-pound, fly-caught, cod from the Yorkshire shore! What are we waiting for . . .

28

IRISH POLLACK 1851

Richard Bowden-Smith

Most capital sea fly-fishing can be obtained off the coast of Connemara, viz., in Bertraghboy Bay, at the Skyard Rocks, at Deer Island, and off the Isle of Mweenish and the Isle of Arran. The whiting pollack that are to be met with there, take a large gaudy fly most boldly. I have with a fly taken some in those parts, as large as nine pounds. I used seven flies at once, and have frequently taken seven fish at the same time. One day I caught 194 with the fly, and the man in the boat with me took sixty-eight with two of my flies. I should have caught a great many more, but the wind blew fresh, and we could not remain long enough among the fish when we met with a shoal, but were obliged to tack backwards and forwards, so as to enable us to be continually passing through them. I once actually hauled in eight fish together, though using only seven flies; one of these fish being caught by the lip and the other by the tail, on the same hook. I am not sure that I could not have killed more fish had I used fewer flies, as a great deal of time was lost in taking the fish off the hooks; but it certainly was good sport pulling in so many together.

I one day went to the Skyard Rocks, twelve miles out at sea. One of the men in the boat, with one of my large flies, soon caught a pollack weighing nine and a half pounds; and before he could take the fly out of the mouth of the fish, the boatman saw a monster close to the stern of the boat take my fly, but after holding him for a few minutes only, the hook broke just below the barb. The water here was shallow, with a sharp rocky bottom, and I consequently did not dare to give him much line; but it was very annoying to lose so large a fish. The men in the boat declared that he was the largest pollack they had ever seen. I found it quite necessary to use six-link twisted gut. Soon after this, I caught one of seven and three quarter pounds; and one of the boatmen, with a hand-line and heavy lead, and a fly that I had given him, caught eighteen fish, the largest of which weighed four pounds. The weather now looked as if it were coming on to blow, and the Skyards not being a place to be caught in a gale of wind, in an open boat, we thought it prudent to make for home. It is almost too far out at sea for an open boat, added to which, such a fearfully dangerous and wild-looking place I never beheld; it would not do to be there with much wind from the south-west, as the whole force of the Atlantic would then break upon these rocks: and it being in the month of October, and the weather beginning to be unsettled, I did not think it prudent to venture there again. A steam yacht would be an excellent thing on these expeditions, for should the wind and tide be unfavourable when you wished to return, you could then do so with ease, when it would be impossible in a sailing boat. Scarcely a winter passes without our hearing of fishing-boats being driven out to sea, and never again heard of.

After this I went to the Isle of Mweenish. It was on the 19th of October; and I had not fished many minutes, when I hooked a fine fellow with one of my largest flies. He was so strong, and run out the line at such a rate, that although the man at the helm luffed, the fish broke away, and I found the point of the hook bent, as if it had come in contact with a stone. A few minutes after this, I hooked a monster, and after twenty minutes' play succeeded in getting him very near the boat; but he then made a dart downwards, just as we thought he was going to give up the fight, run out about 120 yards of line, and got away. I felt certain that some part of the tackle had broken; but on examination, I discovered the hook to be perfectly straightened. Soon afterwards I took eight other fish, which were all small. There was one other rod out, and two hand lines; the rod was baited with a sand-eel, and the lines with heavy leads and my flies, but none of them had a pull: this I attributed to my snood or casting-line being of twisted gut stained gray, whilst one of the hand lines had a coarse hemp snood, and the other had harp-string gimp, and the rod had on a sand-eel for bait. It was as bad a day for this sport as could be; the hills were white with snow, and there was a cutting north-east wind. The boatmen said that they scarcely ever recollected an instance of fish taking any bait in such weather. Later in the day, however, I caught ten other small fish, and the harp-string gimp with the flies caught eight fish, one of them weighing five pounds. The hemp snood with the flies caught only one fish, and that a small one; and the rod with the sand-eel did not catch a fish.

The next time I went out it was to the Isle of Arran, when I killed sixty-nine fish, all with my flies. I hooked one tremendously large fellow, which run out the whole of my line - 200 yards. Unfortunately the boatmen were not quick enough in bending on a sea-line to my rod; they were nearly a minute about it, with the fish pulling most furiously all the time. The moment they had done it I threw my rod overboard, when away it went at a rapid rate for a considerable distance, but it was too late; the mischief, I suspect, had been done before I threw the rod overboard. We saw, from the sudden stopping of the rod, that something was wrong; and on getting in the tackle again, we found that the wheel-line had broken about ten yards above the fly.

My last two days of sea fly-fishing were the 10th and 11th of November, in Bertraghboy Bay. A gentleman, who was desirous of witnessing this sort of fishing, accompanied me on both occasions. In the two days we killed 420 pollack, but none of them were large. I once hooked seven at one time, and killed them all; the smallest weighed three and a half pounds. I also caught two small cod with pollack-flies.

As the weather now began to get rough and stormy, I did not venture out again; for the sea gets up very quickly in those parts, and if it blows fresh from the North, it is almost impossible to regain the shore, should the tide be ebbing at the same time.

When I hear of gentlemen fitting out their yachts for Norway and Lapland, and even to as great a distance as Nova Scotia, for the purpose of salmon-fishing, I cannot imagine why this part of Ireland has not attracted their attention; and can only account for it by the fact of its being in a wild part of that country, and very little visited or known. When I say wild, I mean that it is situated in a part of Ireland which is uncultivated, and consists principally of lakes, barren heaths and magnificent mountains: for I found the peasantry there, though very uncivilized, a particularly civil and inoffensive race, and apparently totally different from the rest of the Irish peasantry; they are supposed to be of Spanish origin.

Your snoods or casting-lines for fly-fishing for pollack must be either twisted gut stained gray, or twisted wire covered with paint of a leaden colour, that will stand the salt water. The casting-line should have two swivels; and when there is a good breeze, sufficient to enable you to use your largest flies, the swivel nearest your wheel-line should be a very large one. You should always be prepared with your strongest as well as finest tackle, that you may be properly appointed, whatever the weather may be.

Sea Flies for Pollock

No. 1   This was a favourite fly with plenty of wind. Tail: about half an inch of gold twist round the shank of the hook, then red feather of cock-of -the-rock. Body: lower part red worsted, upper part blue worsted or shag, gold twist, orange hackle lower part, bright dark crimson hackle upper part. Wings: under wings cock-of -the-rock's red feather, tipped with white, upper wings two white feathers from under the wing of wild fowl stained yellow. Head: large blue jay's hackle twisted on.

No. 2   Tail: gold twist, then some strips of swan or white turkey mixed, stained red, orange, blue or green. Body: same as No. 1. Wings:

under wings mixed colours, of swan or turkey stained, upper wings brown turkey tipped with white.

No. 3   Tail: gold twist round shank of hook, then mixed, small scarlet hackle, small blue ditto, silver-pheasant black and white feather, ditto stained orange. Body: same as No. 1. Shoulders: blue jay. Wings: lower wings stained, mixed, scarlet, blue, orange, upper wings mottled feather of peacock's wing, light buff with black bars.

No. 4   Hook reversed. Body: same as No. 1. Tail: mixed. Wings: two white feathers from under wing of wild fowl, stained green. Head: blue-stained hackle twisted round.

No. 5   Used when the weather is bright and not much wind, and made on large trout-hooks, two-link twisted gut. Tail: two turns of gold twist, then a small cock's hackle stained blue for tail. Body: rich red worsted, gold twist, rich bright red hackle. Wings: mixed; stained mallard, red, yellow, green. Head: guinea-fowl hackle twisted round.

I have given the above as specimens of a few only; but I have made the pollack-flies of every description of bright and fancy colours.

Your snoods or casting-lines should be nearly three yards in length, and should have two swivels, the larger one should be placed about four inches below the wheel-line, and the smaller swivel about the middle of the casting-line. The largest swivel should be two inches in length, and proportionably stout.

Your rod for this fishing should not be more than three yards and a half long, with a strong stiff top, and very large rings; and the rod should consist of two pieces only, spliced, as the sea-water would soon destroy a rod with ferrules. Your lines should be of hemp, some of them very stout, for rough weather, and finer ones for calm weather. The manner of using your rod when under an easy breeze, is this:- you dip about half a yard of the top of the rod in the water, holding the rod perpendicularly, and when you feel a fish strike, you immediately reverse your rod and play your fish as on any other occasion. Of the stained hackles, I think the dark orange were decidedly the best.

Those who are fond of hand-line fishing, or setting the spillet, which consists of a long line with 100 or 200 hooks attached, and which, after having baited and set, you leave for some hours, will find the following baits very good:-

Lug-worm: for cod, haddock, ling, fluke, bream, tamlin, conger, sole, whiting, flounders, dabs, &c.

Whelks, alias cow-horns or buckey: for turbot, ling, haddock, cod, conger, &c.

Sand-eel: for pollack, turbot, flat fish, cod and ling.

Garden worms: for flounders and most flat fish.

Scallops: almost too soft to be put on the hook, but they will take fish.

Mussels: for ling, bream, cod, whiting, rock-cod, haddock, mackerel, gurnet, &c. To keep this bait steady on the hook, you will find it a good plan to tie a bit of thread round it.

Herrings: for cod, turbot, hake, ling, mackerel, whiting, gurnet, and many other fish.

Red and gray gurnet: for hake, and a few other fish.

Sugar-loon: for haddock, whiting, cod, ling, bream &c.

Mackerel: for turbot, ling, cod, haddock, mackerel, &c. In fishing for mackerel, always use gut and fish as fine as you can.

Sea Fly Fishing for Bass

The bass will take any gaudy fly very boldly. Your casting-line should be of twisted gut, and your tackle very strong, as the bass is a very powerful fish. On the south-west coast of England, I have taken them with the fly, as large as fourteen pounds. The fly is thrown as in trout-fishing. At low water, and near the mouth of a river, try for them near the edges of the weeds and long grass. A boat is generally necessary for this purpose.

Gray Mullet

Gray mullet will take a small fly: fish for them near the mouth of a river, when the tide is beginning to flow, at which time they occasionally come in with the tide in large shoals.

Perch

Although this is not a sea-fish, it is often to be found at the lower parts of rivers, where the tide mixes with the fresh water; and you will find that a small flat fish, not quite so large as a halfpenny, is a capital bait for them. I have also taken them with a gaudy salmon-fly, by sinking the fly and occasionally suddenly drawing it quickly.

From *Fly-fishing in Salt and Fresh Water.*
Richard Bowden-Smith, 1851.

Editor's Note:
Although the author seems to have caught his pollack by trolling a weighted line, his fly-patterns are quite elaborate and, I feel, warrant inclusion. In bass fishing he certainly 'threw the fly'.

PART VI

COD, GARFISH
&
OTHER SPECIES

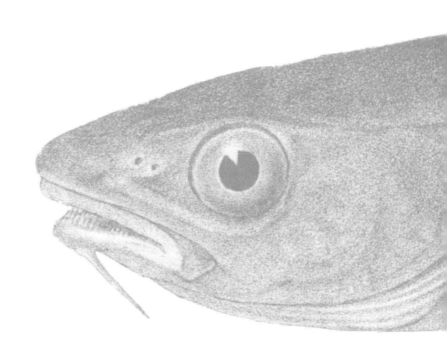

29

FLYROD COD IN THE BALTIC

Martin Jørgensen

Cod, *Gadus morhua,* are a much underrated quarry for the flyfisherman. In Denmark and Norway, where they are very common, they are sometimes even considered an annoying disturbance in the much 'finer' fishing for sea-trout.

But cod are excellent quarry for the angler whose gear and mind are tuned in to it, and the abundance and size of the fish can easily justify deliberately targeting this species.

The reason for the cod's bad reputation is probably its lack of fighting power. And true; don't expect long runs and jumps from a cod, but don't expect that you can just drag in a cod of 3-4 kilos (6-8 lb.) either. It will give quite a fight and make the experience worth remembering.

Cod is a fish that spends most of its time near the bottom. In many places cod are considered impossible to take on a flyrod, because of this fact. But there are two things to remember here: shallow water has a bottom too, and then, when dark falls, even cod will leave the bottom and seek food close to the surface.

Cod will feed on almost anything: from herring and sand-eels to crabs and clam-worms. The cod is not a great and fast hunter, but it is greedy and determined, and will relentlessly pursue its prey. When you look at a cod, its tail- and body-size will reveal that it is not a fast swimmer- either in short sprints or over longer distances. But the large neck, head and mouth tell a story too: when a cod opens its mouth, it creates a surge that can pull in almost anything in front of it.

Tackle for cod

Flyfishing for cod calls for heavier tackle than for most other Northern European salt-water fish. You will often need to cast a sinking line with a heavy fly and, once you have a hook-up, you will need the force to pull a large and bottom-seeking fish to the surface. An 8-9 weight 9' rod - preferably with a fairly slow action - with a sinking or sink-tip line is a good choice if you want to take on larger fish in deeper water. If you fish from a boat or a float-tube, you will need a fast-sinking line, maybe of the Deep Water Express type. Shooting heads can be a good choice, not for the casting-distance, but for the ease of casting the heavy line and fly. The leader can be almost as short as you please. Two metres is sufficient.

These fish will not be put off by the sight of the line. The tippet should reflect the size of the flies and the fish. 0.25mm, 0.28mm or even 0.30mm (1X, 0X or even thicker) is a proper choice.

Flies

Cod feed on almost anything and are extremely opportunistic. They will take almost any sea-trout fly, almost any of the traditional American salt-water patterns, and in fact almost any hook with a colourful, flashing or moving material attached. In the traditional deep-water fishing for cod, the fish often fall for large hooks drawn through a piece of red or orange plastic tube. The flies should be large - size 2 to 5/0 - and heavy. Lighter flies, or flies with floating materials, should be weighted with lead, dumb-bell eyes or bead-chain eyes.

Dressing a large-gaped hook with a layer of lead and a large tuft of red or orange marabou will yield an excellent cod-fly. Crab-flies are a good alternative as many cod are filled with small crabs. If you want to try fishing for smaller surface-active fish at night, use traditional sea-trout night-flies such as muddlers. These will also be likely to attract a sea-trout now and then. Dressing special or sophisticated flies for cod can generally be considered as something done for the sake of the fisher more than the fish.

Tactics

Cod can be caught all through the year. They will stay in the deeper parts of the ocean in the extremely cold and very warm parts of the year, but still be reachable most of the time. The best time for the flyfisher is from the early spring to the early summer and then again in the autumn. In the warm part of summer you can often experience smaller cod feeding frantically in the surface at night. They take a surface fly with great enthusiasm.

The best flyfishing is found in depths of at least 3-4 metres (9-12') and even deeper, so fishing from a boat or float-tube can greatly enhance your productivity. But fishing from the shore - especially from rocky coasts with deep water close to land - will often put you into very good cod fishing.

Except for the night-fishing for surface-active fish, the surest way to get a cod is to fish close to, or even on, the bottom. This calls for two things: sinking flies and line, and a bottom that has few rocks and little sea-weed.

It seems that touching the bottom itself, stirring up material and making noise, is a key factor in attracting fish. A very slow, jerky retrieve, directly on a sandy or muddy bottom is lethal if there are fish in the area. Faster retrieves over the bottom or higher in the water typically seem to attract the smaller and more agile fish.

Cod are very clumsy hunters, and you may find that a fish will attack your fly many times before getting hooked. Have patience. If a hook-up fails, just let the fly sink and then give it a small jerk. That is likely to stimulate another strike.

Cod will often school, and this means that once you find the fish, you should consider fishing the exact same spot, because it's likely to hold more fish.

Once hooked the cod will immediately dive towards the bottom with surprising strength. On sandy bottoms this offers no problem, but on rocky and weedy bottoms the fish will often get stuck or tangled if they are allowed to reach the bottom. When fishing from a boat it is fairly easy to hold the fish off the bottom, but if you are wading, you need to put a lot of vertical pressure on the fish. Once near or in the surface that cod will live up to its poor reputation as a fighter and seem to completely lose the urge to live. It might make a faint try or two, but normally you can can land even large fish by grabbing them over the neck just behind the gills.

Seasons

Cod can be caught all year round, but some parts of the year are better than others for flyfishing. The winter, when cod are traditionally caught on large lures over deep water, is not ideal for the flyfisher. The fish will stay deep and be slow. However, as soon as the sun warms up a bit, the fish will become active. Even though the water is may still be close to freezing point, there can be activity on sunny days. Spring is an excellent time for cod fishing, both from boats and from the shore, but once the water gets warmer, it's necessary to move out over deeper water in the daytime. At night the fish will be very active in the shallow water, and surface fishing near the coast can be really productive.

Later in the season, in the autumn, the fish will once again be active all day, but once the water gets much colder the cod will lose it's hunger and become more passive.

30

COD, POLLACK & COALFISH IN NORWAY

Jan Hansen and Asgeir Alvestad

Two world records on one day

In July 1996 the three friends; Leif Nygård, Geir Stene and Asgeir Alvestad went far north to Sørøya in Troms to enter a sea-angling match. Their plan was to spend a few days 'pleasure-fishing' after the competition. The competition, which Asgeir won, was based on the use of conventional deep-sea tackle; large spinners, pirks and bait. It went well in spite of rather rough weather conditions.

After the weekend, Monday dawned with calm weather - time for some experiments. Leif, Geir and Asgeir set out in a small boat. The two spin-fishing companions were soon knee-deep in cod. Asgeir was in the bow with his big-game flyrod, constructed especially for saltwater fishing. On the reel a super-fast sinking line and a lot of backing. Using casts of some 20 metres, and then feeding-out backing, he brought the fly down to around 20 metres in an approximate water depth of 70 metres.

It was almost impossible to get the fly through the numerous coalfish swimming under the boat. They were eagerly taking the fly. Often, once a coalfish was hooked, it would be chased by large cod that were swimming around under the coalfish. The skin was often stripped from the coalfish by the time it was brought aboard. On one occasion Asgeir managed to haul a large cod over the rail, the coalfish still firmly trapped in the cod's mouth and in the mouth of the coalfish? - The fly. The cod weighed 11.5 kg and the coalfish was around 3 kg. A few minutes later a coalfish of 4.5 kg was captured. This is still the Norwegian fly record for this species.

At last Asgeir managed to find a "hole" free from coalfish and managed to let the fly sink deeper. After a while a cod took the fly. This was not a lazy fish, but a fit predator, fully able to catch fast-moving prey-fish weighing several kilos. The cod made several runs of more than 70 metres and fought, according to Asgeir - 'like a well fit salmon'. Finger hurting from "reelstrokes", the special big-game flyrod proved its worth. To cut the story short, twenty minutes later the world-record fly-caught cod was hauled aboard. Weight? 15 kg.

To cope with this really special kind of flyfishing you depend on calm days where there is little wind and currents. This has nothing to do with the presence of fish, but is simply a necessity to keep the boat and the water from moving at different speeds, which inevitably make it impossible to let the fly-line sink deep enough to reach the fish.

Though the story above may well lead more people to use flyfishing equipment from boats on the open sea, this kind of fishing is little practised at present. The normal way of flyfishing for cod is from the shore. You can have reasonable success at flyfishing for cod by fishing for sea-trout all year round. You will probably bring back a larger number of cod than sea-trout. To go for the cod and be sure of capturing some of the larger ones you must know a little about the cod and its feeding habits.

The cod feeds in shallow water according to water temperature and the need to grow fat before and after spawning. This will bring it near the beach in November (water temperatures from 2 - 6 degrees) and around Easter which is the time for spawning. Around Easter the water temperature rises to November level again after the winter. At these periods the cod is said to be 'tail above'. It is now often seen searching the bottom with the tail in the surface, head-down, nose in the mud and vegetation, much like a pig rooting for truffles. At this time the fish are caught on streamers, or imitations of sand worms or shrimps. Asgeir advises this colour scheme for cod-flies, according to the temperature. White below 7 degrees C; 7-9 degrees, green; 9-10 degrees, red; and then yellow into the summer.

The cod varies in size and quality along the coast. There is an old saying that goes 'never eat cod on days without 'r'. I eat my catch of cod the year round, but admit they taste best around Easter. But that is also when I catch the largest ones, often around 3 kilos. During summer here in the southern part of Norway the cod are often smallish . Whatever the time of the year, -a cod of 16 kg is a rarity in the south, but reasonably common in the northern and western part of the country.

Coalfish

The coalfish is even more likely to be accidentally caught when fishing for sea-trout than is the cod. It swims closer to the surface than cod, especially during summer, and coalfish caught accidentally during summer months tend to be bigger than the cod.

Bigger by no means carries any suggestion that this fish is more tasty than the cod. Coalfish taken in the south will more often than not carry worms and need to be cleaned soon after its landed.

The delicacy of finding such things inside it may have something to do with my distaste for it. I much prefer cod. Taste or not, the coalfish is a good fighter and a specimen of more than two kilos will be difficult to handle. The coalfish tends to reach larger sizes and better quality the farther north you get.

Asgeir's fly/colour scheme indicates the need for white flies below 6 degrees C, then yellow/green until around 10 degrees. Black colours are often productive during the summer.

Pollack

Sinking lines are a must if the pollack is on the menu. Apart from that, most of the year you will find pollack where you find sea-trout, places with good currents. The flies used for sea-trout can be left on when going for pollack. This species tends to thrive best in warmer water which points out the southern coast as the place to go. These fish must be experienced. For their weight, they are among the Norwegian coast's most strong-fighting fishes. Their fierce strikes are followed by long strong dives for the depths. A new report claims a fly-caught pollack of 7kg caught in the fjord outside Kristiansand.

Again, Asgeir has been at the right place at the right time: Tromlingene in May. Went out to try the sea-trout and test out a few things. We started casting from the edges of small islands outside Tromøya, situated close to the city of Arendal. The fly was an orange coloured Dog-nobbler. We caught a pollack on every cast. The day totalled twenty-five, most of which were released. The ones brought home averaged around two kilos.

31

BALTIC GARFISH

Martin Jørgensen

The garfish, *Belone belone,* is a very common visitor to many Northern European countries. It is normally a pelagic fish whose migration pattern is not known in detail.

But one thing is for sure: these fish will return to spawn in shallow and rich areas along the coasts of many places in Europe. The pattern of their behavior is well-known in this respect, and normally they are very reliable, and will return precisely within days each year. In the outer Baltic area the season starts at the end of April and the beginning of May, and the gar can be followed towards the south and east after this time. They will disappear again in less than a month and not return before the autumn, when their appearance is less synchronized and the fishing is much more sporadic.

Even though they come to spawn in the spring, they still eat, and because they are fast fish and avid hunters, they are a joy to catch. For their weight, they are probably one of the strongest species found in our waters. But they do not grow big. A half-kilo fish (1 lb.) is average, while a fish of 1kg (2 lb.) is huge.

Tackle for garfish

The limited size of the fish should be reflected in the tackle. A five-weight rod is an excellent choice, and even lighter is possible if the wind allows it.

The most suitable line is a weight-forward floater. You do not need long casts, and the fish are moving just below the surface. Garfish are not easily scared, so a fairly short leader of approximately 2-3 metres (6-9') will be fine. The tippet should be 0.20 millimetres (3X) or 0.18 millimetres (4X) - not so much to hold the fish as to turn over the flies under windy conditions.

Flies for garfish

The flies for garfish vary a bit. Many fishers will recommend silvery streamer-patterns in sizes up to 4 and 2, but if you really want to catch many fish, you should go down to sizes 10, 12 and even 14. These small hooks will set much better in the hard bill of the fish. Garfish have very good eyesight and will easily spot the small flies from great distances.

One of the most successful colours for garfish-flies is orange, and almost any small, orange fly will catch them. A size 12 unweighted Woolly Bugger is an excellent choice, but some people use flies as simple as orange yarn, wound-on or tied to a small hook. An orange San Juan Worm will probably serve you well. Use very sharp hooks such as specimen-hooks or even small dry-fly hooks. These will penetrate the hard bill and give a nice, clean hookup in the corner of the mouth. The traditional stainless salt-water hooks are hard to get in the smallest sizes, so be pre-pared to trash some rusty flies.

If you do not have any small flies handy, you can also try traditional pat-terns: streamers, scud-patterns and even shrimps in larger sizes. The garfish will probably attack them, but setting a larger salt-water hook can be quite difficult.

Tactics

Garfish are mostly active in the daytime, especially on mild, sunny days. This makes the first warm spring days in May ideal for a garfish outing. Choose a day with light wind as it enhances your possibilities of seeing the fish in the water.

They can be found everywhere from the deeper parts of the open ocean to the inner fjords. Normally you can spot them either moving over light bottoms in shallow water or tumbling in the surface during their mating ritual.

They are not willing to bite while engaged in that ritual, but both right before and right after. Also, mating fish will be a sign of other fish in the vicinity, and it's a good idea to stay in an area with surface action.

If you see no fish, try looking for a sandy bottom with a depth of 0.5 to 1.5 metres (1 to 5 feet), interspersed with patches of sea-weed, sand-bars, stone reefs or other significant 'landmarks'. The fish will often follow these natural corridors on their way. You can also look on a map to find places like points or narrow sounds that the fish have to pass on their way into the Baltic. These are bound to hold garfish.

If you see fish, just cast to them and let your fly sink a bit. Then retrieve slowly, maybe in small jerks. The figure-of-eight retrieve comes in handy here. Contrary to what many people think, this fast-moving fish is not only stimulated by fast-moving food items. The fish will go for the fly and often miss a couple of times. Have patience and strike lightly on any feel-ing of weight in the rod. Keep on retrieving even if you have felt or have missed a fish. When you have fish on, be prepared for some wild runs and jumps. Even a half-kilo garfish will take line off a five-weight rod. Also be prepared to lose a few fish. They are hard to hook properly.

Garfish are excellent food - don't be scared by their iridescent green bones, they are absolutely harmless - but keep in mind that you can only eat so many fish, and release the majority on a good day.

32

FLOUNDER

Martin James

One fish that is plentiful in European waters is the flounder, *Platichthys flesus,* a thick-bodied flatfish with powerful jaws. A bottom-living flatfish which moves in and out with the tide, feeding on worms, cockles and crustaceans, especially shrimps. Though reputed to have a small mouth they are often caught by shore anglers fishing with big baits such as crabs, and herring and mackerel strip. The flounder spends its life between the tideline and the 25 to 30 fathoms mark, but they are often caught several miles upstream in freshwater rivers by anglers legering worms or gentles.

The tide had been flooding for about an hour, when I arrived on the banks of a small twisting West coast estuary near Carnforth in Lancashire to fish for the flounder. It was time to put my new TS series fast-sinking line to the test. A couple of feet of 16 lb line was needle-knotted to the fly-line. You don't need a longer leader on a sinking-line. In fact if you use a long leader you can have problems. I tied on a size 1/0 Clouser Minnow. Pulling off some line it was quickly roll-cast, a quick back-cast ,then shoot. It worked a treat. The line straightened and sank very quickly. As I retrieved I could feel the minnow bouncing on the bottom. My tackle was working. An hour or so later a flounder hit the fly, my first! To be honest it is hard work with these lines, and several times the fly hit me in the back with a thump. But these lines do get the fly down to the fish.

I fish the Clouser Minnow in short quick pulls allowing the fly to settle between pulls. This helps the fly to kick up small puffs of silt which I suspect the flounders find attractive, and hopefully it gets the fish following and then grabbing the fly. When fishing small river estuaries I try to get the fly to drop down in the centre channel. I work the retrieve so the fly is then retrieved along, and then up, the side of the channel. You must expect a take at any time but do not slow your retrieve if you see a fish following. They are easily spooked.

Some of the best flounder fishing conditions are in autumn when there is a high pressure zone sitting over the country. Those flat calm days with several hours of bright sunshine, high water around noon, are perfect for flounder fishing.

The other species of flat-fish that come in range of the saltwater flyfisher is the plaice. Though not as plentiful as the flounder there are some areas of the coastline where you have a realistic chance of catching plaice, which often feed on sandeels. One area of Britain which springs to mind are the shallows of Walney Island. Given conditions of calm clear water on a neap tide in summer the saltwater fly-rodder should be able to catch not only plaice but also bass and codling.

33

FLYRODDING FOR FLATTIES

Barry Ord Clarke

The flatfish are, as a group, formidable predators. Disguised by some of nature's most effective camouflage and equipped with lightning fast, alien-like, telescopic mouths and periscopic eyes, these fish patrol the sea bed taking everything from marine worms to mussels, razor clams and small fish.

The key to successful flyrodding for flatfish lies in choosing the right locations. Flatties are, because of their unique body form, natural bottom feeders. Their preferred habitat is, generally speaking, sandy, although there are variations in favoured feeding grounds according to species, time of year and state of tide. Plaice are extremely fond of small mussels and can be fished from the shore by locating mussel beds within casting distance at low tide, and then returning to fish at high water. Sheltered bays with a good water depth can also hold sandy pockets which are favoured hunting grounds for plaice and flounders.

A most important piece of equipment when it comes to fishing with fly in the sea is a car. Mobility is everything! If you find what would seem to be a suitable area but don't come into contact with any fish, move on. Keep moving until you find fish. If one fish is caught it's fairly safe to assume they are there in good numbers. By using coastal maps, showing sub-surface contour lines, and inspecting fishing grounds at low tide, you should build up a picture of where to locate the fish. Such places as piers, estuaries and river mouths with brackish water are ideal for picking up flounders and dabs, but check the local fishing regulations first. Some places (for example Norway) don't allow fishing at river mouths because of migrating sea-trout and salmon. The best time of year for flyrodding for flatfish is mid to late summer, especially during periods of prolonged hot calm weather, although it is possible to fish the whole year round. On the whole, the most favourable conditions are blue skies, clear water and bright sunshine.

Most of the coast-line in Norway is accessible by car with small single-track lanes every few kilometres off the main roads, weaving their way through forest and farm-land down towards small sheltered bays. Where I live, near the town of Skien, the coast-line is typical of that found just about over the whole of southern Norway. A sea-swept solid granite shore-line scattered with hundreds of small islands, smoothly sculptured by glacial ice to resemble the backs of half-submerged whales heading south. There isn't much in the form of foliage that can manage to set fast its roots and survive the strong winds and extreme cold of winter, except sltorn, a small thorny bush, and the occasional stunted wind-swept oak, its virtu-ally horizontal branches pointing northward. So finding room for your back cast isn't normally a problem. Tides are small here; usually less than one metre.

My first encounter with flatfish on fly, took place during the summer of '86. Two fishing friends and I decided to take an evening trip to a well known local sea-trout fishing spot about 25 minutes drive from home. This isn't such a common thing to do during the height of summer, but because of the extremely hot weather we had been experiencing, the brown trout fishing in the small mountain tarns was extremely slow. We arrived at around 10 o clock in the evening and waited for the sun to go down. It's a great tradition in Norway when fishing, and especially hunt-ing, that you make a fire and cook coffee. For most outdoorsmen here, even if the hunting and fishing trip was successful, they wouldn't call it a good trip without the ritual coffee cooking. I say coffee cooking, because that's what it is. This is not your normal Gold Blend out of a jar, but a thick, black, bitumastic substance, made by heaving a mountain of coarsely ground strong coffee, along with pine needles and various other organic debris, into the boiling water of a billy can. And I might add that this makes a double espresso taste like a cream tea. The coffee is ceremonially drunk from traditional hand-made wooden cups, each fashioned from a knot of birch wood.

As we sat around the fireside, fish and fishing-trips past, present and yet to come were discussed, while all the time we were carefully watching the mirror-flat water for any signs of sea-trout breaking the surface. When fishing actually commenced, around 10.45pm, all we had observed were small pollack. Pollack can be a real nuisance in when present in big num-bers, taking every fly that is presented. An hour later, and spaced about 15 metres apart, all fishing the top of the water with floating lines, none of us had touched anything except masses of tiny pollack up to 300 grams. It was clear that we weren't going to take any sea trout on this trip. It was then that I decided it was time for a change of tackle, and try to fish the fly deeper, out of reach of the pollack. At this time, still living in England but spending all my summers in Norway, one of my fly boxes was well stocked with the usual reservoir lures, of which some happened to be Boobies.

My Norwegian companions had not seen anything like the Booby before, and had no faith that I would ever catch (in their own words) sly, wild, Norwegian fish, on a fly that didn't resemble anything from nature, and was designed only for brain-dead stockies.

So, with sinking line, a bright orange Booby, my long practised English reservoir tactics, and the nods and sniggers from either side of me, I began to cast, wait and retrieve. After I had made half a dozen casts and a couple of adjustments to my leader I was into my first fish; a decent cod of around 3lb. After an hour passed and with two more cod on the shore, I moved to a small island accessible only at low tide with chest waders. To the south of this island was a long sandy ridge that progressively deepened as it ran further out. Because of the absence of kelp here I shortened my leader even more and fished deep, close to the sea bed, with the hope of taking some larger cod. My first cast snagged half way through my retrieve; I thought that I had been a little too ambitious when trimming my leader. Then, as I lifted my rod, I felt that unmistakable indication of life at the end of my line. I connected, and the game was on. At first I was sure it was another cod behaving strangely, but after 30 seconds or so I had no idea what it was. I had never had a fish behave quite like this before. Swimming back and forth from side to side, constantly shaking it's head, causing the rod tip to bounce up and down. And then when I tried to gain some line it just felt like a dead weight, with spurts of powerful resistance. This continued for a couple of minutes until I managed to bring the fish up, and within gaffing distance. The gaff I use for saltwater fishing, is one that I acquired in a Norwegian tackle shop constructed from a well-oiled telescopic car aerial with a 2/0 stainless steel fishing hook attached to the business end. It can be carried in the pocket and just flicked out when needed. I saw to my amazement when the fish rolled over just under the surface and flashed it's white underside in the light of the moon, that it was some kind of flat fish. It wasn't huge, but it was my first flattie on fly. A fine deep red-spotted plaice, a little over 2lb. My Norwegian fishing friends ate humble pie, and I feasted on lemon-buttered barbecued plaice.

Since that first accidental flatfish on fly, I have developed the Booby more for saltwater fishing, trying to make it more durable and attractive to flatties. A Booby fished in combination with a Hi-D line is probably the most effective way of flyfishing at an accurately controlled depth. It gives control over the distance from the sea bed at which your fly is fishing, enabling you to fish the Booby with a slow figure-of-eight retrieve just a few centimetres from the sea floor, creeping it over mussel beds and sandy bottoms. Equally effectively, a longer leader can be used to fish the fish just above the level of the sea-weed. If you would like to try to take several fish on one cast, you can use a dropper system with two or even three Boobies placed about 40 cm apart. Because flatfish are often found in numbers a "full house" isn't that unusual.

Using a # 7/8 Hi-D shooting head combined with a fast action 9-10 ft rod, you should be able to cover sufficient water in most weather conditions. The use of a line tray can also be extremely useful if wading, as this will increase your casting capability and will also cut down on line tangles. Your leader material should be of a heavy salt water type, and at least 8 lb, and even up to 12 lb. If fishing droppers, a stiff leader material greatly reduces the risk of wind-knots.

When tying Boobies for saltwater fishing, I recommend the use of anti-corrosive hooks. Two of the best of these are the Partridge of Redditch J.S. Sea Streamer, and the Mustad 79586 DD Salt water.

I have found that Boobies tied in vivid red, pink, olive, black and white, in sizes 8 and 10, with longish tails of around 5-8 cm, made of marabou, and supplemented with a few strands of something flashy like crystal hair or flashabou are the most productive. The body is normally ostrich herl or chenille in a matching colour. I also use fluorescent plastic beads as an attractor "hot spot". These are slipped along the hook shank before securing the hook in the vice. You then tie in the tail and push the bead or beads, back over the thread windings that secure the tail and the rest of the fly completed as normal. The buoyant eyes from which this pattern takes its name should be made to look like eyes as most predatory fish use the eye as an attack point. This can be achieved with the use of a non-solvent varnish (varnishes containing solvents have a tendency to melt polystyrene and foam) or if you use the rubber from a balloon or condom as the envelope for the eyes, waterproof markers can be used. Care should be taken when attaching the eyes as balls of different sizes will cause the fly to swim badly or even spin.

Fishing the Booby is a game of patience and experimentation. After making your cast, you must give your line sufficient time to sink to the sea bed so that your Booby is at the correct height from the bottom (leader length). Normally when fishing from shore not more than 35 seconds is required. Whatever you do, don't be tempted to place your rod on the ground and go and do something else while you wait for this time to expire. On one occasion while fishing with two friends in Norway, I decided to answer a call of nature and returned to find my rod under the water line and disappearing slowly towards Denmark. Fortunately I recovered the rod and landed the fish. It is quite common for cod and pollack to take the Booby 'on the drop', as it is sinking. One of the great things about fishing in the sea is that no matter how precise you are in your specimen hunting you are never quite sure what you are going to catch!

Once your line is out and in position on the sea-bed, you can begin the retrieve. A very slow figure-of-eight with frequent short pauses. Takes can, of course, occur any time, but just at the beginning of a retrieve, after a pause, is when many fish will hit the fly. One of the advantages of fishing the figure-of-eight retrieve is that you are in constant contact with your line. This is very important especially when making the pauses. After a while, when you become experienced in fishing this method, you should be able to read the sea-bed through your line, feeling your way across the bottom. If your retrieve is speeded up the Booby will dive and probably snag. If you find you are snagging weed, extend your leader by 20cm and try again, then repeat this until it swims freely.

Flatfish in general, but especially the plaice, have a inclination to take the fly deep into their throat, and then hold fast on the bottom for a short while before moving off. So a rule of thumb is "if it stops strike". Because of this tendency for the Booby to be taken very deeply your fly is sometimes only retrievable with surgery. I recommend that you always carry a well-stocked flybox, with at least a half dozen of each pattern.

Skitt fiske!

34

PIKE AND IDE IN THE BALTIC

Claus Bech-Petersen

The Baltic, which spans nearly 400,000 square kilometres, offers some of the best saltwater flyfishing for brown trout in the world, with good numbers of double-figure fish. However, few people take advantage of the other species this large sea has to offer. The rivers that enter the Baltic pour 15.000 cubic metres of freshwater into the sea each second, and because of these huge rivers the Baltic remain brackish year round. In north the salinity is only 3.5 0/00, very close to freshwater. The three Danish sounds act as the border between the brackish water in the Baltic and waters of the North Sea with a salinity of 35 0/00. The low salinity in the Baltic means that you will find several freshwater species here. The northern part of the Baltic contains true freshwater species like grayling and whitefish which can be found cruising the shores of the sea. Further south there are zander and perch, but of most interest to the flyfisher are probably the pike and ide. Pike grow large in the Baltic (one Danish fisherman caught a 45 pounder a couple of years back), and the ide is, though small, an ideal dry-fly fish in the summer months.

Monster pike!

Denmark has a small population of saltwater pike, but the fish are regularly killed by intruding salt-water, and the best fishing is found in Sweden and Finland. The archipelagos on the eastern coast of Sweden are famous for their pike fishing, especially the islands of Gotland and Åland and the area around Stockholm. These attract thousands of fishermen in spring when the big pike come close to shore to spawn. Many of the fish are of course small (which means that the population is healthy) but twenty pound pike are by no means uncommon and many much bigger fish are caught each year; some even by novice anglers.

In Finland the best fishing is on the small island of Åland (which, by the way, is the oldest de-militarised zone in the world). I first fished for the Åland pike in 1995 on a flyfishing assignment for my newspaper. It was in early November and actually a little late in the season. The best autumn fishing is found from August to November. We encountered a storm that made it difficult to fish and there were only a few sheltered bays where we could fish effectively. On the second day we fished with a professional guide, Vidar Håggblom, who specialises in pike. Vidar owns an entire island with private fishing and here, between the skerries, we found our pike. The photographer Steen got the first fish. It weighed only a few kilos, but Steen, an experienced flyfisherman, who has fished saltwater on most continents, was surprised by the strong and stubborn resistance the pike gave him. Despite the storm we caught fish on all the perfect drifts over the shallow bays and along the shore. By late afternoon Steen was getting the hang of it!

The sun was setting when Vidar pulled the boat close to a small island. The water was shallow and the fishing slow and we suggested wading in stead of casting from the boat. Vidar was surprised by the request as nobody wades the shores when they have access to a boat, but promptly accepted. The water was devoid of life and after a few casts along the shore I turned around and used the wind to shoot the line as far out as possible. A few minutes later, the fly was intercepted - and released again as a pike turned away in an enormous boil of water. Two casts later it happened again. A pike stopped the fly but despite a heavy, hook-setting pull with the line-hand, the hook came back without the fish. It was not comforting when Vidar told he had caught and released an eighteen pound pike on the very same spot the day before . . .

Despite the storm we got thirteen pike that day. The largest fish were about six and a half pounds, and even though we were satisfied, the guide was not. He had expected at least five more, and a few bigger fish, above eleven pounds. The fishing season for pike in the Baltic generally peaks in spring, just before and after the pike spawn, and in autumn, when the water cools and the fish return to shallow water. The spring fish, which are caught from March through May, are the biggest, but in the cold water they can be difficult to fool. But these spring pike, which are filled with new generations, are heavy and just after spawning they seem to strike at almost any bait or fly if presented slowly in front of them.

At Åland, and in some places in Sweden, you need a boat to fish the best bays, but several places on the north-eastern coast of Åland the fish can be found in water shallow enough to wade. Åland is very popular among Danish fishermen and many have got their first 20 pounder here. Summer fishing for Baltic pike is not that common and most fishermen wait until mid-August before they again turn their attention toward the pike. At this time of year the pike are much more active and until November they can be caught at many of the same locations as in the spring, although they tend to lie closer to deep water. The flies are more or less the same; big and flashy or big and white. The herring is a major food source in many places. Useful flies are 4-8 inch long white Deceivers, large poppers in autumn and a few flies in the classic pike colours; white and red or orange.

The tackle I have used in the Baltic is basically the same medium-heavy outfit as I use everywhere else: A nine-foot rod that carries an assortment of 10-weight shooting heads. Floaters and intermediates seem to be most useful but occasionally you might need a fast-sinker.

My flies are dressed to cast easily and a lighter rod could be used if it was not for the 30 pounder I always hope for - but haven't met yet. Leaders are short and heavy and the shock tippet is Orvis special braided wire, which accommodates standard knots for nylon.

Ide stalking with the dry fly

Swoffing, as the Australians term saltwater flyfishing, is usually a serious affair with heavy rods and large flies. One of the few exceptions is the little ide, which throughout the Baltic is found in brackish water. In his book *Small Fish and Big Fish* the Finnish author, Juhani Aho, devoted an entire chapter to 'the secretive ides', as he called them.

Aho had, like me, a hard time learning the whereabouts of the ide. One day you will find the fish all over the place. The next day they are gone. But luckily they are easy and fun to catch, when you have found them. The ide in the Baltic live in the sea most of the year and migrate to freshwater to spawn in April, May and June. For the saltwater flyfisherman they are most interesting during the summer, when the fish have recovered after spawning and forage all day in the warmer water.

My experiences with ide come from the western shores of the Danish island, Sealand, where the ide roam all summer. It can sometimes be difficult to predict where they are, but frequently they are easy to locate, as they can be seen rising or rolling at the surface as they take small crustaceans and insects.

And on a warm summer day fishing for ide reminds me of the trout-stalking I have had in New Zealand lakes: Shorts and boots, light 5-weight rods, sun glasses and a small box with a selection of dries and nymphs in sizes 10-14. When an ide breaks the surface or reveals its shadow you react fast and place the fly a foot in front of it.

Baltic ide are not big. Most of the fish weigh between one and three pounds, and a trophy fish would be five or six pounds. But the numbers - it is not unusual to catch 10 or 20 fish on a good day - make up for the size.

The most pleasant fishing for ide is on calm days, where a light 3-weight outfit is ideal. Despite that I seldom use anything but my light saltwater rod which carries an 6-weight shooting head. Coupled with a monofilament shooting-line (20lb b.s. golden fluorescent Stren) the rod easily casts a light sea-trout streamer 90 feet on calm days, so with this combination I still have a chance if sea-trout or steelhead show up. Ide are not particular when it comes to flies. For dry flies, a selection of Humpies, Irresistibles, Black Gnats or Wulffs in sizes 10-14 would be quite adequate. My nymphs are most often simple hackled wet flies or hare's ear types in the same sizes. Ide seem to have a thing for a touch of red so a Red Tag is always worth a try.

35

IRISH SHARKS!

Rudy van Duijnhoven

Blue shark on the fly

The blue shark circled angrily round the boat, looking for the second mackerel in a row that had been pulled from his teeth. Right behind the boat my white and blue streamer happened to be in it's path and it slowly moved in closer to it. When the shark's nose almost hit the streamer, it opened it's mouth and the full 30 centimetres disappeared within the blink of an eye. A few quick strikes with the rod drove the 7/0 hook home and the fight was on. The blue shark dove straight head-down at high speed and only a few quick movements of the skipper and myself cleared the line so the reel could start it's fast spin. In the mean-time all the people on the boat cheered and were at least as pleased as I was.

The shark reached a depth of some 60 metres before I could stop it. The double handle on the short #12 flyrod proved a big help in pumping the fish back up. The fish dove twice more before skipper John Brittain could work a rope over its head and the shark could be pulled on board. Cameras did their work with the necessary speed, so the fish, which weighed about 35 lb, could be returned quickly.

August 1997 saw René Flohil and myself set out to sea for the second year. The previous year, when fishing near the mouth of the Shannon, strong winds prevented us from going out far enough for sharks, and we had to restrict ourselves to bass and pollack that we fished for close to the cliffs and near the outlet of a power station. This year the weather was much better, little wind and only occasional showers.

We were to fish from Clifden skipper John Brittain's boat 'Blue Water' - a new boat of the Sygnus type - one of the largest of its kind along the entire coast. John Brittain is a flyfisher himself, and was keen to see if it would be possible to land one of those big west-coast blue shark on the fly. Five other anglers, who were to be using conventional shark tackle, made up the group.

After catching the mackerel that we needed for the rubby dubby, we motored to a spot some one and a half hours from Clifden and with a depth of around 100 metres. On conventional gear the other anglers each caught a blue shark within the next two and a half hours, with the lady of the team catching the biggest one, of course.

After this delightful period, it was our turn. The Fenwick #12 flyrod was rigged with a System Two 1213 reel filled with 500 metres of 30 lb Dyneema backing, Amnesia running line and a leadcore shooting-head. A length of nylon-coated, steel wire was knotted to the leader with the fly connected by a strong link-swivel. The fly was a blue and white streamer tied on a 7/0 hook.

Blue shark came into the rubby-dubby trail regularly, but they then had to be teased to the boat before they would take a fly. A dead mackerel, without a hook, was cast into the rubby-dubby trail, using a casting-rod. When a shark took, the mackerel was jerked away from it. After this had been done several times the hungry shark was circling close to the boat, looking for the mackerel. It took a while for us to get teaser, shark and fly synchronised, but eventually I did it. A mackerel was pulled out of a shark's grasp, and when the fish started searching for it, my streamer was directly in its path.

We returned my fish and then it was René's turn. Another shark was soon attracted to the teaser. Upon seeing the boat, however, it turned away at great speed and disappeared out of sight. René made a few casts anyway and on the second one his hand was almost pulled through the first guide of the rod. After setting the hook and clearing the line a similar fight ensued. But as this fish was heavier - around 55 lb - it took much longer to land.

This one blue shark on fly tackle probably meant more to René than all the others he has caught on conventional gear over the last ten years.

When later that day we motored back to Clifden, the two of us were more than pleased. We had proved that blue shark could be caught on the streamer and flyrod. John Brittain had had his doubts at the start of this expedition, but that same evening he asked me whether he could buy my #12 outfit from me...

These were the first two blue shark ever caught on the fly in Irish waters! It had been tried before, but ours was the first success.

PART VII

SALMON IN THE SEA

36

SALTWATER SALMON

Richard Davies

Most of us who enjoy flyfishing for salmon hope to arrive at the river when it is fining down after a spate and at such times the fish can be flattering. However, before the main runs have entered the river, usually due to low flows, the only chance of seeing a fish, let alone catching one, is in the sea or estuary. This may not be the disaster it appears since salmon can be tempted in salt water around our coastlines. When you do tempt one, get ready for one of the fiercest fights you'll experience.

Flyfishing for salmon in the sea is not something we come across very often. There are a few known places around the British Isles where it is possible. There may however be many more awaiting discovery or exploitation. I say this because in my opinion the local geography is more important than the flyfishing techniques employed.

In this chapter I would like to describe to you the tackle, technique and, most importantly, some of the physical conditions required for catching salmon in the sea. It is here that there is scope for exploration and hopefully success.

It should be made clear that I am not talking about sea-pool fishing, which is fairly common and relatively well-documented. Neither am I talking about deep-sea fishing, where the chances of encountering returning adult salmon are remote. I am talking about somewhere in-between, where the water is salt but near the river mouth.

I cannot take all the credit for what I am about to describe. I am merely fortunate enough to live and work on a system where salmon have been consistently caught in saltwater a full mile from the top of the tide sea-pool. So much success has been had here that even when the river is in good fettle we still chance the tide.

Here I would like to mention Clive Bruton who, in early July 1978, caught three grilse and lost a larger fish at the estuary of the Hebridean Fhorsa River. This was the event that enthused so many fishermen to follow in his footsteps. Indeed it is after him that this part of the fishing is named - 'The Bruton Stream'.

Since that day the method has been refined by my namesake Richard

Davis - the previous owner - and then by my predecessor and mentor Jonathan Morsehead.

There is nothing magical or super-successful about fishing for salmon on the tide. There are, as with all salmon fishing, more frustrating experiences than euphoric ones. On the day of writing this passage six rods covered several hundred fish with various flies and casting angles in seemingly good conditions and yet no-one moved a thing. This is not normal, but then salmon seldom are.

The length of this chapter prohibits a full, in-depth description of saltwater salmon fishing. It may however help our understanding if we briefly examine the workings of the Bruton Stream.

The prevailing wind, substrate and currents at low, flowing and ebbing tides are shown in figures A, B and C respectively.

At low tide the fish normally congregate in the bay around the various reefs. At this stage fish are seldom caught or fished for unless they settle near the shore in shallow water, enabling the angler to see and cast over them. We will discuss the issue of spotting fish later.

In a normal year the prevailing wind in the Hebrides is south-westerly and fairly strong. This has caused the river flowing over the beach to be blown to its far north and east extremes as shown in figure A.

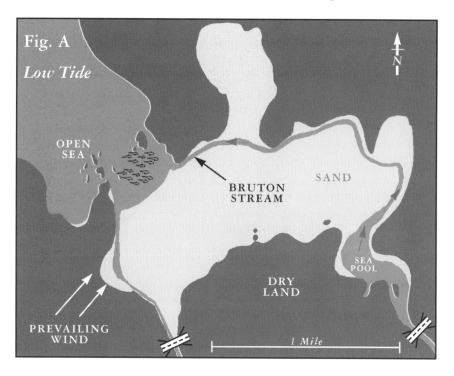

Fig. A
Low Tide

N

OPEN
SEA

BRUTON
STREAM

SAND

SEA
POOL

DRY
LAND

PREVAILING
WIND

1 Mile

It follows that this river channel (forged in sand) will always contain the deepest water at high or low tide. At low tide, and in low flows, the water in the channel is only a few inches deep and, significantly, this channel has no holding pools. The channel itself is about three feet deeper than the beach.

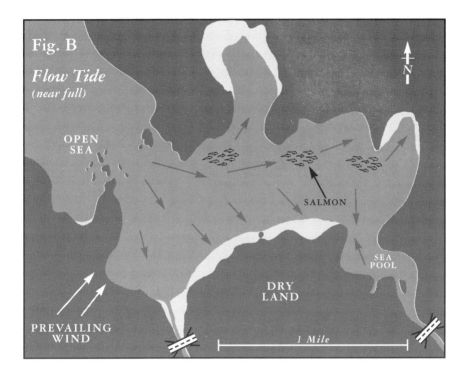

Salmon waiting in the bay, excited by the smell of their own river, follow the tide in, sticking to the deep channel (see figure B). Only on a very big spring tide, or when the river is in full spate, will the fish venture as far as the river proper where they behave accordingly. For the majority of the time they have to drop back with the tide because of the lack of holding pools. They do so reluctantly, slipping back in shoals at the last possible moment. I believe this behaviour, coupled with the presence, however small, of fresh water is why salmon are most often willing to take on the ebb-tide.

Let me explain: while the fish are moving around the bay or tidal river channel they can be likened to fish running in a spating river, notoriously poor takers. If however, they pause for a while, holding station against the tide-rip, it becomes possible to tempt one to the fly. This holding, or resting behaviour most often occurs on the ebb tide (see figure C). Again, this can be compared to fish in fresh water, forced to stop running by a dropping river when, for a short time, they can be fairly easy to catch.

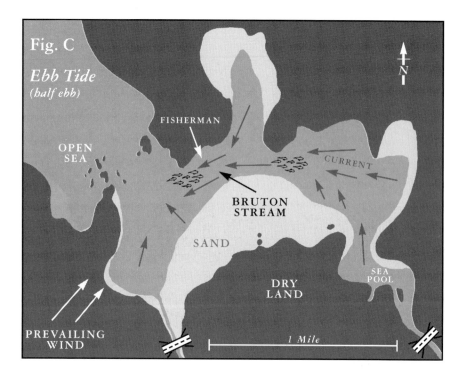

Salmon usually hold in the Bruton Stream on the ebb-tide. The presence of a freshwater lens brings fish up, head and tailing, and gulping in the fresh water that floats on the salt. It could be said that at this stage they are in fresh water, but they are merely rising to taste it and returning to the sea water below. This gulping, or head and tailing, increases as the ebbing tide drops quickest, between two and four hours after a normal high tide. It is during this phase that the rip in the Bruton is strongest, and this is the time to concentrate fishing effort. This does not imply that a spring tide with a faster rip is better for fishing because a larger tide falls quicker and leaves a shorter fishing window. It seems a medium tide is best - when a good rip and a reasonably long window of opportunity can be had. Not so long ago, on one such medium tide, (around 4.2 metres) two rods took eight salmon.

Knowing that salmon rise or fall with the tide, and sometimes hold station, is one thing. Knowing where they are is a different matter. Spotting shoals harbours its own problems.

Seeing salmon in the water if you are high above them is not too difficult, especially in clear shallow water with a sandy bottom. Estuaries containing shallow water tend to be from small spate streams and realistically these are the only likely places for another Bruton Stream.

Salmon tend to shoal and thus appear as a large ghost-like blob that moves and changes shape. The darker the blob appears the more layers of fish there are, and the nearer they are to the surface. When near the surface they are more willing to take because of their excitement at the smell of fresh water. I like big, black blobs!

Waiting for a while to see a fish jump from a blob, to identify it as a shoal and not weed, is time well spent. But relying solely on seeing a fish jump to decide where to fish can be very inaccurate. It may lead to time lost casting just a few yards from a shoal rather than over it. This is because salmon often leap as part of a circling behaviour. See figure D.

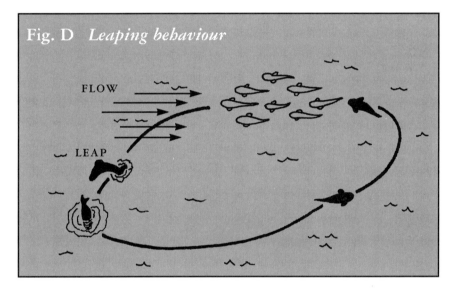

Fig. D *Leaping behaviour*

FLOW

LEAP

It is helpful to have someone positioned on a high point spotting the blobs for you as this is virtually impossible from water level, even with polaroids. In fact, without being able to see the fish, and without success, it is easy to lose interest.

It is becoming clear by now that saltwater flyfishing for salmon has many contributing factors which make it possible in certain places and not in others. Because of the limitations in spotting fish, and the requirement of an estuary with few or no holding pools, it is unlikely there are many ìBruton Streamsî around the coasts of Europe. I believe small spate rivers with long meandering shallow estuaries are the most likely candidates. Fortunately these are the rivers where, without rain, a 'Bruton Stream' is most often required, since without water salmon cannot run them. On large rivers with short or deep estuaries fish can slip into the lower pools and are fished for normally.

Once a pattern of salmon movements has been established in an estuary it is possible to begin predicting where they will be at certain times and when they rise to gulp in the fraction of fresh water present. This is when to start fishing. I use a single-handed Wychwood ìLong lineî ten-foot 8/9 rod with a No. 10 floating line on a System 2 reel. Occasionally, if the weather and sea are settled and very small flies are being used, I might use my ten-foot Loomis IMX No. 6 rod loaded with a No. 7 floater on an Orvis Battenkill reel. If you need to cast a little further and have large salmon to play you may want to use a larger double-handed rod. The double-hander is also a useful tool on a blustery day. I struggle on with my trusty ten-footers because I like the feel of a fit salmon leaping and bending them double - it's just not the same with a larger rod.

The System 2 is, in my opinion, a great reel. Reasonably priced, corrosion resistant and, importantly, has a reliable smooth drag - essential when fish can run over a hundred yards of line off. Believe me, salmon in the sea fight harder and take line faster than those that have expended a lot of energy ascending a river, testing tackle and angler to the limit.

I rarely use anything other than a full floating line because summer salmon and grilse tend to come up to the fly willingly. The air and sea temperatures in the Hebrides are generally favourable for such co-operative behaviour. Occasionally, the fish will not rise to the surface, and sunk lines have been tried, without success. When they stay deep it is usually because hot sunshine has warmed the sand to a high temperature before the tide has come in. The flowing sea water then absorbs this heat from the sand and the surface water can reach as high as 24 C (warmed water rises to the surface). Water temperature as high as this is very uncomfortable for salmon. A few degrees higher can be fatal, and it is therefore not surprising that they won't come up to take a fly. It seems that if they aren't coming up to the freshwater lens then they aren't going to take below either. This opinion was reinforced when, on one occasion, they wouldn't come up to the fly, or take a sunk fly, and a spinner was tried. Their response was negative - the shoal scattered and were not seen again until the next tide. I wouldn't however be totally discouraged by our lack of success with a sunk line. As many of you will already know, anything is possible in salmon fishing - and no sooner do I or anyone else say it's unlikely than it becomes imminent! Sunk-line tactics may be successful at your 'Bruton'.

Above all, use a rod, reel and line you feel comfortable with. If you need to cast a long way in order to cover fish consider a shooting head line. Don't stick to the orthodox if it leaves you fishless. Be a thinking fisherman not a 'classic' fisherman with an empty creel.

The next item of tackle, and arguably the most important of all, is leader material. I would always advise to err on the side of caution. Here, where the fish average around 6 lbs and the occasional 10 pounder is hooked, 14 or 15 lb test of around twelve feet is ideal. Salmon as fresh and uneducated as those in saltwater do not seem shy of a thick leader provided it is presented well. Strong line enables the odd wind knot to be overlooked, fish to be played out quicker and helps us present a fly better into or across a wind. My main reason for using it is to avoid breakages. What's the point in a meticulous approach and careful thinking fishing if you risk losing the prize - leaving a hook in its mouth? It is better not to hook a fish at all than do that, so please don't be tempted to fish with a light line. Not wanting to exhaust a point I will not dwell on it any longer, other than to share that I once saw a highly regarded angler leave hooks in three salmon within half an hour because he insisted on using too light a leader. He was rightly red faced.

Fly selection is a personal thing. Fly pattern does not seem to affect your chances in the Bruton Stream to the extent that size and fishing speed can. On a typical day, with, say, an eight to ten inch wave, light cloud cover and a nice tide-rip, a size 10 fly fished down and across would be O.K. A slower rip and calmer sea would imply a size 12 or 14 with a slight retrieve. Conversely, a very rough day might warrant a size 8 long wing, or even a small tube-fly. If you would like advice on pattern then I'd have to say keep it simple. Silver stoat, silver blue, squirrel & blue and Fhorsa blue are my trusted patterns. All easy to tie, which is handy, as you'll need to tie a few more than normal due to corrosion - especially if you are as lazy as me and forget to wash them in warm, fresh water after use.

One important bit of advice as regards fly selection is to select only one fly if there are any obstructions, particularly seaweed. A dropper, or even worse, a point-fly trailing around the kelp behind a lively seven-pounder is the stuff nightmares are made of. If, however, the substrate is clear of weed and sandy you may like to fish two, or even three, flies. Droppers are occasionally used at the Bruton - the most exciting to use being a black and silver muddler, well greased. It can be almost unbearable to watch it bobble through the wave waiting for that heart-stopping lunge from a fish. Unfortunately it does not always work as planned and a large proportion of fish that move to it are not hooked. If you are a numbers fisherman stick with trebles.

Fish in the traditional down-and-across style remembering that the fish will be facing the current, (whether ebbing or flowing), from whichever direction and however slow it is (see figures B and C). The slower the flow the squarer to the current you cast. Ensure that you generate a high line-speed so as to present the fly with the leader fully extended. This will increase your chances of success dramatically in salt, or freshwater. It is surprising how often a well presented fly is snapped up within the first three or four pulls. This is especially true if you are fishing efficiently and covering fish for most of the time the fly is in the water. Perhaps the fly landing attracts the attentionof the fish and, if it were not moving in an attractive manner from the word 'Go', the fish would lose interest.

It might sound as though flyfishing for salmon in saltwater could, during periods of low flows, become the norm at many of our river mouths and coastal areas. Do not, however, expect to find 'Bruton Streams' at every river mouth. It is not going to be easy finding coastal points or channels within casting and wading range of the shore, where salmon congregate at certain stages of the tide. (You could of course fish from a boat, but you still have to locate the fish). Unless you are lucky it can be like looking for a needle in a haystack - and one that moves around as well. This is probably why there are so few known 'Brutons'. We are indeed indebted to Clive Bruton for his fortunate discovery at the mouth of the Fhorsa.

It is only right that I issue you with a few words of warning about coastal fishing for salmon and sea-trout. Migratory fishing rights extend to a mile beyond the low-tide mark in Scotland. Written permission is required to fish for salmon or sea-trout within this limit. In England and Wales an Environment Agency migratory fishing licence is required. The Crown owns much of the foreshore, and permission is not usually required to fish in saltwater in England or Wales. However some estuaries and most tidal rivers are in private hands and need written permission. It is therefore wise to check prior to your fishing trip and save any embarrassment. And remember that fishing licence!

A further word of warning: tidal areas are very dangerous. Never wade anywhere you do not know well and never wade as the tide is coming in. Too many fishermen are drowned every year and no fish is worth the risk. A fishing lifejacket is an invaluable piece of tackle for any fisherman but essential for the tidal wader.

You should feel comfortable and confident with the way you are fishing and the tackle you use. Without confidence unfamiliar forms of fishing are rarely given a fair chance and without a fair chance, success is rare. Lack of success leads to lack of confidence. This is a familiar 'catch 22' situation for many salmon fishermen and is the single-most cause for there being so many 'classic' fishless fishermen. Have faith in your experiments. Work hard at it. It's fun! Figure out the fish movement patterns. Learn to recognise where a shoal lies and then concentrate your efforts at those times when fish are holding near the surface. Use various fly patterns and sizes, or experiment with various angles and speeds of retrieve, until you unravel the mystery that is flyfishing for salmon in saltwater.

Last of all, GOOD LUCK.

37

SALTWATER SALMON, AND SEA-TROUT

Sidney Spencer

Questing among anglers for aspects of fishing which are little enough known or written about to excite interest today, I found in the salmon and sea-trout persuasion a very live and unsatisfied curiosity about salt water fishing. Orkney and Shetland voe fishing for sea-trout features fairly well in the literature of the sport and most sea-trout anglers know too that sea-trout can be caught in the vicinity of river-mouths round the coast and specially in the West Highlands. But I feel that the scale on which this type of fishing can usefully be carried on is not understood as it ought to be, and salt water fishing for salmon immeasurably less so. There would be much more salmon fishing in the sea were it not for the widespread belief that salmon will not take in salt water, and for the fact that not all river mouth environments are suitable: the point is not that the fishing must be conducted at a river mouth but that there must be a fish-attracting inflow of fresh water to perpetuate the shoaling habit in fish moving inshore from outer waters.

I could take you to places where you could throw a fly among shoals of salmon at the choicest states of tides without moving a fish so that you would say 'they' were right and salmon do not take in salt water. And I could take you to others - selecting tide and time and wind conditions of course, where your first cast among the fish would produce a fierce pull and a take. You would say, 'Why haven't I heard about this before now?' It is not however quite as simple as, in order to make my point, I have made it out to be. Whether one seeks sea-trout or salmon the subject is one that requires study. All worthwhile fishing methods require study of course, but this one does not involve the mechanics of fishing nor, within small limits, special equipment. It does require meticulous study of the habits of the fish, and of the local conditions, especially the tides. If your are fishing river or loch you take great care and appreciable time to investigate to the point of thorough understanding, the run of the river bed, the effect on current and therefore on holding places, of bends and spurs of rock, gravel bars and so on. On the loch you study the bottom contours, the trend of the hidden currents and much else besides.

In salt water fishing, for salmon especially, local topography will require this same degree of attention, though the identification of holding places has no significance because you are looking for and will be fishing to, travelling fish. It is the finding of taking places where salmon will come to fly or a spun bait that is vital. And the difference between some shore-line point where salmon can be taken from passing shoals and those where the fish ignore anything you care to show them embraces a whole unique range of frustrations. Substitute for the shore point, if you wish, a boat well handled and skilfully held in position on an interception line, but you will, if my own experience is any guide, only succeed from a boat if there is adequate wind and wave. I have found sea-trout markedly less nervous of a boat than salmon which is odd. I regard sea-trout in fresh water as the shyest fish but their shyness is something they acquire progressively as they leave their salt water environment behind them. In the sea they are easier to fish from shore because they will take in a vastly greater variety of conditions than will salmon, they are less defined in their travelling routes, and they are somewhat less critical of tide height. They will also take in a greater range of depths though tending to prefer shallow or medium depth water and they will take in confined spaces among rafts of weed and very close inshore. The sea-trout is at home in the estuary and nearby waters, the salmon is an ocean feeder and whilst he too is, of course, a fish of two environments there is a greater difference between his ocean life and the inshore and river portion of it than there is in the similarly dual life of his smaller cousin. To the difference between their sea lives I attribute the difference in their reaction to any fly or bait presented to them and in this context it is worth remembering that while sea-trout carry their feeding habit into their estuary and river life, the salmon does not. He ceases to feed at some stage unknown to us but certainly before he enters shallow water.

This is the heart of the matter, in my view. If you are going to catch salmon in the sea you have to fish to them in deep water; they will not take where you can take sea-trout easily - in shallow estuaries. I am not contending that 'deep' inshore water compares with the real deeps of the open sea feeding grounds, of course, but simply that arrival in coastal water seems finally to inhibit the feeding urge. I find it very hard to answer the question 'What do you call deep water?' because for one thing, moving fish are travelling with the tide in a constantly changing depth. Let us say that you will not catch salmon in any area which is exposed or very shallow at low tide and that I personally have had little success, at any point where, at half-flood there has been less than say, twenty feet of water. Here is where our study of local shore contours comes in and here is where the fortunate fisherman is he who can fish for incoming salmon where the river they seek enters at the head of a steep-sided and therefore (usually) deep sea loch. Many on the western seaboard of the Scottish and Irish mainlands are like this but the islands generally are less suitable because of the machair or other low ground fringing the Atlantic coast. They have other attributes however - in a few cases some salmon fishing in brackish enclosed waters or coastal lochs to which the tide can penetrate.

Granted that you have access to a deep-water channel traversed by companies of fish making for their river immediately prior to their run dates, the preliminary to an attack on them has to be observation from some vantage point at various states of tide. I would begin by being in position at the first of the flood to see what number of fish came in during the whole of the tide and what route they followed, that is to say, how far off shore, how close-in on points - whether they pause to cruise round the mouth of any small stream and so on. Next to be decided is whether the fish are, in fact, running the river. You probably know this by other means - the local bush telegraph for example. If they are not going up, they will come down the estuary and go seaward again with the ebb tide and that should, therefore, be awaited. The best of the salt water fishing comes, naturally, when salmon are collecting about river mouths but are unable to run for lack of water; they then move in and out with the tides and will do this until the river rises and draws them up and away. Meanwhile their tidal movements will be on the surface and you get repeated chances to show them the fly. If, on the other hand, the adjacent river is big and pushing fresh water far down the loch, there will be decidedly less surface shoaling though possibly more individual plunging. Generally the fish are travelling faster, deeper and unseen.

In short, therefore, we need a period (which at the time of maximum run need only be short to permit and accumulation of salmon) of warm, dry if not fine weather. I have found that weather really matters little so long as the river is low but wind from a warm quarter is necessary. It need not be strong so long as it will raise a brisk ripple. Salmon will come to a fly in a calm but they will not take it. The leaders of a group, company or shoal will turn aside to follow a fly or bait put across their path but without a ripple will turn away just as you think they are about to take. They are interested but not enough. This is the maddening part of sea fishing for salmon - so often they show interest and so seldom take. The answer has already been given - fish over deep water and in a good breeze.

The critical features are simply location and weather conditions; the actual fishing is simple. Rod, reel and line can be whatever you use on the river but do not use your best outfit; I find that however carefully you wash reel and line in fresh running water after fishing in the sea, you simply cannot wholly offset the corrosive effect of the salt water on metal components and the reel is particularly susceptible. So I use my second best outfit and wash very thoroughly as soon after tidal fishing as possible.

Brightness seems to be the basic requirement in either fly or bait. Flies of the general air of the Silver Doctor, Dusty Miller or Dunkeld category have served me very well and in a rough wave I would go up to fours in size. Alternatively a three-hook lure, say two inches long Dunkeld type in dressing will take very well. The cast can be 8/5 or 9/5 or of eight or ten pounds breaking strain. I do not feel that small flies and light casts enter into this fishing at all because in the conditions which demand them - shallow, calm or lightly ruffled water - salmon will not take although sea-trout will. Spinning, on balance, will take more fish than fly fishing and I like a multiplier with ten-pound line and wire or nylon trace with a blue and silver one-and-a-half inch Devon as well as anything. I do not think bait size is critical though you should err on the small side; the water is commonly very clear. A small spoon, gold inside and hammered silver outside will kill. Rod, much as I personally like the seven- or eight-foot single-handed type, is best rather longer. Sea-caught salmon, especially grilse or small fish, are excessively soft in the mouth and with a short rod have to be held much too hard as they are brought into the net.

So often the last plunge into the fringe of wrack along the shore requires the 'holding off' that only the nine- or ten-foot rod can provide. And it is small consolation, having hooked a fish out of a passing shoal after a long wait, to lose it at the net and recover only a fly hook or triangle ornamented with a small strip of mouth tissue or an inch of maxillary.

Before I turn to sea-trout, two last points and first the tide. Half-flood seems to bring most fish but this can vary with local conditions. In most places it pinpoints the maximum willingness to take whereas the ebb, in general, finds the fish in different mood. It is almost as though, having failed in their natural objective of running the river they had lost heart and interest and on their way back to deep water have much less regard for fly or bait. I do not say they have none, and in some places the local fishermen favour the ebb.

My second point concerns sea-pools of which the variety is infinite. If they are deep and wholly salt at full tide they are worth fishing though fly size may have to be adjusted downwards and cast weight proportionately. If, however, as so often happens they are shallow and sandy or pebbly the chances with salmon in my experience are small and you should turn your attention to sea-trout. Salmon, however, have no book of rules or, if they have, they often ignore it and an odd fish can be taken from the unlikeli-est places at times. An undercut rock in a sea-pool will often be occupied by a fish coming in with the tide and such a fish may not go back with the others as the tide falls. Given a wind on the pool, you may catch that fish later irrespective of pool height. But one cannot call this salt water fishing: indeed at low tide the pool will not be even brackish. There are a few places in the Hebrides where lochs close to the sea are invaded by the tide and whilst of most it is said that neither salmon not sea-trout will take when the loch is brackish, there are exceptions. For my part I have found salmon terribly stiff in mixed water conditions but sea-trout very much better to the extent that they will take in river mouths where salt and fresh water mingle in distorted spirals over the sand.

But true sea fishing for salmon must be done out where the sand is hidden by sheer depth; here fishing to the leaders of questing shoals as they go up-tide tightly packed, an individual here and there plunging ahead, just beyond the floating weed, can be very exciting indeed. The fish are unbelievably strong and active and 'hands' are needed; hard holding will provoke violent acrobatics, uncontrollable runs and perhaps pulled-out hooks. Too light a hand will result in fish weeded and lost.

Sea-caught sea-trout in play, and size for size, are similar. Mouths are even softer than those of the salmon and the fish have a much greater ten-dency to dive into weed. The spinning rod is usually too stiffly-actioned and rather than spin for these fish I use the two- or three-hooked lure in the salt water, and flies - preferably on the small side - in sea-pool and tidal lengths of the river. Sea-trout, however, differ from salmon in one important respect and that is the variety of salt water conditions and local-ities on which they can be taken. Brief reference has already been made to the voe fishing of the northern isles. The technique can be used equally well wherever sea-trout feed in sea lochs along the fringe of the weed. Fly rod and tackle are used to cast standard pattern flies - Butcher, Blue and Silver, Alexandra and others in the attractor class and the size can be what you would normally fish in neighbouring freshwater lochs. The worm on Pennell or Stewart tackle, cast like a fly - but more smoothly and careful-ly in the back cast! - and worked rather slowly, can be deadly, though I do not think any superiority over the fly outweighs its disadvantages. The worms do not live long in the salt water and even with toughened baits there is the nuisance of frequent re-baitings.

In the open estuary sea-trout will take flies of the type indicated. Lures made up from strips of teal with silver bodies and blue hackles, those with peacock strips for wings, silver bodies and red hackles, and indeed almost anything with flash and bright colours. The weakness of the lure is its

fragility. Elaborate mixed 'wings' are unnecessary and soon fray to nothing - the simpler a lure is the better. As with salmon some ripple on the
water is a great help. Sea-trout will cruise in small lots or big shoals in
very shallow water which is often crystal clear. In calm conditions these
fish can be shy but they will take under any reasonably concealing ripple.
The shoals are easily seen and if the fishing point has been carefully chosen it can be possible to cast to each of them as, ruffling the surface in a
fairly compact mass, pushing the collective bow-wave ahead of them, they
come abreast. Usually the majority of such passing groups will be within
reach - they seem to hug the edge of the weed on wrack-fringed shores
though much depends on shore declivity. Again, I prefer the locale where
the loch is narrow and shores steep rather than the estuary where water is
thin on sandy channels. Incidentally this sandy channel fishing, common
and very productive in some of the Western Isles, demands the maximum
local knowledge of tides and quicksands. It is emphatically not a game to
be taken lightly.

Conditions for sea-trout fishing in sea-pools vary enormously because of
the variety of the so-called sea-pools themselves. So very often the lowest
pool in the river is invaded by the tide and this, properly the sea-pool, is
shallow. The sea throws up a bank of gravel where the fresh water goes
into the salt and this holds up a stony reach of thin water in which sea-
trout (other than finnock, herling, whitling or what you will) do not stay,
going back again with the tide. I know one such pool which after each
summer tide is literally floored with finnock and never a good sea-trout
among them. Other pools providing depth and cover, even at full ebb, are
different propositions entirely and should be fished at any state of tide.
Some fish will stay and I would fish for them as in a normal river-pool
with normal flies and lighter tackle than I would use for the open water
of the estuary or down along the shores of the sea loch. All sea-pools
within my experience tend to fish best at dusk and after.

There is another kind of salt water fishing for sea-trout which in some
ways is the most interesting and exacting of all. Unfortunately the
number of localities suitable is very limited because proper conditions can
only arise where an enclosed area of seawater forming feeding ground for
the trout is filled and emptied by the tides through a narrow channel.
There are a few such places in the Outer Hebrides and some on the north
Irish coast. It is important at this stage to understand that broadly the
fishing I have been describing thus far has been based on sea-trout within hours or days or weeks of their summer or early autumn running times,
but that we are now considering what is mainly a spring and early summer fishing - in short a fishing for sea-trout while they are living their

normal feeding and growing life in their sea environment. Most of the fish one meets will, it is true, run their rivers in the next two or three months but in the spring they will be mixed in the sense that some will be newly down from their previous river run and are thin, others fat now with three or four months' rich sea feeding behind them or perhaps with a whole year of it. Some slight discrimination in taking spring sea-trout from the sea is therefore needed.

The tidal channels on which one should select a fishing point - preferably with local guidance - can be anything from small river widths upwards depending on the size of the enclosed area and the topography of the surroundings. It can be the tide outlet for a whole sea-loch or an expanse of slob land submerged at full tide, or a freshwater loch which is penetrated by the tide in large volume. A mere backing up of fresh water will not suffice because the river which fills your selected channel at flow and ebb must really be a river with a swirling current - the kind of tide race that looks dangerous and can easily be just that. In the places I have in mind large numbers of sea-trout rove up and down with the tide as it fills the channel and may be found to take on both tides. My experience in Ireland has been, however, that the strongest rush of water comes with the ebb as the basin empties and that it is the outgoing fish that take best. They are fierce fighters in the strong current and a renewed warning about holding too hard is not out of place here because, again, mouths are soft and hooks pull out. Tackle can be heavier than for static-water fishing and the fish are not shy. I would not hesitate to fish a two-inch lure but a spun bait is best of all - a blue and silver Devon of say, one-and-a-half inches for simplicity and a natural sand-eel for choice. Plenty of line is needed because fish and current are strong and the over three pounds class are very liable to make long runs. I use an eight-foot single-handed spinning rod, a multiplying reel with 150 yards of line and seven- or eight-pound nylon or wire. In this fishing, you do not see the fish as in estuary fishing, you fish the stream as you would a river, the only difference being that here the fish are passing and you rely on putting the bait across their paths; in the river they are, for the most part, in their lies and stationary.

These spring sea-trout from the rivers of the sea fight to the last and any carelessness will lose many at the net. The final dive for the weed as the net is extended is especially dangerous. Again, though it is true of playing all fish everywhere or at any time, 'hands' are an enormous asset.

From *Newly from the Sea*. 1969.

PART VIII

FLYFISHING
AROUND EUROPE

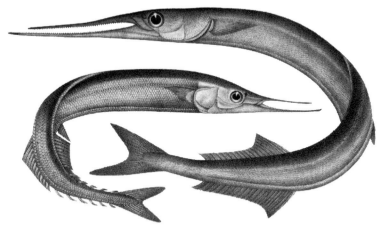

38

NORWAY

Claus Bech-Petersen

The last Scandinavian frontier

The beautiful Norwegian fjords are popular spots for sea-anglers from Scandinavia, but these rich waters are still unknown to most flyfishermen. This is despite the fact that they teem with fish and trophy-sized fish of most species are caught from the rocks every year.

I had often fished the fjords while touring Norway, or while waiting for the salmon to run into the swift rivers. I had caught good fish this way too, but my approach always seemed too casual. This was because I always hope for the best and seldom load saltwater tackle when my mind is set for salmon or sea-trout.

But the idea of a serious fly-tackle attack on the fjords had been lurking in the back of my head for a while when I left Copenhagen in July 1996. The car was filled with depth sounders, high-density shooting-heads, and huge, shiny flies. The goal was to catch some fish and, more importantly, do the necessary research for future trips.

I got more fish that I expected, and even though they did not make me an expert on saltwater flyfishing in Norway (I doubt if anyone is), I learned a great deal, especially from long discussions with local fishermen and the owner of the hotel where I stayed. In spring and autumn big cod, pollack and coalfish move into the fjords. They swim three to ten metres deep. If you are prepared to use a depth-sounder and spend a couple of hours, it is not difficult to locate them.

Our host at the hotel in Risør was an avid fisherman and he had marked the charts with the best locations when we left shore the first day. Even though Sørfjorden at Risør is shallow by Norwegian standards, the water was 25 metres deep only 100 metres from the shore. This is much too deep for effective flyfishing, but a shallow reef covered with mussels looked promising. After a couple of minutes the first fish took the fly five or six metres below the surface. It was a small pollack, maybe four or five pounds. It was quickly followed by another fish before the school disappeared. But despite the instant success, it seemed that the fish had left the fjord, maybe driven away be the fierce summer heat. Unfortunately, a strong wind was blowing from the sea all week. Most days our little dinghy was too small to challenge the waves.

The outermost part of Sørfjorden is shielded by a small group of islands. It was in the quiet waters behind these islands that we found our fish. Most days we simply drifted with the wind, casting large bucktails wherever we found shallow reefs that were less than six metres deep. And there were plenty of fish. Almost all the reefs contained good numbers of garfish, the odd pollack and coalfish as well as cod between three and eight pounds. Not big fish by local standards, but well worth the effort.

Six-metre-deep water is not too difficult to fish with modern fly tackle, but the real challenge came one day when the depth sounder indicated good numbers of fish in a small rock crevice ten metres below the surface. A few casts with a spinning rod told us they were cod, and during the next hours we landed countless fish on our flyrods. In advance I had been rather sceptical of fishing this deep, but I just exaggerated my usual sinking-line techniques from the Danish sounds. That worked just fine, at least as long as the boat did not drift too fast. The trick was to let the shooting-head sink for at least 60 seconds before retrieving the fly; a six inch variation of Bob Clouser's modern classic Deep Minnow. When the fly reached the bottom and was pulled a few times, it was grabbed by a five to seven pound cod. They all fought like mad and tested the limits of my nine-weight tackle. These fish were not giants, but I was still happy that I did not hook a twenty pound cod on that rod. I am not quite sure that the expensive, but fragile graphite fibres could have lifted such a fish from the bottom.

The fishing we did from the shore was quite typical for southern Norway in July. A lot of small to medium sized fish and often some cod in shallow water when the sun sets late at night. Further north, in the sub-Arctic parts of Norway, the water does not get nearly as warm. There, you can find big cod and coalfish in shallow water in the middle of the short summer. But in Risør the season peaks around Easter, where cod up to fifty pounds are caught from the shore, and schools of coalfish and pollack between two and twelve pounds can be found in water shallow enough to be covered with a flyrod. And especially the coalfish, the poor man's salmon, puts up a terrible fight for freedom when it feels the hook penetrate its lips.

Dances with mackerels

The first schools of mackerel that arrive in southern Norway tend to swim deep and out of reach of the flyfisherman, but after a few weeks they spread into the fjords where they chase herring fry in the surface. There are tens of thousands of mackerel in each school. From the end of July until the middle of September, when the fish return for deeper waters off-shore, you can watch them hunt the terrified herring-fry that break the surface in panic. Seagulls join the party from above. Under these conditions, called seagull fun in Denmark, the mackerel is a perfect match with trout-sized tackle and size 2-6 streamers. Most of the fish are between one and two pounds, but they grow fast on the herring diet and just before they leave in September there are a significant number of bigger fish. Our host Poul got a five-pounder in 1995.

We arrived too early and only got to taste the hors d'oeuvre. A few mackerel took our flies when we covered a school by accident. One of them accepted my deeply-fished bucktail and took off with a big part of my backing. (I never saw it again). After ten minutes of tough battle the leader broke and left me with dreams of really big fish, maybe four pounds, and a commitment to return next summer to fish for these fish that probably are the strongest and fastest in Scandinavia.

I stayed at Risør Gjestehus (phone +47 37 15 50 02), a small family-owned hotel with boat-rental and a primitive camping ground right next to the fjord. The owner Poul is an avid fisherman and knows all the hot spots.

Note:
No licence is required for saltwater fishing in Norway, whether for sea fish or salmonids. Migratory salmonids taken must exceed 35 cm in length. In North Norway the size limit for sea-trout and arctic char is 30 cm. There is no close season for fishing in the sea. It is not permitted to fish within 100 metres of the mouth of any river. If in doubt about this enquire locally.

39

SWEDEN

Olof Johansson

The long Swedish coastline offers plenty of opportunity for the saltwater flyfisherman. On the west-coast the water is nearly as salt as in the North Sea and the fauna is truly marine in nature. The south and east coasts, bordering the Baltic Sea, offer a mixture of marine and freshwater species. The further north you go in the Baltic the less saline the water becomes. Very few marine species of fish can live in the far north in the Gulf of Bothnia.

Fishing is easily accessible. There is no fishing license to pay and no permit is needed if you want to fish with sportfishing tackle along the coast. On the other hand, a visitor will find that he is more or less left to help himself. There are few guides and service for the fishing tourist is often hard to find, except at a few places. Local tourist officers are often ignorant about fishing possibilities in their area. Fishing tackle stores are usually better at providing useful information.

The northern part of the west coast facing Skagerak is rocky with fjords, islands and rocky skerries. It is always possible to find sheltered waters and to fish even when the weather is far from ideal. South of Kungsbacka the coast of Kattegatt is open and shallow.

Tide is no problem on the west coast. Even during spring tides there is only about 30 cm difference between high and low water. In the Baltic there is no tide at all. Greater changes in water level are caused by changes in wind and barometric pressure.

The south coast, around the province of Skåne, is also shallow and open. The same goes for the big islands, Öland and Gotland (where you can find very good fishing for sea-trout). You need good weather there for flyfishing.

The long coast from Blekinge up to the Finnish border offers all kinds of different fishing environments, from sheltered bays with rich vegetation to barren, rocky islands.

Sea-Trout

Flyfishing for sea-trout began about 40 years ago. For a long time it was pursued by only a small group of specialists. Most anglers preferred to fish with the spinning rod. Over the years more and more anglers realised that flyfishing was not only much more fun, but was also frequently more productive than spinning. Today flyfishing is well established on all parts of the Swedish coast.

The sea-trout on the west coast are comparatively small. A fish over two kilos is a good specimen. A fish over five is exceptional. There is size limit of 40 cm and a closed season from September 15th to the first of March. Best fishing is from beginning of April until Midsummer. Fishing can also be good during cool spells in July and August, but at this time it is necessary to fish at night.

The sea-trout of the east coast is quite different from the west coast fish. They grow faster and stay in the sea longer before running the rivers to spawn. A trout of four kilos is just average. Sea-trout over ten kilos are caught every year and the record stands at 15.6 kilos. The south and east coast offer the best chances from October till the middle of may. Mild winters with little ice can give good fishing. When the sea warms up at the end of May the fish tend to leave the coast and follow the herring schools out into the Baltic.

Sea-trout fishing in the archipelago of Stockholm has improved greatly thanks to stockings with smolts and to rehabilitation work done in the spawning streams. The most serious problem - and it goes for the whole coastline - is fishing with gill nets. The Swedish Anglers' Association has worked for a long time to have stricter laws for netfishing passed. Some progress has been made, but still too much of the results of the conservation work for sea-trout is being harvested by the netters.

There are lots of named fly patterns that have proved their worth with sea-trout. Most specialist however seem to trust their own patterns. You need some baitfish imitations. Sand-eel and herring are very important for the Baltic sea-trout. The west coast trout also eat small fish, but a large part of their menu is made up of small shrimps, ragworm and other invertebrates. For a short period in April, when the ragworms spawn along the west coast, the trout can be very selective. Very long, slim imitations of ragworm can then be deadly.

You often see trout rising. A few anglers claim that they have had success with dry flies fished at night.

A floating, intermediate or sink-tip line is most useful. Many flyfishermen use 5 or 6 weight rods, but this light tackle is really quite inadequate. You need an outfit that can punch out a long line in adverse wind conditions. Sometimes you must also be able to throw a big fly. I would not bother with anything lighter than a 8-weight rod and a 9-weight is probably even better.

A good place for sea-trout is fairly shallow, but is not far from deeper water. During the night the fish often move into water that is only just deep enough to cover their backs. The bottom should provide some cover - big stones and patches of sea weed. During the winter the fish tend to congregate in estuaries. When the water warms up in the spring they move out to more exposed waters where they like to hang around rocky points and streamy sounds.

Cod

My first experience with saltwater flyfishing was with cod in the early 1960s. Both during spring and autumn lots of cod move into very shallow water close to shore. A cod caught on a heavy rod in deep water is not a very impressive fighter. But these shallow-water fish could really turn on both power and speed.

Too bad that commercial fishing has almost wiped out this coastal type of cod. Nowadays is far easier to catch a sea-trout from the coast than to hook a decent sized cod.

Pollock

The pollack has also been hammered hard by the commercial fishing fleets. We used to have fantastic sport with surface-active pollack over rocky reefs off the west coast. Unfortunately these opportunities are very rare now. My friends and I fished with floating lines and big Muddlers. Often we would cast to fish that we saw breaking the surface. The strikes were hard and made the water boil, and the fish fought with lot of power and temperament.

You can still have this wonderful experience along the Norwegian coast, where many tidal streams hold big schools of both pollack and coalfish. More than one flyfisherman has fled empty salmon rivers, to sample this great fishing resource, and few have regretted it.

Garfish

This is a favourite among many flyfishermen. Schools of garfish move in to shallow water, close to shore, in order to spawn. The first show up in early May and best flyfishing is from the middle of May to middle of June.

They seldom weigh more than one kilo, but they fight very well with a lot of aerial display. Streamer and small tube flies, often in light colours and with some blue and silver crystal-fibres work well

Mullett

The mullet is a fairly new addition to the Scandinavian fauna. Thirty years ago only a rare one was caught in gillnets each summer. The first caught on rod and line was recorded in 1977. Since then thick-lipped grey mullet have become well established along the Swedish west coast and great schools can be seen in harbours and on shallow flats during summer months. The dominant theory is that warm water discharge from nuclear power-stations and petrochemical plants have provided warm water refuges, where the mullet can survive the coldest months of the year.

Flyfishing for mullet must be one of the most difficult challenges. I have tried many times but have never been able to trick one into taking my fly. However, a few specialists have managed to take mullet with some regularity on small, drab flies. Most mullet caught on fly are however hooked by anglers fishing for sea-trout. That was the case with the Swedish fly-record, a fish weighing 5.196 kilos.

Flounder

I don't think anyone fishes intentionally for flounder with fly, but they are often a by-product of sea-trout fishing at night. Strangely enough this flatfish is often seen rising and splashing on the surface in hot pursuit of small fish and shrimps.

The flounder is not the only flatfish that will take a fly. There is a Swedish fly-caught record for turbot, a 2.54 kilo fish caught in the entrance to Gothenburg harbour.

Whitefish

This is another fish that can give variety to night-time sea-trout fishing at some places along the west coast. They seldom weigh more than one kilo. Whitefish along the east coast are both bigger and more common, but are not yet exploited by flyfisherman.

Pike

The waters of Skagerak and Kattegat along the Swedish west coast are too salty for pike, but the east coast is famous for its pike fishing. The large archipelago off Stockholm must rate among the best pikewaters in Europe. There are plenty of pike and they grow big and fat on the rich diet of herring.

More and more flyfishermen have discovered what a fine challenge the pike is. Chances are good of hooking big fish, especially during April when they move into shallow bays for spawning. The Swedish record for pike on fly is 13.95 kg, a fish caught on the Baltic coast near Stockholm.

Most anglers fish from boats, but many prefer to use a float-tube or chest waders. A powerful rod is a great help, both to cast the large flies and to control heavy fish. A normal sink-rate line is most useful. Leaders should test around 6 - 10 kilo and, of course, a tip section of pliable steel wire is necessary.

The first flies for pike were crude creations. In many cases just a bunch of flashabou on a 2/0 hook. As flyfishing for pike developed, flytiers came up with much more elaborate and artistic flies. A basic design that can be used with great variation is Lefty Kreh's Deceiver.

Ide

This fish looks a lot like a chub and grow to about the same size. It is common along the east coast and provides the opportunity of interesting flyfishing. They shoal in the shallow bays where they take both dry flies and sinking imitations of small crustaceans.

Grayling

The coastal waters in the Gulf of Bothnia can provide wonderful flyfishing for grayling. The northern part of the coast, between Umeå and the border with Finland, is especially, holding lots of grayling with a good average weight. Flyfishing for grayling is a well established sport there. Don't miss it if you travel to this part of Sweden. Try it on a quiet summer night, when the sun just dips below the horizon for a few minutes, the sea is flat and shimmering and only the small dimples of rising grayling disturb the surface.

40

DENMARK

Rudy van Duijnhoven

Denmark and more especially the island of Funen, has in recent years become the Mecca for sea-trout anglers from all parts of Europe. Rivers on the island have been restored and fish-ladders built around obstructions so that once again the sea-running brown trout can reach their spawning grounds. Millions of sea-trout have been stocked into the coastal waters around the island, where the fish find enough food to grow to into double figure weights within a few years. Flyfishing for sea-trout along the sea-coast has been practised in Denmark by local flyfishermen for at least thirty years. But it is during the last ten years has there been an enormous revival in interest in this species.

Fly-rods used for sea-trout are usually in the nine to ten foot range, for line-weights seven through nine. The floating line is used most of the time, preferably a weight-forward, bass-bug- or saltwater-taper fly-line. The reason for this is the wind that is nearly always present along the sea-coast and because one often has to make long casts to get any takes at all. For this reason some specialist anglers use a system of shooting heads as well.

The leader can be short, around three metres, with a 12 - 15 lbs. tippet being just about right. Some anglers prefer to knot a small, floating dropper to the leader in order to draw some extra attention.

Shrimp-patterns as well as small baitfish-imitations are preferred by most anglers. There is an excellent flyshop in Odense by the name of 'Go Fishing', the staff of which are more than willing to help visitors with advice on hotspots and fly selection.

A few years ago a pattern was developed by Belgium angler Patrick Daniels that imitates the ragworm, Nereis, a sea animal that is especially active in the early part of spring. This pattern, called the 'Fons Terror', incorporates a long, narrow strip of mink fur to imitate the swimming movement of the ragworms. It seems to be especially successful in that time of the season.

In search of the Silver Arrows

Fonsvang Hotel on Funen is an excellent starting point from where to begin expeditions for sea-trout. Special courses are given here in flyfishing for sea-trout, and all the other facilities that one might expect at a fishing hotel, and more, are present.

In recent years it has become possible for the visiting flyfisher on Funen to be accompanied by a guide. Some thirty people, selected by angling bodies and representatives of the tourist industry on Funen, can help with advice and actually go fishing with guests. "Where do I have to fish, during what time of the day, with what and how". Questions for which the guide will have an answer. And with those answers a lot of precious time can be saved, time that would otherwise be wasted searching for good places to fish and testing different fishing methods. One guide can accompany up to five fishermen, so the costs can be shared. A fishing guide will cost 500 Danish Krones for the first two hours, 150 krones for every following hour. A guide can be booked at a hotel or at any other place which displays the blue leaflet, *Sea trout- Eldorado on Funen, Langeland and Aero*. Another leaflet, *100 Fine Funen Fishing Hotspots*, has proven it's worth over and over again. Not every hotspot around the island is of course mentioned; the local people had to be left some room too! But those fishing grounds that are easily accessible and offer enough parking space for a number of cars, are clearly described. One can use the maps to choose a fishing spot where the wind comes from the side (which is preferable), or into one's face. But more than average waves coming towards the shore can discolour the water in such a way that the chances of success are reduced. Whereas the sea-trout are mostly fished for during the day in winter-time, the nights are usually more productive in the warmer periods of the year.

Long Island

This is the name that the Danish people themselves give to Langeland, the oblong island to the south-east of Funen. Due to the direct connection by boat with the city of Kiel, the island is very busy with German tourists during the summer season. Beyond that season it is still remarkably quiet, the numerous fishing places are usually abandoned.

Just as on Funen, the garfish will come close to the shore once the water has warmed up sufficiently. While wading it often happens that a school of garfish, hunting for small bait-fish, passes between the fisherman and the shore. The flyfisher has a good chance of catching this fast hunter. The Danish fishermen often advise the use of imitations of small baitfish for the garfish, whereby the bend of the hook has to be as far as possible towards the end of the fly. But even this results in rather a lot of lost and missed fish. Shrimp-imitations on hook sizes eight and ten often produce more properly hooked garfish. Fish these flies with a floating line, a leader of ten or twelve feet with a tippet of 10 or 12 lbs nylon. After casting we fish this imitation back with short, five centimetres long strips and a pause every now and then. When the water surface is flat-calm one can see the schools of garfish approaching. A swirl here, a jumping baitfish there; when a fly can be put close to them a take is almost sure to follow. Do not be wrong about the size of these fish, gars of 80 and 90 centimetres are among them. Fish that can be quite spectacular on light tackle.

Our base for the fishing trips on Langeland and also for the east part of Funen was the Rudkobing Skudehavn Hotel, situated close to the bridge that connects Langeland with Funen. The hotel consists of a main building with a restaurant, bar, sauna, solarium, swimming pool, etc.

Addresses:

Fonsvang Hotel, Ronaesbrovej 5, Fons, 5580 Nr. Aby, Denmark. Tel. +45 64 42 18 14, fax. +45 64 42 32 74.

Anglingshop 'Go Fishing', Brogade 6 - 8, 5000 Odense, Denmark. Tel. +45 66 12 15 00, fax. +45 66 14 00 26.

Rudkobing Skudehavn Hotel, Havnegade 21, 5900 Rudkobing, Denmark. Tel. +45 62 51 46 00, fax. +45 62 51 49 40.

Fyntour (Tourist Office for Funen), Svendborgvej 83-85, 5260, Odense S, Denmark. Tel. +45 66 13 13 37, fax +45 66 13 13 38.

41

GERMANY

Wolfgang Küter

Regulations for saltwater fishing

Saltwater fishing in Germany is not free. Anyone fishing in the German sea will need the general German fishing-licence (Jahresfischereischein). This can be obtained at local administration offices, the costs will differ from county to county but will usually be about 15 DM per year. As this is rather cheap nobody should fish in the sea without the licence.

For Germans, obtaining the licence is somewhat difficult, as they have to pass a written examination before they are allowed to buy it. For visitors from abroad the exam is not necessary. A licence for up four weeks can be bought from any local administration. When fishing in private waters a permit is required from the owner, but for sea-fishing the general German licence is enough.

General situation of flyfishing in Germany

Flyfishing is not very common among German anglers. Most angling here is for coarse fish; waters holding trout or grayling are rare through much of the country.

Salmon and sea-trout died out in most German waters decades ago. Only in a few rivers in northern Germany did small sea-trout populations survive.

Today there are restocking programs, mostly with sea-trout, in a number of north German rivers. The authorities are also trying to reintroduce salmon to some rivers; the Rhine system with some of its tributaries like the Broel and Sieg being the best known example.

Saltwater flyfishing in Germany

With this background it becomes obvious that saltwater flyfishing is not widespread. However it is on the increase. The main reason for this is that the sea-trout restocking programs by Danish and German anglers and other organisations have led to a good population of sea-trout along the German and Danish coasts of the Baltic sea. Many keen sea-trout anglers, having started out as spinfishers, have started to use the flyrod occasionally.

The first few pioneers started to fish with fly for sea-trout in saltwater in the mid 1970s, but as sea-trout were scarce at that time hardly anyone followed their tracks. More flyfishers appeared along the German coasts about 3-4 years ago, when sea-trout fishing became more popular as sea-trout populations increased.

All this happens mostly along the Baltic coast; the North Sea is hardly fished with the fly.

Species

The sea-trout is the main target for all saltwater flyfishers here. The population of cod has considerably increased in the Baltic sea since the beginning of the 1990s and so today cod are frequently caught with fly in saltwater when fishing for sea-trout. Garfish are caught from May onwards when the water warms up a little. Hardly anybody concentrates on cod or garfish with fly; everybody wants to catch sea-trout.

Tackle and flies

Very much the same as are used in Denmark. In fact most successful Danish tactics are copied successfully here.

42

HOLLAND & BELGIUM

Rudy van Duijnhoven

A bridge over bass water

The opportunities to fish with the flyrod along the Dutch coast are rather limited, mostly due to it's shallow nature and the fact that the water often just is not clear enough to allow flyfishing for different species. Shad can be caught in the summertime at places where freshwater is released into the sea like the Haringvliet Dam. Garfish are an exciting quarry but often out of reach from the shore. Luckily the number of sea-running brown-trout in our coastal waters has seen a steady increase over the last few years. But last August (1996) when I went onto the water of the Oosterschelde in a small boat with two friends, we came across a type of fishing that holds some exciting promises for the future. The bridge that connects Schouwen Duivenland with Noord Beveland in the south-western part of Holland is some five kilometres in length. There are high and massive piers at intervals of 100 metres and these piers are placed well below the surface on four pillars. The water around such a pier can be any-where between 7 and 25 metres deep and sea-bass are known to live here between May and the end of October, depending on the temperature of the water. Because high prices are paid for these fish, they take a heavy beating from both commercial fishermen and poachers (so-called 'sport-fishermen' that sell their catch as well). But there are still enough fish left to make it worthwhile for the flyfishermen to test his or her skills against these fish.

The bass feed primarily on small baitfish and sandeels in August and we knew that we would need weighted flies to get deep enough down in the heavy tidal flow, so we had tied up a number of patterns that we thought would fit our needs. Our rods were rigged with Teeny Nymph-lines T-300 and T-400, the standard choice for a lot of our sea-fishing in deeper waters around Europe.

It is not permitted to anchor anywhere near the bridge, so we would need electric outboard-engines to hold the boat more or less in one place. Sea-bass are so spooky that even the passing of a boat with a normal out-board-engine puts them off the feed, so we used this engine only to get within some 80 yards of the pillar we wanted to fish. René Flohil, who had fished this water a lot with Sassy Shads and other artificial lures (but not yet with the flyrod), believes that they are even scared by the use of a depth-/fish-finder. Which is why we only used this after we had fished a pier, just to see whether or not there was anything down there.

Two more things are necessary for this fishing, very little wind and to be on the water just when the outgoing tide starts to run. The entire period of the outgoing tide is usually good, during the incoming tide we hardly hooked any bass at all here. As can be expected the water has to be clear enough as well for the bass to be able to see our offerings. This was unfortunately not the case during our second outing, when boats busy netting mussels had muddied the water rather a lot. On this day we only found the water close to shore to be clear enough for flyfishing.

After René had put us in the right position, we cast our flies towards the pier and fed extra line so the line could sink as deep as possible. We lost some flies on the pillars when the heavy flow pushed our flies against it, but as most of the bass stayed among those pillars we felt that we had to risk it. (Towards the end of the outgoing tide they will hunt further away from the pillars too).

And when, during our single or double-handed retrieve of the fly, that pull came from deep down our hearts jumped with delight. Only deeply-bent rods would prevent the fish from going back behind the pillars so we gave as much pressure as we dared. René then moved the boat out of the trouble-zone, where we could continue the rest of the fight and the landing of the fish without too much trouble. And when that silvery fish finally lay in the net, we felt we had got ourselves a trophy. One that any flyfisher would like to earn. We only 'kept' the bass on slide-film and we returned them, unharmed, as soon as we possibly could.

Getting back into position was only matter of time and our search for this excellent sport-fish continued. We landed bass up to 62 cm, which might have been six pounds in weight, but we hooked and lost much heavier fish than these, fish that managed to throw our barbless flies within a matter of seconds. But we now know where they are and how to fish for them, so it is just a matter of time before we 'bump' into each other again.

43

ENGLAND AND WALES

Paul Morgan

Flyfishing in saltwater in Britain differs in many important respects from that in other parts of northern Europe. Our lengthy and varied coastline is subject to a greater range of tides than almost anywhere else in the world, and the salinity of British sea-water is much greater than in parts of Scandinavia.

Our quarry species, too, despite considerable overlap, are generally different to those in the north. In the brackish waters of the Baltic Sea, and to a lesser extent in the northern North Sea, the sea-trout is king. There, the sea-trout feed and grow, and can be fished for in much the same way as one would fish for lake trout. On the western coasts of Scandinavia, like the north and west of Scotland and Ireland, pollack and coalfish dominate the flyfisher's catch.

The principal sportfish of the coasts of England and Wales is the loup de mer, the sea bass. Historically we have been at the extreme north of the geographical range of the bass. The south coast, the south-west and Wales are the traditional bass grounds. However, in the hot summers and mild winters of recent years their range has extended so that they can now be caught all around the coasts of Great Britain. The shores of Yorkshire and Northumberland, formerly known only for cod, pollack and coalfish, are now the haunt of bass and mullet.

The traditional shore-fishing methods of fishing for bass were surfcasting, and in rocky areas spinning and floatfishing prawn or livebait. Flyfishing has always been a minor, but locally important, method. In my local river-mouths there has been an unbroken tradition of flyfishing for bass for over a hundred years.

The method has been given a boost in the last few years. Sporting methods of sea-angling were pioneered by Mike Ladle and his colleagues in the 1970s. In particular this encouraged us to fish for bass with plugs and lures. In my own case, I found that I could fish the very shallow, rocky, weed-filled shores which were impossible to tackle by any other method. My floating plugs caught bass where no other angler dared to fish. A natural progression led to the use of the fly - a method even more suited to this kind of snaggy terrain. The huge growth in American saltwater flyfishing has publicised the methods, tackle and flies, and today flyfishing is the preferred method of a large proportion of Welsh coast anglers.

Local lore has it that the bass follow the prawns inshore in April. They become plentiful in May and remain until the end of the year. Within twenty miles of my home there are large and small estuaries, cliffs with rocky gullies, surf beaches, and shallow weedy shores. Bass are found, and can be caught on the fly, in all of these habitats at some stage of the tide. The main limitation on flyfishing is the weather. Prolonged westerly winds make wading impossible and colour the water. In these conditions you could try the estuaries but you would be better heading inland for trout or sea-trout.

I have discussed bass fishing in Wales as an example of British bassing. Other notable areas include the Thames Estuary, all of the south coast of England from Kent to Cornwall, South Wales, North Wales especially around Anglesey, and Morecambe Bay.

Most of the bass caught on fly are under the legal size limit of 36 cm. They can vary in size from a just few inches in length to fish of over ten pounds in weight, but bulk of the catch will be schoolies of between one and two pounds. Bass conservation is discussed in detail elsewhere in this book. Right now the situation looks promising. Good breeding years and protection of nursery areas in estuaries, together with the softening of the climate, promise a healthy population of large bass in the future. But, bass are very vulnerable to over-fishing, by either commercial or angling methods. Please be aware of this.

Mullet are at least as widespread as bass, and like bass they are becoming commoner in the north than they once were. They, too, are present from spring to late autumn. Very visible, they are frequently mistaken for sea-trout or bass. Many hours are wasted by anglers who think that they are fishing for sea-trout! As can be seen from the articles on mullet fishing, innovative anglers find the mysterious mullet a constant challenge. As flyfishers open their minds to new ideas, I believe that the use of scented or flavoured flies, chum or groundbaits, and combinations of flies and baits will bring more frequent success to mullet fishers.

Sea-trout, while present all around the coast of Britain, are more difficult to catch on the fly in the south. The methods which are successful in the Scottish islands and further north are seldom successful here. Sea-trout are almost always present around the mouths of the Welsh rivers that I fish. While I have occasionally caught one spinning, I have not caught a Welsh sea-trout on fly in the sea. It is difficult to come up with a convincing reason for this, but it seems certain that our sea-trout are already set on their spawning migration and have virtually stopped feeding. It is certain that, unlike Scottish and Irish sea-trout, English and Welsh behave more like salmon. Once in freshwater they very rarely feed and this fasting apparently begins even before the fish enter the river.

Where sea-trout are caught in saltwater in Britain, it is usually by fishing estuaries at low water, using river tactics.

Salmon are even less frequently caught in the salt than sea-trout. If either of these species are deliberately targeted, or if one is caught and retained, an Environment Agency game-fishing licence is needed. No licence is needed to angle for other sea fish.

Most of the other species mentioned in this book will also be caught in British waters. Mackerel are the most frequently caught. Unfortunately their season is short. Some years we catch none at all from the shore. Their presence is more consistent the further south and west you go.

Garfish are found around most of the coast from April onwards. They often show themselves at the surface. In my experience they are difficult to tempt and difficult to hook. I must keep trying!

Horse mackerel or scad are widely distributed and keen to take a fly. Together with bass, mackerel and garfish they have contributed to some of my most interesting mixed bags.

Some of my fellow writers have succeeded with flyfishing for flatfish. I, unfortunately, have failed completely. I have spent time fishing for the common and predatory flounder, dragging the bottom with weighted crab and shrimp imitations. All for nought! Well, not quite. Every time I have tried flyfishing for flounders I have caught lesser weevers. These small fish are quite voracious, engulfing a fly almost as big as themselves. The poisonous spine on their dorsal fin can inflict a seriously painful wound and could even put you in hospital. I think it likely that flounders, like the turbot and halibut of the north, despite being predatory, make use of their olfactory as well as visual senses. As we experiment more with scent and taste with flies, we may have more success.

The main target for boat anglers in Cardigan Bay is the tope. Although they are not usually known to take artificial lures, I have heard of one taken on fly. It may be that they could be targeted in the same way as blue sharks are in Ireland. These methods are in their infancy and much remains to be learned.

In Scandinavia it is not uncommon for cod, and even flounders and other bottom-dwellers, to rise to the surface at dusk and take the angler's flies. Unfortunately, I am not aware of anywhere in Britain where this occurs.

In summary, what we have in Britain is a mainly summer-time, saltwater fly-fishery, aimed principally at the most sporting of gamefish - the sea bass. Mackerel, garfish, scad, pollack and coalfish are proven fly-takers and locally important. Mullet, the flatfishes, wrasse and other species are mainly being targeted by a few specialists.

There are an increasing number of us who flyfish the salt in preference to freshwaters. And there is tremendous scope for the casual or holidaying angler to flyfish in the sea. Armed with reservoir gear, a weight-forward line and a few white lures; blessed with fine weather and a few hours freedom, any flyfisherman can try it with a good chance of success.

44

IRELAND

Rudy van Duijnhoven

Hardrock lovers on 'The Green Island'

Waves breaking on rocks that arise from the sea and rolling over others, water flying high into the air against a background of impressive cliffs. In the deep blue water in front of and in between the rocks large pollack hide among the kelp, waiting to attack anything not too big that comes within their reach. The west coast of Ireland offers both spectacular scenery and exciting fishing for those flyfishers willing to experiment here.

"To go where no one else has gone before". A well-known line from the adventures of the Starship Enterprise, but also a line that held a lot of truth when we; Harry, René, and myself, explored the rocky shores near Kilkee with our flytackle in the summer of 1996. A local fisherman told us at least that he had never before seen any flyfishermen here.

The differences in colour of the water made it easy to see where the deepest water could be found. This is where we cast our fast-sinking shooting-head lines (the Teeny Nymphline T-300 is what we used most of the time) and let them sink there for half a minute or so. The leaders that we used on these lines were short, only five feet in length, with a tippet of 10 or 12 lbs.

Our 9 and 10 foot 8-9 weight rods were the right tools for casting those lines, but even with these, not every fish we hooked could be stopped from diving back into the kelp and among the rocks. The pollack fought hard and deep and landing them on the rocks where we were standing was not easy. The streamers that we used were mostly Deceiver- and tarponfly type flies, the last ones with longer feathers for the tail and weighted with brass eyes. White, silver, blue and green seemed to be the most productive colours.

When the flyline had reached the desired depth we used both single and double-handed retrieves to lure the pollack to our flies. When fishing among rocks and in seawater that is constantly moving one can expect to lose some flies on the kelp and rocks, but only deeply fished flies produced takes. Pollack that did not take the streamers right away, often followed them up to the surface, where they would then make a last dash at them.

One can use the waves for landing the pollack. We pulled them in close to the rock where we were standing and then waited for a wave to lift the fish onto the rock. This is the safest way to land fish among rocks; climbing or reaching down for them is too dangerous.

The low tide period was the most productive for us, but it did mean that we constantly had to watch behind us to ensure that our route back was not cut off by the rising water. We did not want to risk anything so we left some of the protruding rocks in plenty of time. We also chose to fish from rocks that projected almost at right angles from the sea. Waves can really slide onto a rock that protrudes at a narrow angle and push anyone standing there off his or her feet.

From the raw nature of the cliffs to the skyline of a power-station is a big step, but here where it releases it's cooling-water into the mouth of the river Shannon, we found other fish that were eager to take our flies. Schools of sea-bass hunted the white water in search of small baitfish and with a long cast and a fast retrieve they could be taken on the fly.

We could only fish this spot from a boat and the catamaran "The Liscannor Star", although not built to be a flyfishing boat, was a good platform for our fishing.

Sea-bass are very spooky fish so the boat was anchored where we could only just reach the outlet with a long cast. Again we used fast-sinking shooting-heads, but on somewhat lighter, six to seven weight outfits. Flies in smaller sizes like those we used for pollack took fish here too, although I fished mostly with Acrylic Minnow-type flies that I had tied with Superhair and treated with Softex. Changing flies seemed to be necessary when the takes diminished. Putting the rod under the arm and retrieving the flyline with two hands produced the most takes. A hooked fish that was brought to the boat was often followed by schoolmates of about the same size. The fish we caught were not all that big, up to five pounds perhaps, but the silvery sea-bass to us are one of the most beautiful fish to catch in the European seas. Handling them takes some care because they have some sharp spines on their fins and on their gillplates.

Our deeply bent rods did not go unnoticed by other boats in the area; the fishermen on them fished for conger with heavy tackle. On the radio on board we could hear them talking about "Dutch guys", "fly-rods" and "bass". We could be sure that this spot would be visited by one of those boats the next day.

We kept a few fish for the evening-table, but released all others. Unfortunately the bass is one of the finest fish to eat and also one of the most expensive. In many European countries it is under heavy pressure by professional fishermen and poachers.

The catamaran is owned by Michael and Anne McLaughlin who also run a fine guesthouse, the "San Esteban" in Doonbeg. The guesthouse is built at a spot with a splendid view over one of the bays and the rooms and food leave little to be desired. Michael and Anne McLaughlin can be contacted by writing to: The San Esteban Sea Angling Centre, Doonbeg, Co. Clare, Ireland. Telephone +353 65 55105. Fax +353 65 55288.

Nick Cosford also recommends the following:

Bob Moss has lived and fished in The Dingle Peninsula for over twenty years. He is a most proficient bass angler. For the past couple of years his experience and knowledge have been available to visiting anglers who want professional guidance.

Bob Moss, Ballydavid, Tralee, Co Kerry, Ireland.

Telephone +353 66 55158.

John and Lynn Quinlan run a picturesque 'Bed & Breakfast' that is sympathetic to the needs of anglers. John is an accomplished angler and can arrange salmon, trout or sea-trout fishing as well as sea angling.

John Quinlan, Thatch Cottage, Kineigh West, Cahirciveen, Co Kerry, Ireland.

Telephone +353 66 74721.

Other information about fishing in and around "the Green Island" can be obtained from the Irish Tourist Board.

Note:

In the late 1980s the Irish government had the foresight to ban commercial fishing for bass. For recreational anglers there is a minimum size limit of 40 cm. No more than two fish can be taken in a twenty-four hour period, and there is a close season on retaining bass from 15th May to 15th June.

The commercial ban is renewable annually and there has been pressure to have it lifted. Understanding the importance of the recreational fishery to tourism the government have so far resisted this pressure.

No licence is required to fish for sea fish anywhere in Ireland. However, in both Northern Ireland and in the Republic of Ireland a licence is required to fish for salmon and sea-trout, whether in freshwater or salt.

While there is free access to fish on most of the coast, some river-mouths may be private.

45

SCOTLAND

Rudy van Duijnhoven

Three 'young' men and the sea.

It was 1995 and the last day of our stay at the Inverpolly Estate in Scotland. Both Theo and Harry had succeeded in landing their first salmon on the fly earlier in the week, while I had gathered enough slides, pictures and video-shots to make two slideshows and a promotional video for the travel agency who had sent me this far up north in Scotland. Today was meant to be a day of experiments; the three of us would go out at sea towards some small islands to find out whether anything worthy would like to take our streamers there.

The blue sky, with only a few clouds here and there, made it feel like summer, still it was the second half of September already. There was very little wind this day, but the large rolls made clear there was nothing but the Atlantic Ocean behind the last island. With our fourteen foot boat and small engine, it took us some twenty minutes to reach the lee of the furthest isle.

Our plan was that one man would use the oars to keep us more or less in one place, while the other two would cast fast sinking lines (both rods were equipped with a Teeny T-300) towards the shoreline. We would let line and streamer sink there for a while and than fish them back towards the boat. After some time we would then change seats, of course.

Our streamers were simple bucktail-patterns, mostly flies that we would use for zander in Holland. Some of the streamers had a large goldbead near the eye, to get them down faster and to add some extra flash. The flies were tied on hooks in sizes 1/0 and 2.

With one other man from the group I had fished from one of the islands for a few hours earlier in the week. We landed some small fish but the larger fish that both of us hooked dived down between the rocks deep below, where they managed to cut the nylon. Fishing from the boat we could hopefully pull the larger fish away from the sharp rocks.

The water was calm here and beautifully clear; we could easily see the bottom in even 15 feet of water. Some distance away from us, a small head appeared from the sea, two shining eyes staring at us. The seal, which is what it was, soon went down again only to surface once more at another spot. As it turned out there were two seals near the island, which after a while disappeared around a corner. They never came close enough for us to be able to take pictures of them; I guess they sensed that the three of us were flytiers...

For the first half hour only small fish, pollack and coalfish, took our flies; in the clear water we could see schools of small fish following our streamers. Then Harry hooked something better; suddenly the upper half of his rod was dragged beneath the surface. After a good fight, a pollack of several pounds in weight, came swirling at the surface. The fish was landed by hand, unhooked, admired (the deep brown colour accentuated in the bright sunshine) and photographed before being released. We had found what we had hoped for!

In the next few hours the three of us hooked and landed some twenty good-sized pollack; fish that performed extremely well even on our eight and nine weight outfits. The heaviest one, which must have been seven or eight pounds in weight, almost pulled the rod out of Harry's hands but he managed to hang on.

These fish apparently came up from the bottom to grab our streamers, only to dive down with them straight away. This made a take look like this: a little tap to mark that a fish had taken the fly and a deeply bent rod the next moment. Whenever a fish managed to get back to the bottom we usually lost it. Those rocks, or rather the shells on them, were really razor-sharp.

While having lunch on the island, with the flood-mark several feet above our heads (the difference between low and high tide is as much as ten feet here), I thought about the other fish that might well be out there at sea. There had to be garfish, mackerel, cod and perhaps sea-bass, all of which will come to a fly if it reaches their level. And what about blue shark? They are regularly caught off the coast of Ireland and that is not too far away. Could they be lured to a boat here too by making use of some rubby-dubby and then be hooked on a streamer-pattern? The answers are there in the future.

The starting of the engine pulled me out of my thoughts. We fished on for a few hours more, tried some other islands closer to the bay and left the water with a feeling of satisfaction. Some questions were answered today, others had been added; in future years I will be back to experiment some more!

NOTE.

As Rudy suggests, the main quarry species for the saltwater flyfisher in Scotland are pollack and coalfish - and, of course, sea-trout. The warmer climate of the last few years has extended the range of bass and mullet considerably and these may now be encountered where they were unknown only a few years ago.

No licence is needed to fish in Scotland, either for sea fish or for salmon or trout.

While access to the shore is not usually a problem; as in other countries river-mouths and estuaries, and even islands, may be privately owned. It is safest to enquire locally before fishing such places.

46

MEDITERRANEAN FLYFISHING

Marco Sammicheli

I live about 100 km from the sea and cannot always choose the best conditions to go fishing, so I fish in the conditions of weather that I find when I can go fishing. That means that sometimes I can have several trips without finding the right conditions and without fish.

In the past two years I have registered three I.G.F.A. saltwater flyrod records for European bass. This, at least, means that we do have a flyfishing bass-fishery. These bass have not been large - up to 2.270 kg - but lately I have been fishing waters where there are real chances of catching bass in the 5-10 kg range. They are regularly hooked by bait fishermen.

Bass fishing can be good in every season. In estuaries November, December and January can produce the bigger spawning bass. In this situation it is said that the best conditions are stable good weather, cold air and a north-east wind. Note that this can easily mean uncomfortable nights.

Except in the estuaries, it is not an easy matter to find bass here. Fishing is always best with a good surf brought on by rough weather. Big bass can be found were you think the water is "unfishable", right in the foam. When you can see foam everywhere along the shore, finding one spot with less foam and deeper water can do the trick. Without surf, bass fishing means mainly night fishing - and that's really a strange thing for the average Italian flyfisher.

A major exception is fishing near estuaries where bass fishing can be highly productive even with a calm sea in the day: currents and rips hold active bass depending on the tide. We have very small tides and the most productive stage of the tide is not always the same: often bass appear suddenly with the changing of the tide.

On Summer nights, on a falling tide, I have witnessed many bass crowding little estuaries connecting saltwater lagoons to the sea, feeding at the surface like trout taking mayflies: almost surely they were taking shrimps. In this situation the fishing can be very difficult, with the bass really selective. Unfortunately in the best saltwater estuaries angling is not allowed.

I fish with an eight-weight outfit, intermediate lines or fast sinking heads, classic flies like Snake, Deceiver, Clouser minnow, in white, black (at night and with muddy water), chartreuse, hooks from size 4 to 2/0.

In the summer months, May to October, we also have other species of fish. This year I hope to catch some of the best: Bluefish, Pomatomus saltatrix. These have increased during the last few years according to the experience of surf-fishers. Some places have a stable bluefish presence in the summer. The average size is 1 to 4 kg with larger specimens often caught from boats. The major problem is to find places where they come within casting distance. It is common to see big mullet jumping and escaping from breaking bluefish. Wire tippets are needed and hooked fish fight hard, jumping out of the water.

Leerfish, Lichia amia. Big specimens are not easy to find but at times they can be seen hunting at the surface, with a fin out of the water, near estuaries or harbours. Fish of over 10-15 kg have been caught from the shore in Tuscan waters. In some places it can be easy to find groups of smaller leerfish, 25-40 cm., hunting near the shore in the late summer. Even little fish can give good fishing on light tackle. This is a really strong fish, a great Mediterranean jack.

Leccia stella, Trachinotus glaucus. Conspecific with the permit and the pompano, this is our little jack, common and schooling, not big, but really powerful for their size. Up to 1-1.5 kg, but most commonly 15 - 20 cm.

Bluefish, leerfish and leccia stella penetrate estuaries and harbours, hunting for mullet and other small or juvenile fish.

Smaller quarry for the flyfisher include:

Garfish or aguglia, Belone belone. Common and exhilarating, they stay in schools on the surface and when hooked always jump. They are miniature spearfish.

Scad or sugarello, Trachurus trachurus. Pelagic carangidae that shoal near rocky shores, harbour walls and saltwater estuaries. They take flies mostly at night or at dawn, and it's possible to hook one fish after another. Averaging 200/400 g., up to 1 kg.

Occhiata, Oblada melanura. A small, up to 30 cm, bream, sometimes common along rocky coasts with rough water.

Barracuda, Sphyraena sphyraena. Smaller than the Atlantic barracuda and difficult to find; best in rocky areas, near estuaries and harbours.

Dentex, Dentex dentex. A sea-bream; large specimens live in deep water but juveniles may be caught from rocky shores.

Weever, Trachinus draco. Can be common on sandy bottoms. Most fish are small, but they can reach weights over 1.5 kg.

These species are quite common, and if they can be found in some con-

centration, and especially if they are visible in the water, it should possible to take them on fly tackle.

Gilt-head bream or orata, Sparus aurata. Like the renowned permit, these bream hunt for crabs on sandy bottoms under the midday summer sun. They grow to a good size, up to 3-4 kg and more.

Ombrina, Umbrina cirrosa. Sciaenid fish similar to meagre or the American croakers or drum. They are found mostly near estuaries and are not common. They average 30-80 cm.

Striped bream or mormora, Lithognatus mormyrus. Not a big fish but a hunter of small bottom creatures on the sand and in shallow waters, sometimes like bonefish but not tailing of course. They are caught in our waters from boats slowly trolling small artificial lures on sandy bottoms.

The I.G.F.A. saltwater flyrod section includes conger. I have never heard of conger captured with fly tackle, but maybe it can be done.

Fishing for mullet is obviously frustrating even if it's possible to catch some at times, mostly by chumming with bread and casting flies imitating the chum. We have plenty of mullet (up to 6 kg) in estuaries and along beaches.

Boat fishing can produce, in the summer months:

Dolphin fish, Coryphaena hippurus Dolphin are common on the west coast but are usually not so large as those found in tropical waters.

Bonito, Sarda sarda. Also common on the west coast but they seldom come into casting distance for shore fishing.

Mackerel, Scomber scombrus. Common and in large schools that produce many hookups with fish up to 45 cm and more.

Frigate mackerel, Auxis thazard. A small tuna often found near the shore, especially near harbour mouths.

Amberjack, Seriola dumerili. Juvenile specimens can be caught from shore, but rarely. Big specimens are common offshore or near rocky points with deep water.

Bluefin tuna, Thunnus thynnus. Common and extensively fished with conventional tackle, mainly by drifting and chumming. Flyfishing is only for small specimens and is still in its infancy.

Albacore, Thunnus alalunga. In 1997 good catches have been reported in the Adriatic sea, flyfishing to breaking schools, with plenty of fish of 10-15 kg.

Little tunny, Euthynnus alletteratus. In our waters it is quite rare for them to come within casting distance for the shore angler.

Skipjack tuna or Oceanic bonito, Katsuwonus pelamis. A small schooling tuna common offshore in southern Italian waters. If found feeding at the surface should provide good flyfishing.

Blue shark, Prionace glauca. Good catches of sharks of around 20 kg have been made flyfishing offshore in the Adriatic sea using chumming techniques.

Swordfish, Xiphias gladius. I know of two little swordfish caught with fly tackle in Tuscany waters, but the famous fishing areas for swordfish are around Calabria and Sicily where they are common.

Spearfish, Tetrapturus belone. Spearfish are found mainly in the Sicilian Straits of Messina where they can be locally quite common.

It would be a narrow vision of the sport that depended on the presence of the trout family for flyfishing. Mediterranean flyfishing is still to be developed and it could be really good. We need more flyfishers exploring the fisheries of the southern coast of Europe and developing a knowledge flyfishing in the Mediterranean. There is a huge potential for saltwater flyfishing in Sicily, Sardinia, the islands of Greece and many other waters as yet unfished with the flyrod.

PART IX

TACKLE
&
METHODS

47

SALTWATER FLY-TACKLE

Paul Morgan

Flyrods

I am not a tackle-freak. I keep things very simple and inexpensive. Most of my saltwater flyfishing has been done with an old fibreglass Geoffrey Bucknall Powercast reservoir rod. Lately I have been using a cheap telescopic carbon fibre rod, and I have often used one of my regular loch and river rods of between 9 feet and 10 feet 6 inches. As long as it will cast a fairly large fly a reasonable distance it will do. (A reasonable distance in this context does not necessarily mean a full flyline's length: much of my fishing is done at ranges of ten to twenty yards).

Most European saltwater flycasting can be acheived with ordinary reservoir trout fishing equipment. Any rod capable of throwing a seven to nine weight line will be adequate for most situations. Only occasionally you might feel the need to throw a heavy popping bug or tandem lure with a heavier flyrod - but this is not compulsory! Few trout anglers will not have a suitable rod already.

Fortunately the saltwater environment does not have the same detrimental affect on rods as it does on reels. The reel-seat is the area most likely to suffer from corrosion, but with sensible care - a rinse in fresh water after fishing - problems seldom arise.

Reels

Inexpensive plastic fly-reels are fine for most European saltwater flyfishing. I have had several like this which I have used for a season or two, then thrown away. I also have a couple of Bob Church Lineshooter reels which I use for all of my heavier-line flyfishing. They are made of carbon-fire, are light, and have a wide spool for low line-memory. I have caught salmon, sea-trout and Nile perch, all into the teens of pounds, on them without any problems. However, I am always apprehensive if I hook a fast-running fish. These reels are not terribly free-running and I expect that I will eventually have to get a "real" saltwater reel with a reliable braking system.

Many good middle-of-the-range reels are resistant to corrosion and would be quite suitable for fishing in the sea. My worry is less about the affect of saltwater than the affect of hard treatment on rocky shores. I still believe that a cheap 'disposable' reel is the best bet, with the option of a really robust and expensive reel if you have money to throw around, or if you are likely to make use of it for tropical flyfishing.

Fly-Lines

Most of my local fishing is in shallow weedy bouldery bays. I almost always use a floating line, usually a weight-forward eight-weight, with a level mono leader of ten-pound breaking-strain. If I want depth I use weighted flies. When fishing smaller flies I use the slimmer double-strength nylon. Although many people find them indispensible, I have never used, or felt the need to use a line-tray when using a floating line. I don't use one when fishing with a sinking line either, but only because I cannot be bothered carrying one more item of tackle.

For fishing deeper rocky shores for cod, pollack and coalfish; for fishing fast strong tides or estuary currents; and for fishing in deep water from boats or piers, a fast sinking fly-line is essential. In these circumstances a shooting-head is probably the best choice.

Flies

I tie my own flies, and scrounge other people's when I get the chance! For much of my saltwater flyfishing, I do not feel that fly-pattern has been all-important. I use simple hair-wings and streamers, mostly white or white/blue Deceivers, tied on stainless-steel hooks in various sizes. I have done very well with epoxy resin minnows, but have not tied them myself. I also have some tiny rubber eels which are wonderful, especially for pollack.

On several occasions I have found myself on the coast without any salt-water tackle. Using whatever freshwater tackle I have had to hand I have had success using white lures, gold-head nymphs, dog-nobblers, killer bugs and standard winged wet flies. Despite my reservations about the need for vast numbers of patterns, I do feel that there are breakthroughs to be made in flyfishing for saltwater fish, and that some of these will depend on accurate imitation of food items.

Other Essential Items

Lightweight neoprene chest-waders have made a big difference to all of my flyfishing; fresh and saltwater. I have several pairs. They have opened up areas impossible to reach with thigh-waders. In many, though not all, circumstances, I also wear a halter-type buoyancy aid. It has never been put to use, but is a comfort when wading deep, on rocks, or in fast tides. Being able to wade deep means that I can wade far out from the shore in shallow bays. It is seldom convenient to wade all the way back to dry-land to land a fish, or change an item of tackle, so I travel light. Little fish can be swung to hand, or released without handling. Big fish are worth the trudge to shore, but I do sometimes lose good fish which I would have landed if I had carried a net. A wicker creel takes some beating for carrying small fish such as mackerel, and is the best tool I know for scooping up whitebait when the water around your legs turns black with herring fry. I suppose that the best receptacle for newly changed flies is a wool-patch on your cap, but I just tend to drop them loose into my shirt pocket. I often get stabbed! I do not return them to their box until I have washed and dried them at home.

When I am actually fishing my bag or pockets contain only a few items:-

Flies in three small plastic boxes.
Two spools of leader material.
A heavy-handled knife, for use as a priest.
Long-nosed pliers, for unhooking deeply hooked fish.
Plastic carrier-bags.
At night; a waterproof torch or head-lamp.

The knife/priest and the pliers are seldom used but are essential. The plastic bags are optimistically carried in case I, or the Fates, decide that I am to keep a fish to eat. More frequently they are filled with mussels for soup or samphire for supper. The torch makes it much easier for middle-aged eyes to change flies and, just as important, ensures that I do not unknowingly grasp a weever fish bare-handed in the dark.

48

MORE SALTWATER TACKLE

Martin James

The saltwater fly fishing rod has to be designed to cope with all types of fly fishing lines from a heavy floating one to a fast sink and all the different types in between under all conditions many of them adverse. At one time you couldn't buy a rod purposely designed for fly fishing in saltwater. One had to use a heavy reservoir trout rod. The problem was these rods soon showed signs of corrosion. The reel-seat would seize up and you were in trouble after a few trips.

My present rods are made by Greys of Alnwick. The two models I use come in two and four pieces designed for casting nine and ten-weight lines. These rods have a fast stiff action which helps to set the hook, casts a good line and when a fish is hooked the rod works extremely well. The fitting are corrosion-proof. The rods are fitted with two good stripping-guides, a small neatly-made fighting-butt, and come fitted with a keeper-ring. These rods won't break the bank but they will do the job and take some punishment.

Saltwater fly fishing reels are not just a reservoir for holding line. They have to be a quality engineered product made from the best materials available and corrosion-proof. My first choice is the Swedish Model 4 Loop. A saltwater-proof model with a fast retrieve that I have used for the past six years at many, world-wide, saltwater venues.

Another reel which hasn't let me down is the Stratos model S350 made in the United States. These reels don't come cheap but are well worth the money spent. Buy the best you can afford. I usually needle-knot about four feet of 15 lb nylon line to the end of the fly line. But only two feet on a fast sinking line. The fly is tied on with a four turn tucked blood knot. It has never let me down so I see no reason to change.

Casting flies for bottom-feeding fish such as flounders and plaice demands fast-sinking lines. Many years ago I used to use a shooting-head system made up of floating, slow-sinking and fast-sinking lines. I wanted something better if possible, and found my answer from the American Teeny Nymph Co with the TS-series of lines. These include a TS 450 550 and 650 all capable of being cast with a nine or ten-weight rated rod. The line I am currently using is the Teeny T S- Series line with a 450 grain weight and a sinking-rate of 8 ips. Its a 100 ft line with a 30 ft sink tip. It's not the easiest line in the world to cast. More a chuck and duck job. I have found the best way is extend the sinking section of the line, roll-cast, lift off quickly, one false-cast and shoot. It requires a little practise but this line gets the fly down quickly.

Often you will find bass and mackerel on the surface chomping into the bait-size fish. This is the time when we need that top quality weight-for-ward floating line. Purchase the best that money will buy.

Some days the fish will be feeding a few feet below the surface below the surface. This is when you will need a good slow sinking line. The Ryobi Masterline Slow Sink Illusion is the best that I've used. It cast's nicely and doesn't seem to be affected by saltwater. Make sure you keep your lines well polished. Pat O'Reilly of the West Wales School of Flyfishing rec-ommends using silicon furniture polish. It works a treat and can give you a few extra yards.

Milk crate and plastic bottle

What a heading. What has a milk crate got to do with saltwater fly fishing? Well it's a very important item of equipment for the shore angler especially on shingle and firm sandy beaches. I first used the milk crate when fishing Puget Sound in Washington State. Standing in the water on the upside-down crate helps to give you some extra reach. It can put several yards on your cast. The plastic bottle is tied to the crate with a length of string, and acts as a float. When the crate is under the water the bottle floats above so you know where it is positioned. It's a very simple idea but very effective and one I often use in the UK. Give it a try.

49

DEEP-WATER FLYFISHING PROBLEMS

Claus Bech-Petersen

Ten tricks for deep water

Most people I know prefer to fish with a floating line whenever possible, but in saltwater flyfishing the ultra-fast sinking lines are often necessary to get the fly down.

Species like cod, coalfish and pollack often lie 5-10 metres below the surface, at least in Scandinavian waters, and this presents a unique challenge to the flyfisher, both in terms of tackle and techniques.

I have used these ten tricks for deep water fishing in Norway and Denmark but they are, of course, useful wherever fish are found in deep water.

1. Use a depth sounder. It will tell you how deep the water is, the structure of the bottom, water temperature and indicate whether there are fish below. I use a portable Bottom Line Sidefinder, which is cheap, lightweight and can be fitted to my float tube.

2. Use the fastest sinking line you can get hold of if you are fishing in water deeper than three or four metres. Even the fastest sinking line - I use a Cortland shooting head, sink rate 6, which sinks one metre in approximately seven seconds - seems slow when you are waiting for it to sink into the depths and there is really no reason to waste fishing time. Some people use lead core shooting heads, which really get down fast, but I dislike them because they are difficult to cast.

3. Cast as far as possible. Long casts increase effective fishing time, because the fly has to sink into the depths fewer times. You should aim at casting distances between 35 and 40 metres.

4. Undersize your line if you are an experienced caster. An 8-weight line on a 10-weight rod gives higher line speed and longer casts, especially if you are casting into the wind. This is, of course, just as useful when fishing on the top.

5. Use a shooting head and a monofilament shooting line. This increases distance and the monofilament allows the shooting head to sink faster than a conventional shooting line. I use Berkeley XT or golden fluorescent Stren in diameters around 0.45 mm.

6. Consider your fly design. Slim flies cast and sink better than bulky

flies and are much better. Heavily weighted flies reduce casting distance and are often a disadvantage. My favorite deep water fly is Vidar Håggblom's Pike Fly, which only consists of a Flashabou tail and a hackle. Even an eight inch long version of this fly casts much better than a medium-large trout streamer and the ultra-slim design makes the fly sink almost as fast as a bare hook. You should also remember that your fly can easy disappear in the sea, so use the largest and most flashy fly the fish will accept.

7. Use short leaders and a sinking head between the leader and the flyline. The sinking head is merely a short section of 30 lbs. lead core line. It hardly affects casting distance and helps the tip of the flyline sink faster, even on density-compensated lines. I use sinking heads that are one, two and three feet long and attach them to leader and flyline with loop-to-loop connections.

8. Count the fly down. Most fly lines are marked with sinking speed, but the salt and the current impede sinking and make the theoretical sinking speed useless in estimating how deep you are fishing. Instead, you should do this: When the first cast hits the water, you may count to 50 before retrieving the fly. In the next cast you count to 60 and continue like this until you feel the fly hit the bottom or get a strike. Then you know exactly how long the fly should sink to repeat the succesful cast.

9. Use the current and the wind to increase effective fishing time if you are fishing fishing from a boat or a float-tube. If you are drifting with the wind or the current, the fly will be covering water even if you do not retrieve it. This means that you can slow down the retrieve to the speed where the fly merely pulsates and twists and still move it quite fast in relation to the fish. Or you can release most of the line you have just retrieved and let the wind and the current straighten the slack before the next retrieve. In both cases you extend the period before the next cast without reducing the effectiveness of the fly.

10. Go fishing with some experienced sea fishermen. They may not be flyfishermen, but their knowledge of the sea and the fish is invaluable and if you explain your special interest and the limitations of your tackle, the odds are that you will have some nice days together - even though they may think you are kind of stupid at first.

50

SCENT, TASTE & THE FLYFISHER

Claus Bech-Petersen

This does not present bullet-proof instructions that will make you catch more fish immediately. Instead, it contains some very un-Halfordian ideas that might show a future way to catch some of the more difficult species in North European saltwater flyfishing.

When Paul Morgan first introduced the idea to this book, I wrote a letter asking him to find a person who had experience using scent as a basic part of the flyfisher's techniques. He didn't find that person and asked me to write an introduction to the subject (and the ideas - for that is all we have right now). What follows is theory - a theory that can keep me working and experimenting in future years.

Today we have reached perfection in tackle and flies. New saltwater techniques are evolving at a staggering speed and our knowledge of most species of fish is greater than ever. But some species are still difficult to catch on the flyrod. They include mullet, flounders and to a certain extent the garfish in spring.

Most of the modern day flyrod species are predatory fish that use their lateral line and their eye sight to locate their prey. These fish can be caught with classic flyrod techniques, because our flies appeal to their eyes (and that is all it takes).

The problem is with species like mullet, which mainly feed on very small food items, using their olfactory sense as a major food-seeking device. Our flies are not geared to that.

Too often the flies smell wrong. Experiments with many different species have shown that even the slightest concentration of tobacco, oil or even human skin can turn fish off. Even a fly with a neutral scent (it that is possible) may not be enough if the fish is expecting a certain smell or taste from its food.

To appreciate this, we must take a brief look toward our bait fishing colleagues. In Greenland it is well known that you cannot catch turbot on even the best artificial bait with any regularity. Knowledgeable fishermen always mount a few slices of fish on their hooks when they fish for turbot. In Denmark every fisherman know that the best way to catch a garfish is with even the smallest slice of fish flesh on a hook. Fresh water fishermen dreaming of eels often inject some anise oil into their bait, because the scent of anise actually attracts the eel. This is not theory. It is fact and has been well known for centuries, even though fly fishermen tend to forget.

But what measures can the flyfisherman take to counteract offending smell and taste, or the mere lack of attraction in a fly?

The first step is to ensure that the smell of the flies does not offend the fish. Cigarette smoke, motor oil and the like should be kept well away from fly boxes so it can't affect the fishes interpretation of the fly in the water. Trout fishermen have always known that an old, worn fly catches more fish than a brand new fly. This might be due to the angler's belief in that particular fly which has caught him countless fish in the past, but another possible explanation is that the fly has been liberated from the offending scents that come from human hands, tobacco and head cement.

And then it might be a good idea to give the fly an attractive smell.

At this point we enter an area between traditional flyfishing and bait-fishing, but I believe that it is up to each and every angler to draw his own lines. At least in Ireland flyfishermen have been known to mount maggots on the bend of sea-trout flies to attract more fish. Similar practices just might help in salt water.

Both new and old flies can be soaked in blood or meat from baitfish, mussels or shrimp so they give off scent when they are retrieved.

Another option is to rub your hands with baitfish before you touch the flies and the leader. This practice is used on charter boats on the Pacific coast in the United States. There is no doubt that the people who rub their hands in fish catch more and bigger fish on their jigs and Japanese feathers than the ones who don't.

The idea of incorporating scent in artificial bait is certainly not new to the manufacturers of plugs and lures, who are working hard to find a way to make their bait release scent at a constant speed. They of course hope that scented baits will be a major breakthrough in the quest for the infallible bait - and the high profits that will accompany it.

But the smell and taste of the flies are only half the story. They might decide if the fish will accept the fly or not, but the first requirement is to actually locate the fish in the wide, wide sea. An echo locator is one way to go. Another is to chum or ground-bait the fish to the boatside.

American flyfishermen have use chumming to attract all kinds of fish for decades and the practice is slowly getting more followers in Europe.

There are basically two ways of chumming. One is a long-term invest-ment where you regularly place food at a certain spot and try to accustom the fish to the presence of food in that spot. This of course attract the fish and make them easier to find. And when the fish get used to eat small chunks of a particular food, they just might accept an imitation of that food even though it does not smell like the real thing. This is what you do in carp fishing but also in fishing for mullet in some areas.

The other method is to use a rubby-dubby bag as when you fish for shark. Normally you would use mashed shrimp or fish and place it in a mesh bag hanging in the water. The waves and the movements of the boat will slowly wash the rubby-dubby from the bag and leave an obvious track for bigger fish to follow. And when they get boatside you just place a fly in front of them.

This method works for more species than you would expect. Flounders and cod will come for a deep rubby-dubby bag, and on the surface it is quite easy to attract both garfish and mackerel this way. A friend of mine has even chummed sea-trout with the juice of mashed mussels.

I have used this technique a little, with varying success. Failure seems to come from too little rubby-dubby, or simply from the absence of fish from the area.

51

BAITS CAST WITH THE FLY ROD

John Bickerdyke

*Sole-skin Bait - Gurnard Skin Bait for Sand Eels - Dog-fish Tail-fibre Fly -
Orkney Feather Baits - Mouse-tail Baits - Artificial Sand Eels. &c.*

Among baits which may be cast with the fly rod that cannot in any sense
of the word be termed flies, the sole skin bait shown in the illustration is,
perhaps, the most useful for bass, sea trout and billet. In fact, all the fish
which will take the whitebait fly will take a sole skin bait. It is easily
made in the following manner: Get a sole skin or a piece of gurnard skin
from a fishmonger, stretch it over a piece of board or glass, and put it in
the sun to dry. The particles of flesh on the skin must be thoroughly well
scraped away. Then cut a piece of the shape, and about the size, shown in
the illustration (A), bend it over the back of the hook, tying the head on
to the shank. Sew around the edge of the belly, and at the same time fix
in a small strip of lead foil or lead wire to make it swim upright in the
water. A shot may be sewn into the tail of it, but it is not desirable to
make it very heavy as it will be an awkward thing to cast.

Gurnard skin bait

A very pretty bait for sand eels is shown in the illustration. This is simply cut out of a single thickness of gurnard skin, prepared as already
explained, and fixed to the hook by whipping the nose on to the shank of
the top hook in the manner shown. The same bait can be made in larger
sizes for pollack and bass. In fact, with a supply of fish skin anyone with
an ordinary amount of ingenuity can make up a large variety of taking sea
baits of various sizes, and find them useful things to have in his book.

Somewhat akin to these fish baits is a kind of fly made of fibres obtained
from the tail of the dog fish. It was communicated to me by Mr Moodie
Heddel, of Orkney. The tail fin of the dog fish is first dried by hanging it

up in the wind out of doors. When dry, the fleshy butt should be cut off close to the edge of the fin, and the dry skin turned down from each side. This operation discloses some ragged fibrous looking matter with a little dried flesh adhering to it. The Orkney fishermen cleanse the fibres by sucking them in their mouths and drawing them through their teeth, but those to whom this operation is repugnant may possibly discover a more civilised way of effecting the same object. The fibres when prepared are a pale yellow, and glisten beautifully in the water. They are about as thick as the bristles in a coarse toothbrush, and the illustration shows their appearance after they have been whipped on to the hook. These baits, which kill well, are worth taking care of; to wash them in fresh water and carefully dry them before putting away is not time wasted.

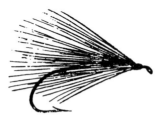

Dogfish Tail Fibre Fly

Feather baits for pollack and coal fish are deemed great medicine in the far north, and account for many large pollack and coal fish, locally called lythe and saithe. I am afraid these hardly come within the term flies, as they are much more often trailed than cast with a fly rod. They are, as a rule, very roughly made, a few turns of yellow worsted round the shank of a cod hook, and a couple of quill feathers on each side, not for wings, but laid flat along the shank to represent the sides of a fish. Black feathers may be introduced, and so may white. There is hardly any limit to the combination of colours which may be arranged. When the fish are feeding eagerly they are not very particular. The following dressings were recommended to me by Mr Moodie Heddel, of Orkney:

(1) Take a large sized cod hook and cover it with a body of orange and black in alternate bars half an inch in width, and lay over the back of the body a few strands of peacock harle, or two whole feathers tied down to the tail. Wings, either white swan's feather or two whole speckled turkey or drake's feathers.

(2) Brown or grey turkey's feathers for wings, one or two curlew feathers placed farther back, and peacock harle on head and tail of body. Beads for eyes, red worsted round the gills, blue worsted along the back and pale yellow, or greenish yellow, on the body.

An Orkney Feather bait

(3) Body, red and black worsted, with gold and silver tinsel. Tail of heron's feather cut out in the centre to make it forked, and a few strips of peacock harle. For wings, two curlew feathers face to face, and, if it is a very long bait, two more feathers, or wings, further back.

These flies may, of course, with advantage be made on very large eyed hooks, but if these are not obtainable of sufficient size, large ordinary hooks can be used fitted with a long loop of twisted gut.

A capital bait for casting with a fly rod, which is a novelty to most sea fishermen, can be made from the tail of a mouse. An ordinary round bend worm hook is used on which a piece of medium sized gut is whipped. The gut is well soaked, then threaded through an ordinary needle. The needle is passed in at the tail, about the centre, threaded through it, and brought out at the thick end, the gut and the shank of the hook following. A few turns of well waxed red silk or twine are required around the thick end of the tail to keep it in place just above the shank. Sea trout and other fish will take this bait, and no doubt regard it as a kind of worm, its hairiness being an additional attraction.

Very light artificial sand eels can be cast with a fly rod, and for sea trout are best worked in that way. They are easily made by means of a piece of grey indiarubber tubing, such as is fitted to very cheap babies' feeding bottles. It can be bought by the yard. It is not only useful for this particular purpose, but also for making the long twisted grey rubber eel for coal fish and pollack, though for these fish the black or red rubber is, I consider, as a rule preferable.

Light artificial sand Eel for casting with Fly Rod

To make the sand eel for casting from the fly rod, increase the length of the shank of a No. 12 or 13 hook about 3in. by whipping on to it a piece of wire, ending with a swivel. Thread a piece of tubing on the hook and bring it down to the bend, where it should be cut slanting, and then sliced to make it vibrate. The end of the tubing next the swivel should then be tied firmly to the wire. The only thing that remains to be done is to paint the eel. The back can be done with two coats of Stevens' blue-black ink, one coat being brought a little farther down the side than the other. The belly can be touched up with silver paint, and the sides left white. These latter should be scraped occasionally to keep them of good colour. Two pink beads can be sewn on to the rubber to represent eyes, with black circles drawn round each in ink. When finished the whole should receive a coat of varnish. Paint and other colouring matter does not last long on rubber, but it is easy to retouch these baits occasionally or to make new ones. For sea trout they are cast like flies, just over the edge of the seaweed, and worked with a sink and draw motion, or drawn along. Those who cannot cast a worm without throwing it off the hook should try this method of fishing in salt water for sea trout, as it is very deadly. The worm, if cast with the fly rod, should be worked with a sink and draw motion - that is to say, as soon as it touches the surface let it sink perpendicularly, then draw it in a slanting line to the surface; then let it have another perpendicular fall, and continue this operation until it is brought close up to the angler's feet.

While this book was in the press, I received from a Scotch correspondent a curious coal fish bait. It consists simply of a hook with a spike of grass in bloom laid along the shank.

From *Practical Letters to Young Sea-fishers.*
John Bickerdyke, 1898

52

SCANDINAVIAN SALTWATER FLIES

Claus Bech-Petersen

I am not a great believer in the theory of selective fish. Fish are not very clever, and wherever I have experienced refusals they have come from over-educated trout, grayling and pike that have been caught and released too often.

That is uncommon in salt water in Scandinavia where most fish are killed when they are caught. And besides, salt water species move around a lot, so even an educated cod is likely to swim somewhere else shortly after it has been caught and released.

Therefore, I prefer as simple flies as possible. Easy to tie, easy to cast, and easy for the fish to see. These are the main points I look for when tying.

The following four flies cover almost all my salt water fishing for non-salmonids at the moment. They are old stand-bys and I would only add a few small flies (dries and wets) for garfish and ide.

Storsilden (The Big Herring)

Hook: Mustad 34011, size 1/0
Body: Flat silver mylar
Rib: Oval gold or silver mylar
Throat: White bucktail, 2 x hook length
Wing: Blue and green bucktail mixed with pearl, silver, blue and green Flashabou
Eyes: Prizma Tape Eyes
Head: Clear epoxy

Storsilden is my standard fly for all predatory species besides trout, cod and pike in salt water. With a total length of four inches it presents a worthwhile meal for most fish. As long as it is not overdressed, it is easy to cast. The long sweeping bucktail wing pulsates in a slow and tantalizing way and even though bucktail has a reputation for being fragile I normally catch 30 or 40 fish per fly before 'retiring' it. The pattern described here is a jazzed-up version.

A simpler version has a white belly and a green wing. It works just as well, but I like the look of this version better.

Vidar Håggblom's Pike Fly
  Hook: Stinger size 2
  Tail: 4-8 inches of blue, green or silver Flashabou
  Hackle: Black cock, tied on the base of the tail

In 1995 my editor told me to go to Finland and test the fabulous pike fishing on Åland, the small group of islands between Finland and Sweden. I happily accepted. This fly was the only one used by our guide, Vidar Håggblom, who specializes in fly fishing for pike in the brackish sea. Today it is the only fly I use for cod. It has never failed me. The three specified colours are the ones preferred by Vidar.

At sunset, when the cod move into shallow water, or when I fish for pike, I often convert it to an 'instant popper' by pulling a piece of ethafoam onto the exposed hook shank. The fly does not get more effective that way, but the sight of good sized cod that inhaling the fly from the surface is quite a come-on to me.

Green Fuzzy Fish
  Hook: Mustad 34011, size 6
  Thread: Clear monofilament
  Throat: Polar Bear Fish Fuzz, slightly longer that the hook
  Wing: Algae Glow Fish Fuzz mixed with 8 strands of green Flashabou

A simple but yet effective imitation of most small fish in the sea. Eight strands of Flashabou makes for a very shiny fly. I often remove a few strands if fishing in in bright, shallow water.

Ultratobis (The Ultra Sandeel)
  Hook: Mustad 34011, size 1 or 2, tied bend-back style
  Thread: Light olive
  Wing: Dark olive over chartreuse over polar bear Ultra Hair. Total
          length is 4-5 inches.
  Eyes: Yellow Prizma Tape Eyes (optional)
  Head: Clear epoxy

The sandeel is one of the most important baitfish in many locations. This fly, inspired by Bob Popovics' Keel Eel, is probably as good an imitation as any. The bend back-style makes the fly semi-weedless.

PART X

BIOGRAPHIES
&
BIBLIOGRAPHIES

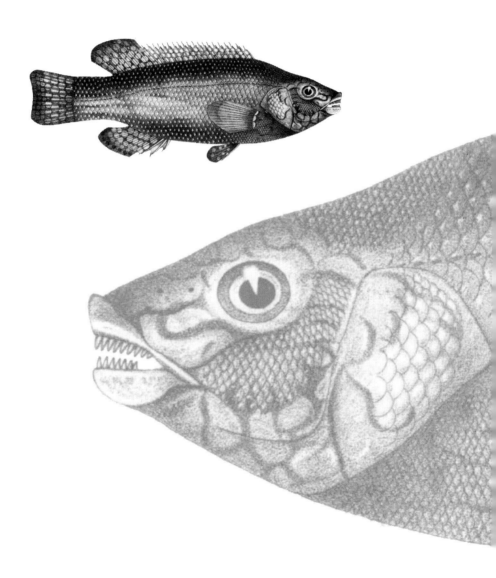

237

CONTRIBUTOR PROFILES

ROGER BAKER

Roger is 47 years old and runs a pub and holiday cottage business in a far corner of south-west Cornwall. He is a member of the B.A.S.S. conservation committee, and National Federation of Sea Anglers bass sub-committee.

He believes that the value of wild bass to sportfishing, recreation and tourism is worth between twenty and fifty times more than it is to the commercial fishing sector, and that with proper management and enforcement, bass could make Devon and Cornwall the bass angling Mecca of Europe.

A life-long angler, Roger has fished in far corners of the world. He finds Cornwall and its Atlantic coast a quiet and relatively unspoilt haven in an increasingly commercialised Britain.

CLAUS BECH-PETERSEN

Claus is thirty-two years old and a journalist. He has worked on all the major newspapers in Denmark, and at present is an editor on the national newspaper "Politiken". He also writes fishing and travel stories for the paper.

He is the author of a recent book on trout and grayling fishing, "Fluefiskeri: efter ørred og stalling".

I could have told you more about him but I am unable to contact him because he has gone off to New Zealand and Fiji, fishing. So, I can't.

I'm not jealous. Honestly.

JOHN BICKERDYKE

John Bickerdyke was the pen-name of Charles Henry Cook, born in 1858 and died in 1933. He was a very well-known angler of his day and his books were widely read. His best known book, "The book of the all-round angler" was continuously in print from 1889 to the 1940s. Its separate parts, on sea, game, coarse and pike fishing, must have sold hundreds of thousands of copies.

His *Angling in Salt Water*, published in 1887, marked the beginning of rod-fishing, other than flyfishing, in the sea as a sport. Prior to that the few references to sea-fishing in angling literature referred mainly to hand-line fishing, long-lining, net-fishing and spearing.

His other books include the Badminton Library volume *Sea fishing, Days in Thule with rod, gun and camera, Days of my life on waters fresh and salt*, and *Letters to young sea fishers*.

RICHARD BOWDEN-SMITH

Fly-fishing in Salt and Fresh Water was published anonymously in 1851. Its authorship has previously been attributed to a Mr Hutchinson, who has been taken to have been a Richard Hely Hutchinson, known to have flyfished off the Irish coast at about this time.

However, I now know of two copies of the book, both of which attribute the authorship to Bowden-Smith. A copy currently in the possession of my bookselling colleague John Scott actually has, written inside, "This book was written by my father, Richard Bowden-Smith, and illustrated by my mother, Georgina Bowden-Smith", signed Walter Baird Bowden-Smith. It includes various other authenticating details.

Unfortunately, at this time I know little of the lives of either Mr Bowden-Smith or Mr Hutchinson.

NICK COSFORD

His Great Uncle Albert built Nick a solid glass-fibre fishing rod when he was six years old. Since then he has done a lot of fishing and caught a lot of fish. Having evolved through coarse fishing, stillwater trout and sea-trout fishing, he is now a dedicated bass flyfisher. Today family life, local politics and work leave little time for fishing and he looks forward to his occasional bassing trips.
Nick lives in Oxfordshire.

GARY COXON

Employed as the U.K. representative for Sage, Gary is an avid flytyer and flyfisher-man. He has demonstrated at shows and game-fairs both in the U.K. and abroad and has fished in many different countries for various species. He is a full member of A.P.G.A.I. (Association of Professional Game Angling Instructors) and teaches flytying and casting at several fisheries in the Cheshire and North Wales areas.

RICHARD A.C. DAVIES

Richard was brought up in South West Wales, surrounded by sewin rivers. He began fishing at the age of eight and by the age of fifteen he was cycling up to eighteen miles to fish the best sea-trout pools. After studying rural resource management at agricultural college he has worked as a gamekeeper, river bailiff and ghillie.

His spare time has been spent studying the finer points of flyfishing, firstly for sea-trout with the help of David Hunt and Dennis Moss, and latterly, after meeting Jonathon Morsehead, for salmon. Memorable catches during the nineties include one of twenty seven sea-trout and finnock in the sea, fourteen sea-trout averaging 2lb (all returned) and six salmon (a record for the pool).

Richard is a licentiate member of the Institute of Fisheries Management (L.M.I.F.M.) and works at Uig Lodge salmon fishery as head ghillie. His other inter-ests include playing rugby for Stornoway R.F.C., photography and writing. He is currently involved in producing a film about summer salmon fishing.

ALAN HANNA

Alan Hanna lives in the island town of Enniskillen, which is located on Lough Erne, the third largest lake in Ireland. A lifelong angler, he pursues all kinds of fish with a flyrod. He is a member of the Fisheries Conservancy Board for Northern Ireland, rep-resenting the interests of independent anglers.

Alan is the author of *Flyfishing for big pike: an Irish approach*, which is to be published by Coch-y-bonddu Books in 1998.

JAN HANSEN

After ten years as a research scientist in computer communications, forty-one year old Jan - technologist, painter & sea-trout flyfisher -has taken a new direction. He has developed "The Norwegian Flyshop", an internet guide to sportfishing in Norway, as well as working as a consultant on the business use of the internet.

"My dearest occupation has become flyfishing at late silent nights after sea-trout both in the rivers and in the sea. Happily there are many interesting spots around where I live in the southern part of Norway. Sometimes I flyfish for trout and white-fish further upstream, but even then I prefer the evenings. The reasons for this is found deep inside somewhere".

Jan.Hansen@flyshop.no.   *http://www.flyshop.no*

STAN HEADLEY

Born in Fife in 1951, Stan moved with his family to Orkney in 1958. His father, Edwin, was a keen trout-fisherman and passed on his love of the sport to him. It quickly became a passion (perhaps an obsession) and his school books were covered with childish drawings of fish and fishing-tackle. Visits to the trout lochs of Orkney in his early years were to set the course of his life in later years.

During his teens he spent almost every spare minute fishing from the rocks for the plentiful saltwater species which abounded in Orkney's coastal waters, particularly pollack, cod, wrasse and coalfish. After a brief sojourn on the UK mainland in his early twenties, where he learnt the finer aspects of fishing via roach, tench and bream fishing in London's Grand Union Canal, he returned to Orkney and re-discovered his passion for trout flyfishing. He quickly became involved with the Orkney Trout Fishing Association, and learnt that competitive flyfishing was a quick and guaranteed way to improve one's experience, knowledge and skills.

He became the Scottish National Fly Fishing Champion in 1990 on Loch Leven, represented his country at international level in 1991 and 1992, and through his membership of the highly successful O.T.F.A. competition team had many successes in the Benson & Hedges International Club Championships.

Stan's travels have taken him fishing to France, Ireland and Norway, and to almost every prime flyfishing location in the U.K.

He has been a prolific writer and commentator on the sport since 1982. His comprehensive guide to Orkney trout fishing has recently been re-written and updated and is a must for any angler wishing to visit this Mecca for trout fishermen. He is the author of *The trout & salmon flies of Scotland*, the first and only attempt to properly catalogue the many patterns in current usage.

The *New Trout Fishing Guide to Orkney* contains a section dealing with seatrout fishing in saltwater, retails for £2.95 plus p&p, and can be obtained through: Headley & Chaddock Publishing, St. Michael's Manse, Harray, Orkney, KW16 2JR.

MARTIN JAMES

Martin James caught his first fish - a rudd - from a Kentish clay pit during a German bomber raid in 1941. Since then he has fished all over the world in fresh and salt water. His expeditions have taken him to the Amazon to fish for monster catfish, to the Pacific Northwest for steelhead and chinook, to flyfish the Arabian Sea for barracuda and kingfish. Wherever angling adventure is to be found Martin is likely to turn up.

He is well known as an angling author and broadcaster, and is a consultant to the well-known tackle firm, Greys of Alnwick. His autobiography *Up against it* tells of his passion for fishing and the countryside, and how he has pursued it despite the debilitating affects of multiple sclerosis.

PETER JAMES

OLOF JOHANSSON

Olof Johansson (60) has been editor of the Swedish fishing magazine Sportfiske since 1974. He has written extensively about saltwater fishing and salmon flyfishing and has published books on both subjects. He has been flyfishing, for a variety of species, in the sea for over thirty years, and is one of Europe's most experienced saltwater fly-fishermen.

http://www.sportfiske-fj.se/

STEPHEN JOHNSON

Stephen Johnson spent his working life as a veterinary surgeon in the valley of the Tweed. However, his family owned the Camasunary Estate on the Isle of Skye. This was where he spent his formative years and where he returned to throughout his life. In 1942 he and his Mosquito were shot down into the Zuyder Zee. During the next three years, incarcerated in Stalag Luft III, he relived the fishing escapades of his early years, writing the notes which would be published after the war as *Fishing from afar.* His later book, *Fishing with a purpose*, which has some overlap with the first, was published in 1969.

Stephen Johnson died only last year, in 1997.

MARTIN JØRGENSEN

Martin Jørgensen is a 37 year old computer magazine editor-in-chief living in Copenhagen, Denmark. He ties plain fishing flies for saltwater as an amateur in his "spare time" - a term which he says, "does not exist in my life".

Martin has tied flies at shows and demonstrations in his home country as well as in Sweden, Holland and America. He has written articles on fishing and tying for magazines in several countries and has published lots of information on the subject on the Internet.

He is a member of the independent and informal Danish flytying and flyfishing group 'The Bananaflies', generally shunning formalisation and commercialisation of his favourite pastimes: tying flies and fishing the open coasts of his country.

martinj@login.dknet.dk

WOLFGANG KÜTER

Wolfgang Küter lives in northern Germany, some 20 miles south of the Danish border. He was born in 1964 and started fishing when he was about 10 years old. After many years of conventional saltwater fishing in the Baltic sea, he started fishing for sea-trout about ten years ago.

He fishes mostly along the north German coast but moves to Denmark when the wind conditions make fishing on his door-step impossible. Normally he fishes close to home because he believes that you catch more fish when you actually fish than when you drive around in the car.

Wolfgang's best sea-trout, caught in 1994, was a fish of 7.8 kg.

He has had occasional articles about saltwater sea-trout fishing published in German fishing magazines.

wolfgang@zaphod.allcon.com

MIKE LADLE

Dr. Mike Ladle is fifty-seven years old, married with four grown up sons, and has been fishing for over fifty of those years. He is Head of Fish Research at the I.F.E. River Laboratory in Dorset and has published hundreds of scientific papers and technical reports. In his spare time he enjoys all kinds of fishing, growing alpine plants, fishing, writing, fishing and fishing. In addition to his many popular features on angling he has written three books, *Operation Sea Angler, Hooked on Bbass* and *Lure Fishing: a New Approach to Spinning*. In the last few years, with his pal Steve Pitts, he has made a number of videos on bass, mullet, pike, cod and lure-fishing. Mike is probably best known as the originator and developer of methods such as buoyant plugs for bass, dry-fly for thick-lipped mullet, baited lures for thin-lipped mullet and plugs for wrasse. Although he has caught many big fish, from pike to roach and from conger to salmon, he is happiest when walking the sea-shore with his spinning-rod and fly tackle. His most memorable catch was over fifty bass taken on plugs, from the rocks, in about five hours - the average weight of the fish was over 3 kg.

Although Mike Ladle's books are now out-of-print, second-hand copies may sometimes be obtained from Coch-y-bonddu Books. Telephone 01654-702837. Fax 01654-702857.

Mike's videos can be obtained from Veal's Mail Order, Bristol. Telephone 01275-892000. Fax 01275-892777.

ROBERT NORMAN LOCHHEAD

I am grateful to Richard Hunter, archivist and angling historian of Perth, for the following. Prior to Richard's research little was known of Mr Lochhead. In order to preserve this hard-won information I think it is worth recording in full.

Born in Falkirk on St Valentine's Day, 1899, to Robert Hill Lochhead (a banker) and Effie Gilchrist née Pattinson, he married Mary Enid Robertson Boyle in Bearsden, Dunbartonshire, on 26th August 1927.

Educated at Glasgow Academy and Glasgow University, he was at the time of his marriage a stockbroker's clerk, having served as an eighteen year old second lieutenant with the Royal Field Artillery for the last seven months of the Great War, during which he was awarded the Military Cross.

Plainly an enthusiastic angler, his 93 year old brother-in-law relates that he was also a good shot and accomplished motorcycle rider who competed in long distance trials and owned a succession of bikes.

The rigours of the First World war behind him, he seems to have spent a few years in the financial sector before the Second World War saw him enlist as a Flight Lieutenant in the Balloon Branch of the Royal Auxiliary Air Force. He was discharged on 3rd December, 1946, with the rank of Wing Commander; a status that seemed to suit his tall military bearing admirably, and by which he became known in the community.

The young Robert Lochhead apparently first learnt to fish with his father on the Spey at Newtonmore and subsequently had the enviable privilege of living for almost twenty years on the banks of the Tay at Birnam, before spending the last four years of his life in Grantown upon Spey. With such devotion to his craft it is hardly surprising that he was effusive in his praise of his wife's tolerance of the considerable time he spent fishing.

This committed angler died without issue on 1st June, 1969. Readers of his book can see his figure fishing on the Tay at Dunkeld on the dust jacket of *With Rod Well Bent*.

PAUL MORGAN

After a succession of short-term jobs during the 1970s, starting as a policeman and ending as a lighthouse keeper, Paul moved to Mid Wales to work a water bailiff. This comparatively settled existence led his collection of angling books to grow to such an extent that, in 1982, he produced a catalogue to thin out the surplus. In 1990 he gave up his employment to run Coch-y-bonddu Books full-time. He foolishly thought that this would give him more time for fishing and travel.

Today Coch-y-bonddu Books employ several staff, have a fine retail shop in Machynlleth and regularly exhibit at game-fairs and angling shows throughout Europe. They are one of the largest mail-order sporting booksellers in the world, selling new and out-of-print books, as well as publishing their own titles.

Paul is considering applying for a job as a water bailiff in the hope that this would give him more time for travel and fishing.

BARRY ORD CLARKE

From early childhood in Oldham, Lancashire, Barry Ord Clarke has been a keen angler. He first learnt to flyfish in Norway, where he now lives with his wife and two young children. He is the fishing consultant to two of Norway's largest sporting estates, Lovenskiold-Fossum and Treschow Fritzoe - some 350,000 acres of rivers and 150 lakes. Barry's principal work is as a professional photographer. He has contributed to international advertising campaigns for organisations such as Saatchi & Saatchi and B.A.A., and his photographs can be seen in London's National Portrait Gallery and on record sleeves. In angling circles he is best known as the originator and co-author of the "International guide to fly-tying materials". He regularly contributes articles and photographs to European angling magazines.

MARCO SAMMICHELI

Marco was born in 1961 in Siena, Italy, where he lives today. He is an active worker in the "fishery conservation and management" sector of the regional chapter of the biggest conservation association in Italy (Legambiente).

After some flyfishing trips to the Caribbean in the early 1990s, he now flyfishes Italian saltwaters almost exclusively, trying to develop flyfishing in the Mediterranean.

Marco holds four I.G.F.A. world records: the all-tackle record for Mediterranean Shad, Alosa fallax nilotica, and flyfishing records for European Bass, Morone labrax, for 6, 12 and 16 lbs tippets.

E-mail: levigamb@comune.siena.it
Legambiente Toscana Gestione Ittifaunistica
http://www.comune.siena.it/levigamb

SIDNEY SPENCER

An engineer, living and working in Devon, Sidney Spencer's heart lay in the loughs and glens of the northwest of Ireland and Scotland.

He wrote three how-to-do-it books in the 1930s: *The art of lake fishing (with sunk fly)*, *Clear water trout fishing with worm*, and *Pike on the plug*.

After a considerable interval, in the late 1960s and 1970s he wrote his best-known books, *Salmon and Seatrout in Wild Places*, *Newly from the Sea*, *Ways of Fishing*, and *Game Fishing Tactics*. There was also a posthumous anthology of his writings on loch (or rather lough-) fishing; *Fishing the Wilder Shores*.

He was a pioneer in stillwater fishing for sea-trout, and in later years kept a caravan on the shores of his beloved Lough Eske in Donegal. He spent as much time there as possible, and there, in 1976, he died at the wheel of his car.

RUDY VAN DUIJNHOVEN

Born in 1961, Rudy worked for thirteen years for a gardening company before studying photography at the Phototradeschool in Apeldoorn, Netherlands. In 1992 started his own business as a freelance photographer and author.

His everyday work now consists of wedding photography, writing articles; illustrating catalogues and magazine articles; making recordings of shows; giving workshops on flycasting and flytying; giving flycasting demonstrations at different shows in Europe.

Since January 1992 he has been flyfishing co-ordinator of the monthly *BEET-Sportvissersmagazine*, published by Vipmedia in Breda (NL). He is also one of the editors of *De Nederlandse Vliegvisser*, the magazine of the Dutch Federation of Fly Fishers, a magazine that is put together by volunteers.

Rudy has large stocks of slides on all aspects of sportfishing. He has had articles and photographs published in many of the major fishing magazines in Europe, Britain and America.

Rudy van Duijnhoven.
Hollands Klooster 18,
6562 JE Groesbeek,
Holland
Tel./fax +31 24 397 44 17
E-mail: rvd.angling.slide@tip.nl

BJØRNAR VIHOVDE

Bjørnar was born in 1971, grew up in Haugesund on the south-west coast of Norway, and lives now at Boemlo a little further north. He completed his MSc degree in 1995. An angler since a child, he has been a self-taught flyfisher since the age of fourteen. He discovered the effectiveness and fun of saltwater flyfishing when he first tried to flyfish for sea-trout. He didn't catch any trout, but caught lots of pollack. Since then he has always carried a flyrod when going to the coast for fishing. He is not only a flyfisher, but also enjoys spinning, baitfishing and deep-sea fishing.

bjorn.vihovde@rubbestadneset.wartsila.infonet.com

SEA-TROUT BIBLIOGRAPHY

A checklist of books wholly or partly about sea-trout or sea-trout fishing.

The date given is usually that of the first edition. The note "usually / occasionally available" refers to the book's stock-status at Coch-y-bonddu Books. In most instances the book's relevance to saltwater flyfishing is noted. Books about freshwater fishing generally, with sea-trout only discussed as one of several species, are not included. While the list is comprehensive it makes no claim to be a definitive bibliography. In particular it omits books published in languages other than English. I welcome additions and corrections from readers.

1. Adamson, W.A. *Lake and loch fishing for salmon and sea trout.* 1961. Hardback. Usually available.

2. Balfour-Kinnear, G.P.R. *Catching salmon and sea-trout.* 1958. Hardback. Usually available. Nothing on saltwater fishing.

3. Bingham, Charles. *Salmon and sea trout fishing.* 1988. Hbk Usually available. Nothing on saltwater fishing.

4. Bingham, Charles. *The game fisher's year.* 1989. Hbk. In print and available. Nothing on saltwater fishing.

5. Bingham, Charles. *Trout, salmon and sea trout fishing: the concise guide.* 1994. Hbk. In print and available. Nothing on saltwater fishing.

6. Bingham, Charles. *Sea trout: and how to catch them.* 1998. Hbk. In print and available. Nothing on saltwater fishing.

7. Bluett, Jeffery. *Sea trout and occasional salmon.* 1948. Hardback. Usually available.

8. Brennand, George. *The fisherman's handbook: Trout, salmon and sea trout, with notes on coarse fishing.* 1958 Hardback Usually available.

9. Bridgett, R.C. *Sea trout fishing.* 1929. Hardback. Occasionally available.

10. Calderwood, W.L. *Salmon and sea trout: With chapters on hydro-electric schemes, fish passes, etc.* 1930. Hardback. Sometimes available. Nothing on saltwater fishing.

11. Cass, A.R.Harris. *Catching the wily sea-trout.* ND. Hardback. Usually available. Nothing on saltwater fishing.

12. Chrystal, R.A. *Angling theories and methods.* 1927. Hardback. Usually available.

13. Chrystal, R.A. *Angling at Lochboisdale.* 1939. Hardback. Usually available.

14. Clapham, Richard. *Fishing for sea trout in tidal water.* 1950. Hardback. Usually available. Estuary fishing.

15. Crossley, Anthony. *The floating line for salmon and sea-trout.* 1939. Hardback. Usually available. Nothing on saltwater fishing.

16. Currie, William C. *Game fishing.* 1962. Hardback. Sometimes available. Chapter on Scottish sea-trout in the sea.

17. Currie, William C. *The Guinness guide to game fishing.* 1980. Hardback. Usually available. Chapter on Scottish sea-trout in the sea.

18. Dawson, Kenneth. *Modern salmon and sea trout fishing.* 1938. Hardback. Sometimes available.

19. Dutton, T.E. *Salmon and sea trout fishing.* 1972 Hardback. Usually available. Short chapter on saltwater sea-trouting.

20. Elliott, J.M. et al. *Sea trout literature review and bibliography.* 1992. Paperback. National Rivers Authority technical report No 3. Compiled by the Institute of Freshwater Ecology under contract to the NRA, this contains an excellent review of the ecology of sea-trout. The bibliography lists about 1000 papers and articles on sea-trout natural history between 1866 and 1991. It is not strong on angling books - most of the sea-trout fishing books in this list are not included.

21. Fahy, Edward. *Child of the tides. A sea trout handbook.* 1985. Hardback. Sometimes available. Sea-trout ecology.

22. Falkus, Hugh. *Sea trout fishing.* 1962 1st edn. 1975 2nd revised edition. Hardback. In print & currently available. The expanded 2nd edition has a good chapter on saltwater sea-trout fishing.

23. Falkus, Hugh. *The sea trout.* 1987. Hardback. Occasionally available. A short story which first appeared in "The angler's bedside book", edited by Maurice Wiggin in 1962. Nothing on saltwater fishing.

24. Gammon, Clive. *The Osprey Anglers series: Sea trout.* 1974. Hardback/Paperback. Sometimes available.

25. Grey, Edward. *On sea trout* (1913) 1994. Hardback. In print & currently available. Essay reprinted as part of two volume limited edition set. Nothing on saltwater fishing.

26. Gray, L.R.N. *Torridge fishery, by 'Lemon Grey'.* 1957 Hardback. Usually available.

27. Harris, Graeme and Moc Morgan. *Successful sea trout angling: the practical guide.* 1989. Hardback. In print & currently available. Good chapter on saltwater fishing.

28. Headley, Stan. *New trout fishing guide to Orkney*. 1997 new edition. Paperback. In print & currently available.

29. Henzell, H.P. *Fishing for sea-trout*. 1949. Hardback. Usually available.

30. Holiday, F.W. *Sea trout: how to catch them*. 1956 Hardback. Usually available.

31. Holiday, F.W. *River fishing for sea-trout*. 1960. Hardback. Usually available. Nothing on saltwater fishing.

32. Horsley, Terence. *Fishing for trout and salmon*. 1944. Hardback. Usually available.

33. Johnson, Stephen P.L. *Fishing from afar*. 1947. Hardback. Usually available. Good chapter on Skye sea-trout in saltwater.

34. Johnson, Stephen P.L. *Fishing with a purpose*. 1969. Hardback. Usually available. Scottish game fishing. Good chapter on Skye sea-trout.

35. Lamond, Henry. *The sea-trout. A study in natural history*. 1916. Hardback. Usually available.

36. Lamond, Henry. *Loch Lomond: A study in angling conditions*. 1931. Hardback. Usually available.

37. Lamond, Henry. *Days and ways of a Scottish angler*. 1932. Hardback. Usually available.

38. Lockhart, Logie Bruce. *The pleasures of fishing*. 1981. Hardback. Usually available. Short chapter on saltwater sea-trouting.

39. Lochhead, R.N. *With rod well bent*. 1951. Hardback. Sometimes available. Scottish game fishing. Nice chapter on sea-trout fishing in Hoy, Orkney.

40. Maxwell, Sir H. *Salmon and sea trout: how to propagate, preserve and catch them*. 1898. Hardback. Sometimes available.

41. McEwan, Bill. *Angling on Lomond*. 1980 Hardback. Occasionally available. Nothing on saltwater fishing.

42. McLaren, Charles. *The art of sea trout fishing*. 1963 Paperback/Hardback. 2nd edition currently available.

43. Moore, T.C.Kingsmill. *A man may fish*. 1960 1996 Hardback. New and usually available. Irish lough-fishing classic. Nothing on saltwater fishing.

44. Mottram, J.C. *Sea trout and other fishing studies*. ND (c1923). Hardback. Sometimes available.

45. Nall, G.Herbert. *The life of the seatrout especially in Scottish waters; with chapters on the reading & measuring of scales.* 1930. Hardback. Usually available. Sea-trout natural history.

46. Oglesby, Arthur. *Fly fishing for salmon & sea trout.* 1986. Hardback. In print & currently available. Nothing on saltwater fishing.

47. Robertson, Wm. *The angling resorts of Scotland.* 1933. Paperback. Sometimes available. Nice short chapter on Shetland saltwater sea-trouting.

48. Scott, Jock. *Sea trout fishing.* 1969 Hardback. Usually available. Chapter on salt-water fishing.

49. Spencer, Sidney. *Salmon and sea trout in wild places.* 1968. Hardback. Sometimes available.

50. Spencer, Sidney. *Newly from the sea.* 1969. Hardback. Sometimes available.

51. Spencer, Sidney. *Ways of fishing: Trout, salmon & seatrout.* 1972. Hardback. Sometimes available.

52. Spencer, Sidney. *Game fishing tactics.* 1974 Hardback. Sometimes available. Hebridean game fishing with a chapter on the salt.

53. Stirling, J. *Fishing for trout and sea trout with worm and wet fly.* 1931. Hardback. Sometimes available.

54. Street, David. *Fishing in wild places.* 1989. Hardback. New copies available. Good fishing reminiscences. Chapter on Shetland sea-trout.

55. Stuart, Hamish. *The book of the seatrout.* 1917. Hardback. Usually available. Sea-trout fishing & natural history. The saltwater chapter is all about tidal rivers.

56. Waltham, James. *Sea trout flies.* 1988. Hardback. Usually available.

57. Wrangles, Alan. Editor. *Salmon and sea trout fishing.* 1979. Hardback. Usually available. Mostly salmon and sea-trout ecology by Gilbert Hartley & John Chandler. Fishing chapters by Conrad Voss Bark.

BIBLIOGRAPHY OF BRITISH SALTWATER FLYFISHING

A checklist of English books which include a substantial section on flyfishing (for sea fish - not sea-trout) in saltwater. The date given is usually that of the first edition. The note "usually / occasionally available" refers to the book's stock-status at Coch-y-bonddu Books. While the list is comprehensive it makes no claim to be a definitive bibliography. I welcome additions and corrections from readers.

1. Aflalo, Frederick G. *Sea-fishing on the English coast*. 1891. Hardback. Scarce.

2. Bickerdyke, John. *The book fof the all-round angler. A comprehensive treatise on angling in both fresh and salt water*. 1888. Hardback. Occasionally available.

3. Bickerdyke, John. *Days of my life*. 1895. Hardback. Scarce.

4. Bickerdyke, John. *Sea fishing. The Badminton Library*. 1895. Hardback. Occasionally available.

5. Bickerdyke, John. *Practical letters to young sea-fishers*. 1898. Hardback. Scarce. Includes the most comprehensive chapter on saltwater flyfishing.

6. Bickerdyke, John. *Letters to sea-fishers*. 1902. Hardback. Scarce. This is the re-titled 2nd edition of the previous title.

7. Bickerdyke, John. *Angling in salt water*. 1887. Many editions up to 1935. Paperback. Usually available.

8. (Bowden-Smith, Richard). *Fly-fishing in salt and fresh water*. 1851. Hardback. Rare. Published anonymously.

9. Darling, John. *Bass fishing on shore and sea*. 1996. Hardback. In print & currently available.

10. Harris, Brian. *The Guinness guide to saltwater angling. Light tackle technique for British waters*. 1977. Hardback. Usually available. A fine book. Numerous references to flyfishing.

11. Holiday, F.W. *Feathering for sea fish*. 1966. Hardback. Usually available. Full of useful ideas for the flyfisher.

12. Ladle, Mike with Harry Casey & Terry Gledhill. *Operation sea angler*. 1983. Hardback. Sometimes available. The most innovative sea-angling book of recent years. Mostly plugging for bass and flyfishing for mullet.

13. Ladle, Mike. *Hooked on bass*. 1988. Hardback. Scarce & difficult to find.

14. Nathan, Bill. Editor. *The sea fisherman's bedside book.* 1982. Hardback. Usually available. A good anthology.

15. Price, S.D. (Taff). *Lures for game, coarse and sea fishing.* 1972. Hardback. Usually available. Includes a chapter on lures for sea flyfishing.

16. Sheringham, Hugh T. and John C. Moore. *The book of the fly-rod.* 1931. Hardback. Scarce. Includes *The fly-rod in the sea*, by Arthur F Bell.

17. Thrussell, Mike. *Fishing for bass: strategy and confidence.* 1989 Hardback. Usually available. Useful and informative.

18. Wiggin, Maurice. *Fly fishing.* 1958 1972 2nd edition. Hardback/Paperback. Usually available. A well-written but rather dated introduction to flyfishing with a short chapter on saltwater.

NEW SALTWATER FLYFISHING BOOKS

A list of some new, currently available books on saltwater gamefishing, mainly but not wholly, flyfishing in saltwater. The majority of these are published in America. None of them are about saltwater flyfishing in Europe. The date given is usually that of the first edition. Price and availability are correct at the date of going to print. Coch-y-bonddu Books carry all of these in stock.

1. Atkinson, Valentine. *Distant waters: photography by...* 1997. Hardback. £25.00 A compilation of worldwide flyfishing illustrated by Atkinson's photographs.

2. Bondorew, Ray. *Stripers and streamers.* 1997. Paperback. £15.95

3. Broderidge, Tom. *Fly fishing the Gulf Coast.* 1997. Paperback. £12.95

4. Brown, Dick. *Fly fishing for bonefish.* 1993. Hardback. £31.95 The most comprehensive guide to the fish, tackle, flies and locations.

5. Cardenas, Jeffrey. *Marquesa. A time and a place with fish.* 1995. Hardback. £39.95 Six weeks alone on the flats.

6. Cederberg, Goran. Editor. *Classic flyfishing waters of the world.* 1993. Hardback. £9.95 Describes forty of the best fishing waters around the world. Scotland, New Zealand, U.S.A., Sweden, Canada, Falkland Islands, Norway, Greenland.

7. Cole, John N. *Fishing came first.* 1997. Paperback. £12.95

8. Cole, John and Pollard, Hawk. Editors. *West of Key West.* 1996. Hardback. £39.95 Flyfishing the flats of south Florida's Lower Keys

9. Combs, Trey. *Bluewater flyfishing.* 1995. Hardback. £49.95

10. Curcione, Nick. *The Orvis guide to saltwater flyfishing.* 1993. Hardback £17.95

11. Dimock, A.W.. *The book of the tarpon (1911).* 1995. Hardback. £39.95 Tarpon fishing in Florida in the early years of the century.

12. Dunn, Bob. *Angling in Australia: its history and writings.* 1991. Hardback. £45.00 The definitive history and bibliography of Australian fishing. A lovely book.

13. Earnhardt, Tom *Flyfishing the tidewaters.* 1995. Hardback. £34.95

14. Goadby, Peter. *Saltwater gamefishing: offshore and on.* 1991. Hardback. £29.95

15. Hanley, Ken. *Fly fishing afoot in the surf zone.* 1994. Paperback. £6.95 Flyfishing for a wide variety of Pacific inshore species.

16. Hersey, John. *Blues.* 1987. Hardback. £10.95 Martha's Vineyard blue-fishing and fishing philosophy.

17. Hole, Chris. *Heaven on a stick. A self-illustrated anecdotal examination of flyfishing and flyfishing retreats around the world.* 1994. Hardback. £18.99 An illustrated narrative of two flyfishing safaris by an Australian ex-naval officer - one around the Southern Hemisphere and one around the North. Fishing in Australia

18. Kaufmann, Randall. *Bonefishing with a fly.* 1992. Paperback. £24.95 Natural history, distribution, weather, tides & movements, spotting, stalking and presentation, guides, tackle and destinations, dictionary of bonefish fly patterns.

19. Kreh, Lefty. *Flyfishing in saltwater.* (1974) 1997 3rd edn.. Hardback. £32.95

20. Kumiski, John. *Flyrodding Florida Salt.* 1995. Paperback. £19.95

21. Kumiski, John. *Flyfishing for redfish.* 1997. Paperback. £17.95

22. Kumiski, John. *Saltwater flyfishing.* Paperback. £15.95

23. Pallot, Flip. *Flip Pallot's memories, mangroves & magic.* 1997. Hardback. £39.95

24. Raychard, Al. *Fly fishing the salt. A guide to saltwater flyfishing from Maine to the Chesapeake Bay.* 1989. Paperback. £7.95

25. Raymond, Steve. *Estuary flyfisher.* 1997? Paperback. £24.95 How to flyfish the Pacific Northwest's many estuaries.

26. Reiger, George. Editor. *The silver king.* 1992. Hardback. £39.95 Anthology of the best of tarpon-fishing.

27. Reiger, George. Editor. *The bonefish.* 1993. Hardback. £39.95 Tales of the flats. An anthology of early bonefish angling.

28. Reneson, Chet & Gray, Ed. *Shadows on the flats.* 1997. Hardback. £29.95

29. Reynolds, John. *Flyfishing for sailfish.* 1997. Paperback. £9.95 The first British book on the subject.

30. Rogers, Neal & Linda. *Saltwater flyfishing magic.* 1993. Hardback. £50.00 A celebration in wonderful colour photographs.

31. Samson, Jack. *Billfish on fly.* 1995.Hardback. £27.95.

32. Samson, Jack. *Permit on fly.* 1996 Hardback. £22.95

33. Samson, Jack. *Salt water flyfishing.* Hardback.

34. Sosin, Mark. *Practical saltwater flyfishing*. Paperback. £10.95

35. Sosin, Mark. & Kreh, Lefty. *Fishing the flats*. 1983. Paperback. £15.95 Flyfishing and spinning/plug fishing for tarpon, bonefish, permit, barracuda and sharks.

36. Swisher, Doug & Richards, Carl. *Backcountry flyfishing in saltwater*. 1995. Hardback. £24.95

37. Tabory, Lou. *Inshore fly fishing*. 1992. Hardback. £29.95 A pioneering guide to fly fishing along coldwater seacoasts.

38. Thoemke, Kris. *Fishing Florida. 600 top fishing spots for fresh and salt water*. 1995. Paperback. £16.95

39. Thomas, E. Donnall. *Whitefish can't jump: & other tales of gamefish on the fly*. 1994. Hardback. £14.95 Tales about all of the American species of gamefish

40. Thornton, Barry M. *Saltwater fly fishing for Pacific salmon*. 1995. Paperback. £19.95

41. Ward, Rowland. *The English angler in Florida*. (1898) New Paperback. £12.95 Recent reprint of Florida fishing classic.

SALTWATER FLY-TYING
AND FLY-PATTERN BOOKS

A list of some new, currently available books on fly-patterns and tying flies for salt-water. The majority of these are published in America. The date given is usually that of the first edition. Price or availability are correct at the date of going to print. Coch-y-bonddu Books carry all of these in stock.

1. Brown, Dick. *Bonefish fly patterns.* 1996. Hardback. £39.95 The most comprehensive guide to the fish, tackle, flies and locations.

2. Fitzgerald, F-Stop. *Secrets of the saltwater fly.* 1997. Hardback. £19.95 Colour photographs of 47 of the most effective saltwater patterns.

3. Kreh, Lefty. Compiler. *Saltwater fly patterns.* 1995. Hardback. £24.95 Paperback. £18.95 Includes a short section and two plates of French and Danish flies for European bass.

4. Meyer, Deke. *Saltwater flies: over 700 of the best.* 1995. Paperback. £29.95

5. Richards, Carl. *Prey. Designing and tying new imitations of fresh and saltwater forage foods.* 1995. Hardback. £22.95 Tying baitfish, crab, shrimp and crayfish imitations.

6. Roberts, George V *A flyfisher's guide to saltwater naturals and their imitation.* 1994. Hardback. £29.95

7. Stewart, Dick. & Allen, Farrow. *Flies for saltwater.* 1992. Paperback. £18.95

8. Tabory, Lou. *Lou Tabory's guide to saltwater food & their imitations.* Paperback. £12.95

9. Wentink, Frank. *Saltwater fly tying.* 1991. Paperback. £19.95

10. Wilson, Donald A. *Smelt fly patterns.* 1997. Paperback. £19.95

FURTHER REFERENCES

In addition to books in the preceding lists, I have found the following books especially useful.

1. Davidson, Alan. *North Atlantic seafood.* 1979.

2. Davidson, Alan. *Mediterranean seafood.* 1972.

3. Day, Francis. *Fishes of Great Britain and Ireland.* Two volumes. 1858.

4. Mansfield, Kenneth. Editor. *The art of angling.* Three volumes. 1957.

5. Marston, R.B. *A list of books... to supplement the Bibliotheca Piscatoria.* 1901.

6. Robb, James. *Notable angling literature.* ND. (c1947).

7. Westwood, T & Satchell, T. *Bibliotheca Piscatoria.* 1883.

8. Wheeler, Alwyne. *The fishes of the British Isles and North West Europe.* 1969.

EUROPEAN NAMES OF THE PRINCIPAL
FLYROD QUARRY SPECIES

BASS, Sea bass. *Dicentrarchus labrax.*

Danish: Bars.
Dutch: Zeebaars.
French: Bar, Loup.
German: Seebarsch.
Italian: Spigola.
Norwegian: Hav-abor.
Portuguese: Robalo.
Spanish: Lubina.
Swedish: Havsabborre.
Welsh: Draenog y môr.

COD. *Gadus morhua.*

Danish: Torsk.
Dutch: Kabeljauw.
French: Cabillaud, Morue.
German: Kabeljau, Dorsch.
Norwegian: Torsk, Skrei.
Portuguese: Bacalhau.
Spanish: Bacalao.
Swedish: Torsk.
Welsh: Codsyn, Penfras.

SEA TROUT. *Salmo trutta.*

Danish: Havørred.
Dutch: Zeeforel.
French: Truite de mer.
German: Meerforelle.
Norwegian: Sjøaure, Sjøørret.
Portuguese: Truta marisca.
Spanish: Trucha marina.
Swedish: Havsöring.
Welsh: Sewin.

SALMON. *Salmo salar.*

Danish: Laks.
Dutch: Zalm.
French: Saumon.
German: Lachs.
Norwegian: Laks.
Portuguese: Salmào.
Spanish: Salmón.
Swedish: Lax.
Welsh: Eog.

POLLACK, Lythe. *Pollachius pollachius.*

Danish: Lubbe.
Dutch: Witter koolvis, Pollak.
French: Lieu jaune, Colin.
German: Pollack.
Norwegian: Lyr.
Portuguese: Badejo, Juliana.
Spanish: Abadejo.
Swedish: Bleka.

COALFISH, Saithe. *Pollachius virens.*

American: Pollack.
Danish: Sej.
Dutch: Koolvis.
French: Lieu noir, Colin.
German: Koehler, Seelachs.
Norwegian: Sei, Pale.
Swedish: Sej, Gråsej.
Welsh: Chwitlyn glas.

GARFISH. *Belone belone.*

Danish: Hornfisk.
Dutch: Geep.
French: Orphie, Aiguille.
German: Hornhecht.
Italian: Aguglia.
Norwegian: Horngjel, Nebbsild.
Portuguese: Agulha.
Spanish: Aguja.
Swedish: Horngädda, Näbbgäda..
Welsh: Carrai fôr, Môr nodwydd,
            Cornbig.

MULLET: Thick-lipped grey mullet. *Chelon labrosus.* Thin-lipped grey mullet. *Liza ramada.*

Danish: Multe.
Dutch: Herder.
French: Muge noir, mulet.
German: Meeraesche.
Italian: Muggine, Cefalo.
Norwegian: Multe.
Portuguese: Fataca, Mugem.
Spanish: Pardete, Cabejudo, Lisa.
Swedish: Multa.
Welsh: Hyrddyn, Mingrwn.

WRASSE. *Labrus spp.*

Danish: Berggylt.
Dutch: Lipvis.
French: Vieille, Labre.
German: Lippfisch.
Italian: Tordo.
Norwegian: Berggylte.
Portuguese: Margota.
Spanish: Maragota, Durdo.
Swedish: Berggylta.
Welsh: Gwrach.

SCAD, Horse mackerel. *Trachurus trachurus.*

Danish: Hestemakrel.
Dutch: Horsmakreel.
French: Saurel, Chinchard.
German: Stöcker, Bastardmakrele.
Italian: Sugarello, Suro.
Norwegian: Taggmakrell,
             Hestemakrell.
Portuguese: Sarda, Cavala.
Spanish: Chicharro, Jurel.
Swedish: Taggmakrill.
Welsh: Macrell y meirch.

MACKEREL. *Scomber scombrus.*

Danish: Makrel.
Dutch: Makreel.
French: Maquereau.

German: Makrele.
Italian: Sgombro.
Norwegian: Makrell.
Portuguese: Sarda, Cavala.
Spanish: Caballa.
Swedish: Makrill.
Welsh: Macrell.

PLAICE. *Pleuronectes platessa.*

Danish: Rødspætte.
Dutch: Schol.
French: Plie, Carrelet.
German: Scholle.
Norwegian: Gullflyndre, Rødspette.
Portuguese: Solha.
Spanish: Platija.
Swedish: Rödspätta.
Welsh: Lleden.

FLOUNDER. *Platichthys flesus.*

Danish: Skrubbe.
Dutch: Bot.
French: Flet.
German: Flunder.
Italian: Passera pianuzza.
Norwegian: Skrubbe, Harbakke,
             Kvasse, Vassflyndre.
Portuguese: Patruça, Solha das pedras.
Spanish: Platija.
Swedish: Skrubbskädda.
Welsh: Lleden ddu.

BLUE SHARK. *Prionace glauca.*

Danish: Blåhaj.
Dutch: Blauwe Haai.
French: Requin bleu.
German: Blauhai.
Italian: Verdesca.
Norwegian: Blåhai.
Swedish: Blåshaj
Welsh: Morgi glas, Sierc.

259

INDEX

An index mainly of people, places and fish. The names of flies and items of tackle, which recur throughout the text, have been omitted.